# Helping Educators Grow

## Strategies and Practices
## for Leadership Development

ELEANOR DRAGO-SEVERSON

Harvard Education Press
Cambridge, Massachusetts

Library of Congress Control Number 2012940000

Paperback ISBN 978-1-61250-491-9
Library Edition ISBN 978-1-61250-492-6

Published by Harvard Education Press,
an imprint of the Harvard Education Publishing Group

Harvard Education Press
8 Story Street
Cambridge, MA 02138

Cover Design: Ciano Design
Cover Illustration: © iStockphoto/Veena Kumbargadde

The typefaces used in this book are ITC Stone Serif, ITC Stone Sans, and Filosofia

*With impossible-to-measure gratitude to all who have helped
me to grow with their different forms of love, care, support, and challenge,
and especially to David and Mom.*

*And with gratitude for the miracle and joy of inspiration that
I find in Stephen, Thomas, John, Jess, and Orin.*

# Contents

# Helping Educators Grow

*How Learning Environments
Can Support Leadership Development*

*We have more possibilities in each moment than we
realize.*

—THICH NHAT HANH

How can we help aspiring and practicing leaders develop the internal capacities they need to teach, learn, and lead in the increasingly complex environment that constitutes the field of education today? One promising
way is to create professional learning environments that invite educational
leaders of all kinds to *experience* the conditions and practices that support
adult growth and development *while simultaneously learning about them.* Increasingly, we are coming to understand that in order to help other adults
learn and grow, leaders need to first grow their own internal capacities—to
expand, in ways both big and small, their ways of seeing, knowing, and being in the world and with others. In my view, helping leaders grow into
their biggest, best selves is the fundamental task and challenge of leadership preparation, because adult development *is* leadership development,
and vice versa. In other words, helping leaders to grow professionally and
personally better equips them, in turn, to support and inspire this essential
growth in others.

In this book, I present a new, learning-oriented model of leadership
development that draws from adult developmental theory and over twenty
years of teaching and research with educators from around the globe.
While I draw from theory—particularly Harvard developmental psychologist Robert Kegan's constructive-developmental theory and my own work

and research about school leadership that supports adult development—this model expands prior work by focusing on specific concepts, strategies, structures, and practices that can help you shape *any* professional learning initiative as a developmental opportunity for individuals and groups in a variety of contexts, including schools, school districts, and university leadership preparation programs.[1] By focusing on the kind of learning that helps aspiring and practicing leaders grow their internal capacities—meaning their cognitive, affective (emotional), intrapersonal (self to self), and interpersonal (self to other) capacities—we equip educational leaders of all kinds to assist others with better managing, together, the complex challenges we face as educators today. If you are a practicing or aspiring school leader, or someone who supports or teaches them, you will find in this book new kinds of tools to use as you work to solve the complex problems inherent to supporting leadership development and adult growth.

Rooted in the study of human development, this new model of leadership development draws particularly from the concept of a holding environment, first articulated in the 1960s by pediatrician and psychoanalyst D. W. Winnicott and later expanded by developmental psychologist Robert Kegan. In his use of the term *holding environment*, Winnicott described the different kinds of "holding" that an infant needs to achieve healthy physical and psychological growth—for example, the physical and psychological care a baby feels when held lovingly in a parent's arms.[2] Later, Kegan used the term to emphasize the fact that as human beings we all need multiple forms of "holding" throughout our lives—guidance, support, nourishment, developmentally appropriate challenges or stretching, and care—and extended its definition to include the kinds of environments that would provide opportunities for personal growth throughout the lifespan.[3]

An example of an effective holding environment for adult growth is depicted in the relationship between Lionel Logue, a "lowly" Australian elocutionist, and Great Britain's Duke of York (more affectionately known by family intimates as Bertie) in the 2010 film *The King's Speech*. Lionel creates a holding environment as he assists Bertie in overcoming a crippling stammer that is the cause of personal anguish and familial humiliation. Lionel's unorthodox instructional methods initially clash with Bertie's rigidly regal demeanor. However, the holding environment Lionel creates ultimately helps Bertie to feel safe and accepted. Once this occurs, Lionel offers developmentally appropriate challenges to assist in Bertie's growth. And the holding environment remains in place as Bertie, who becomes the King of England just as his empire stands at the brink of war with Nazi Germany, grows to demonstrate new capacities.[4]

In this book, I further extend the meaning and application of the holding environment in several ways, with the goal of helping educators shape professional learning initiatives of all kinds as holding environments that simultaneously support growth at individual and group levels. Indeed, by learning about the importance of supporting adult development *while directly experiencing* the principles and practices that compose this new model of leadership development, leaders are better able to *feel* the power and promise of being well held (in a developmental sense) individually and collectively, and also learn directly how to build, sustain, and nourish these kinds of growth-enhancing environments in any teaching, learning, and professional development initiative.

It seems helpful to say a little bit more about the distinction and relationship between supporting growth at individual and group levels. Often, as teachers, we are called upon to specifically care for—or "hold"—an individual colleague or student. In these person-to-person exchanges, during which, for example, we offer advice, direction, or a friendly word, we are working directly to support that other person's growth. But as school leaders, or as facilitators of professional learning initiatives for aspiring and practicing leaders of all kinds, we are working to support not only individual growth but also the growth of a larger group of adults. Accordingly, this book presents a new model for leadership development that can help you attend to *both* kinds of vital growth, the individual and the collective; in its very nature, the model incorporates the important truth that professional and personal growth can be even more meaningful and dynamic when achieved *in and through* the company of others who are also learning and growing.

Why is this important to leadership development today? And why might you want to read this book? Well, we need to help practicing and aspiring leaders develop their own internal capacities. This important work *needs* to happen in our schools, our professional learning communities, our school districts, and our university education leadership preparation programs. And we know it's challenging. Those of us who work in education participate in professional development initiatives in schools, districts, and teams all the time. We attend sessions in schools and districts geared toward supporting adult learning—meaning the learning of teachers, principals, assistant principals, coaches, superintendents, and the other dedicated adults in their care. Still, even though we would like these sessions to be places where adults are learning and growing in the profound ways just described, often they are not.

In addition, we offer leadership courses to help leaders prepare to meet the complex demands of the twenty-first century. (You will read more about this shortly.) We know we need to help leaders develop their internal capacities in order to meet the increasingly complex challenges inherent in schooling. All too often, however, we teach leadership development in the same way we teach world history: by presenting just the facts, just the content. But we have learned that focusing on content is not enough to help aspiring and practicing leaders deal with the uncertainty and the complexity of leadership. We often teach aspiring and practicing leaders *what* without showing them *how*, and without creating the conditions for them to grow from the process or experience of being in, and learning from, the course and the learning environment.

So, we know how important it is to help leaders grow and learn in professional learning initiatives of all kinds. But how do we do this? We can and must do better. One promising strategy, as this book suggests, is to understand that in order for practicing and aspiring leaders to help other adults grow, they need to first grow their own internal capacities and then learn *how to help other adults do the same.* What practices can be employed? How can we reshape and enhance professional learning initiatives and university classrooms so that practicing and aspiring leaders can grow and learn within them? That is what this book is about.

Put simply, this book, and the new model for leadership development it presents, will show you how to shape professional learning initiatives that support the growth of teachers, principals, assistant principals, coaches, specialists, and all hardworking adults who dedicate their hearts and lives to education. It is about enhancing the ways in which we design professional learning environments, and how we teach and learn in them, so that all adults can grow and learn to better meet the pressing demands of teaching and leading today. It will also show you how the principles of constructive-developmental theory and the new model of leadership development presented here can be used as platforms from which you can design, lead, and sustain the urgent and very personal work of supporting adult development across a variety of contexts at both the individual and group level.

At its most fundamental level, then, this book is about supporting growth, and the key understanding that adult development *is* leadership development. As I will share in greater detail throughout, I define *growth* as increasing the cognitive, emotional, intrapersonal, and interpersonal capacities that enable us to better manage the complexities of leading, learning, teaching, and living. Leaders who sustain this kind of growth themselves are then better able to support it in others. Second, this book presents a new model of leadership development for shaping professional learning environments that support adult growth, both individually and collectively, in the sense just described. In other words, it is a model for creating learning initiatives that invite adults to nurture their own development in the company of others so that they can be better equipped to support the development of the adults in their care. Third, the insights presented in this book can be (and have been) applied across diverse settings: leadership development and professional learning in K–12 schools; school districts; university education and leadership preparation programs; classrooms; teams; professional learning communities; leadership academies aimed at supporting the growth of teachers, assistant principals, and principals; and in mentoring relationships, coaching relationships, and other relationships.

## THE IMPORTANCE OF SUPPORTING ADULT DEVELOPMENT

Each one of us nurtures important relationships with adults in our personal and professional lives. We also have hopes and goals for our own personal growth, development, and work. But we may not be aware of how important it is to consciously create opportunities for growth as part of leadership development in the world of education. Why is it so essential to support all practicing and aspiring educational leaders?

There are so many reasons, as I imagine you know. First, I'll emphasize again that supporting adult development *is* supporting leadership development. Investing in adult growth *is* investing in growing leaders; in other words, it is caring for and enhancing our efforts to support leadership development. We must invest wisely. After all, the responsibilities of leadership require us to build our own internal capacities, because these capacities enable us to more effectively support others' growth and development (we have more to draw from internally and therefore more to offer other people). Growing our internal capacities also enables us to better manage the myriad demands of living, leading, learning, and teaching in today's complex, demanding, and ever-changing educational world. This kind of growth helps us to take a bigger, broader perspective on our selves, others, our environment, and the relationships among them.

Second, supporting adult growth is directly and positively linked to increasing the academic achievement of children and young people.[5] Studies have shown that teaching adults in general and school leaders (e.g., principals and the principals they mentor) in particular about adult development practices while they experience the benefits of being in a professional learning environment that supports their own growth makes a real difference in their schools' performance over the course of a year. For example, research from the National School Leaders Network program, directed by Dr. Elizabeth Neale and in which a central part of the curriculum focuses on adult development, has indicated that learning about adult development (i.e., theory and content) and the practices that support it while actually experiencing those practices has a positive impact on school performance and test scores.[6] For these and other important reasons, learning how to build, nurture, and sustain the kinds of environments that support adult development can enhance our own growth and prepare us to better support the growth of others.

In my previous work, I focused on introducing what I call a new *learning-oriented model for school leadership* that is composed of four pillar practices that can support adult growth. These pillar practices—teaming, providing leadership roles, engaging in collegial inquiry, and mentoring—are methods that I have employed to support the growth of adults' internal capacities in many contexts, domestically and internationally. While my earliest work sought to understand how school principals support teachers' growth, my later work expanded its focus to include the ways in which teachers, assistant principals, superintendents, coaches, district leaders, and university professors who teach aspiring and practicing leaders employ these practices to support adult growth in a variety of settings. In this book, I again expand prior work by presenting a model of how we, as professional learning leaders, can support growth and leadership development in aspiring and practicing leaders by creating professional learning environments in which adults *experience* developmental principles and practices *while they are learning about them*. This, as you will see, is vital but challenging work. While more traditional forms of professional development often seek to increase adults' fund of knowledge or skills (*informational learning*), this model emphasizes the importance of learning that involves changes in seeing, understanding, and being that better equip educational leaders to meet the many complex adaptive challenges they face (*transformational learning*). Next, I discuss in greater detail the important distinctions between informational and transformational learning and between adaptive and technical challenges.

## Informational Versus Transformational Learning

When talking about adult learning and professional development, people often prioritize informational learning, meaning the type of learning that heralds an increase in skill or mastery of subject matter or specialized content. While informational learning is important and even essential to good teaching and leading, the type of growth and development we focus on in this book involves transformational learning, meaning learning that actually changes *how* we make sense of our experiences. Transformational learning—that is, increases in our cognitive, affective, interpersonal, and intrapersonal capacities that enable us to better manage the complexities of learning, teaching, leading, and living—changes the shape of our thinking and the very way we see and understand the world. It is substantively different from the increases in funds of knowledge that characterize more informational learning opportunities. Throughout this book, I use the terms *transformational learning* and *growth* interchangeably.

More specifically, informational learning concerns increasing the amount of knowledge, skills, content, and information we possess. You can think about this along the lines of encyclopedia knowledge: it increases *what* we know, and is thought to bring about changes in adults' attitudes, skills, and even their competencies (e.g., navigating different forms of technology, knowing how to analyze data scores to assess changes in students' academic achievement, or acquiring skills to create budgets). This is very important because we need specific knowledge and skills in every domain of our lives; however, this kind of learning alone is not enough to help us manage the adaptive challenges we face in practicing leadership. While informational learning is necessary and has a crucial purpose in the twenty-first century, limiting ourselves to this kind of learning will not enable us to manage all of the challenges in our schools, nor to build internal leadership capacity within school systems and university contexts.

Transformational learning, on the other hand, concerns changing *how* we know—how we take in and interpret information and experiences. To support the process of transformational learning, we need to first understand an adult's current *way of knowing*, since it shapes how a person interprets or makes sense of all experiences. It is the window through which he or she sees the world; to understand it, we must meet a person where he or she is in a psychological sense. By offering developmentally appropriate supports and challenges, we can help a person grow. When transformational learning or growth occurs, there is a qualitative change in the *structure* of a person's meaning-making system, or way of knowing (a concept I discuss in greater detail in chapter 1). When people have undergone transformational learning, they are able to take a broader perspective on themselves, others, and the relationship between the two.[7] Moreover, as this book and new model make clear, transformational learning also equips practicing and aspiring leaders with greater internal resources from which to draw when supporting others and their school communities.

## Adaptive Versus Technical Challenges

Another thing we know for sure is that every day in today's complex, ever-changing world, enormous and new kinds of implicit and explicit demands are placed on practicing and aspiring school leaders. This is true for principals, assistant principals, teachers, superintendents, district leaders, and, yes, university education leadership professors, who dedicate themselves to educating children, youth, and adults. The current educational climate calls for new approaches to supporting adults and their growth so that they can meet these leadership demands and be even more effective leaders. Despite the immense benefits of traditional leadership preparation in universities as well as on-the-job learning, improving the quality of teaching and leadership in today's world requires a new model that explicitly prepares leaders to better manage the complex challenges they face in schools.[8]

Harvard psychiatrist and leadership scholar Ronald Heifetz, whose research and practice focus on building the *adaptive capacity* of organizations and societies, makes an important and powerful distinction between what he calls "technical" and "adaptive" challenges, and he suggests that leaders are increasingly encountering adaptive challenges.[9] Technical challenges, he explains, are situations in which we *can identify both the problem and the solution.* And, even if we do not ourselves have the skills, expertise, tools, or training to address such a challenge, we can identify the problem, and we can find someone, perhaps an expert who has experience with this kind of challenge, who knows how to fix or address it.

As Heifetz points out, however, many of the complex challenges we encounter each day in our educational world are not easy to pinpoint or identify. In other words, we, as educators, are facing profound and weighty challenges that Heifetz classifies as adaptive. These are situations in which we cannot even identify the exact problem, *and* neither we nor anyone else has a clear solution to address it. Needless to say, these challenges are more difficult to resolve, and managing them requires greater internal capacities on the part of leaders.

As you know, the work of educators has become palpably more complex in the twenty-first century. Building school capacity, implementing the Common Core, managing complex reform initiatives, meeting accountability demands, caring for students' diverse needs, closing the achievement gap, and working effectively in an era of standards-based reform are some of the pressing issues facing all educators today.[10] As scholars and practitioners have emphasized, navigating these murky and obscure adaptive challenges requires not only new approaches but also often greater *internal developmen-*

*tal capacities*. In other words, because there are no known solutions, addressing these ambiguous and complex issues requires new tools and enhanced cognitive and emotional capacities; we need to be able to "solve the problem in the act of working on it," and to live and learn our way through the ambiguity and complexity.[11]

Importantly, research has shown that most adults in the United States do not yet have these kinds of capacities; in fact, only about 20 to 25 percent of us do and can exercise them spontaneously.[12] This means that we need to grow and develop in order to manage adaptive challenges more effectively—and we've learned that we cannot do this kind of growing alone. As you will see, one key premise of the new model for leadership development presented in this book is that we can help each other grow to meet these mounting educational challenges by shaping professional development environments that truly support adult development and growth.

## IT'S REALLY ALL ABOUT THE KIDS

In the summer of 2011, I enjoyed the privilege of teaching a cohort of approximately eighty aspiring principals in our Summer Principals Academy Program at Teachers College, Columbia University, in New York. My course, a core requirement and one of the foundations of this leadership preparation program, is called School Leadership for Adult Development, and in it we discuss many of the ideas, theories, and practices involved in supporting adult development that I share in this book. In the class, just as in this new model for supporting leadership development, participants learn content about adult and professional development as they experience the practices they are studying. In other words, the *content* of the learning is incorporated into and reflected by the *context* of the classroom.

Nevertheless, during the first day of class this past year, many of the program participants wondered out loud why they were enrolled in a course on school leadership for *adult* development when their interest was in helping *children* achieve more in their academic and personal lives. I expressed gratitude for their courage in sharing their concern and responded, "I, like you, am all about the kids—that's what initially brought me to this work and continues to energize me. And, because I *am* all about the kids, I am *also* all about the adults and supporting their growth and development." The two, I have learned, are profoundly intertwined.

For more than two decades, as a teacher, learner, coach, and developmental psychologist, I have been studying adult development and learning, teacher and principal development, the value of adult development in educational leadership, and the ways in which learning-oriented school leadership can make schools better and more supportive for all who work, learn, and grow there. All of this work is inspired by my hope of making educational leadership preparation programs and schools better places for adults *and* youth. This hope is borne of a larger goal: to make the lives of others a little better and more fulfilling and to help others become all they can be, regardless of age, situation, or circumstance.

I began my professional journey in support of others with the great honor of serving as a middle and high school teacher, school counselor, program director, staff developer, and athletic coach in schools. I had the privilege of teaching and serving in several different school contexts in multiple locations in the United States. Initially, in my personal observations and experiences as a teacher, I noticed that children's well-being and academic achievement seemed to be positively influenced by teachers, assistant principals, and principals who felt well supported in their own professional and personal development. In other words, I noted that when the teachers, myself included, felt *well held* in a psychological sense—listened to, heard, and cared for and about by the administration—it seemed to have a direct and positive influence on the children. The reverse, unfortunately, also seemed true. I began to wonder why it was so hard to support adult development in schools. How could we do better? What might happen if we did? How might it influence children and youth—their well-being, their achievement?

I set out years ago to better understand this important and promising connection as well as to explore why it was so challenging to support adult development in schools, school systems, and education leadership preparation programs. How might school leaders and university education leadership professors do this important work better? What practices might best support adult development? How can we teach them most effectively? These questions led me to pay careful attention to the kinds of leadership and professional learning environments that create the conditions for nurturing adult development. I went to graduate school to learn more about these very questions and have dedicated myself to working with, and learning from and with, leaders like you ever since. This book and the new model it presents synthesize and incorporate lessons I've learned from my journey over the past two decades. My hope is to share with you the best of what I've learned, as well as the specific strategies, structures, and practices I've refined over the years working to design and facilitate professional learning environments that effectively support adult growth and inspire participants to do the same. As I mentioned earlier, creating these kinds of supportive conditions allows practicing and aspiring leaders of all kinds to grow, learn, and build the internal capacity needed to better meet the increasingly complex demands of teaching, leading, and living today. Just as supporting adult development *is* leadership development, supporting adults at all levels of the school system is one key way to effectively support students, too. The model presented in this book, I believe, can help us do just that.

## TESTIMONIES FROM THE FIELD

A real-life example of the promise of shaping professional learning environments that support adult growth might be helpful to ground this new model in practice. Recently, I facilitated a series of learning workshops for New York City educators. All participants were responsible for supporting the development of adults within schools and the school system as a whole. At the opening of the workshop series, a veteran educator of twenty-six years presented her view of why supporting adult development is so important to leadership and education today, especially given the complex challenges that educators of all kinds must face together.

"Our work is adaptive work," she explained, emphasizing that she and her colleagues needed more than skills to meet new challenges, like implementing the Common Core standards. As everyone listened carefully, she continued, "What I mean is that changing curriculum maps, lessons plans, instructional units—the content—is important, but it's not enough." She then shared her view that leaders need to support both teacher practice and the teachers themselves. As she put it, "We must do both!" Ultimately, she explained, concluding her opening remarks, they had gathered together for these workshops "to learn how to build capacities by understanding how to support adult development and use practices that will help adults grow."

After this wise educator shared her introductory thoughts, I reinforced her point about the purpose of our workshops. I began by welcoming everyone warmly and voicing my appreciation for their time and the opportunity to learn together. I then told them, as we will discuss in greater detail throughout this book, that building our own capacities and those of others is a key responsibility of leadership, and a key challenge of our times. However, I reminded them, as I now remind you, that growth often involves letting go, which can be painful. As a leader at a different districtwide workshop insightfully shared, "Growth involves shedding. Developing ourselves and growth in leadership require shedding—not just for teachers, but also for all of us in the district." It is my belief and hope that this kind of "shedding," in a developmental sense, can allow us to find even bigger ways of being with and for each other in our classrooms, schools, teams, and the world. This new model of leadership development will enable us to create professional learning environments that support adult growth and, in turn, can guide us to perform our work even more effectively and to live even better in today's world. To help us further down this path, I offer in this book a model that can help you create professional learning initiatives, like these workshops, that aim to support adult growth as a form of leadership development.

Importantly, and as you now know, in these and other professional learning initiatives, participants not only learn about content, adult developmental theory, and practices that can support adult growth, but they *experience* the learning environments as contexts in and out of which they themselves are growing. Over and over again, leaders I have had the honor to work with and learn from express that they are "much better able to support adult growth" after participating in these kind of learning experiences. As one such leader recently shared, "I've experienced it here. I know it can work!"

Along these lines, it might also be helpful to think about these learning environments as a chain reaction. When leaders—principals, assistant principals, teacher leaders, district leaders, or coaches—participate in and experience the kinds of learning environments supported by this model, they are better able to create similarly supportive environments for other adults. My most sincere hope is that this book offers a helpful map for creating developmental learning environments in schools, peer-to-peer learning groups, teams, professional learning communities, school systems, university education leadership preparation programs, and in any teaching, learning, and professional development environment dedicated to developing leaders, as well as in life more generally.

## OVERVIEW OF CHAPTERS

Throughout this book, I present the key components of my new, learning-oriented model of leadership development. In the chapters that follow, I highlight different aspects of the model to help you learn about building developmental learning environments that support growth and leadership development in a variety of contexts. I also offer ideas, practical tools, and examples for supporting one's own growth and development, not just as a leader but also as a human being.

Figure I.1 depicts the structure of my theoretical model for leadership development. This model also mirrors the organization of the book.

After chapter 1, where I further discuss the origins of the concept of a holding environment and how my model extends it, I will describe each of the concentric circles and its components chapter by chapter. We will begin with the innermost circle and move outward from there. While the concentric circles are distinct in the model, they are also interrelated and

**FIGURE I.1**

## Theoretical model for leadership development

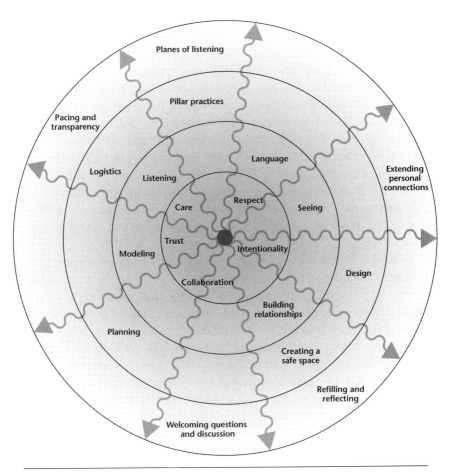

connected to each other in intimate and important ways. Indeed, you can think of them as being woven together in a way that creates dynamic and robust opportunities for growth, and that authentically reflects the core elements depicted in the center of the model. Each chapter in this book focuses on key ideas from one of the concentric circles, or "growth rings," as I like to think of them.

## Chapter 1, Feeling "Held": Constructive-Developmental Theory and Adult Growth

In this chapter, I present the theoretical underpinnings of my learning-oriented model for leadership development, with particular emphasis on constructive-developmental theory. I focus on this theory because it informs my approach to shaping learning environments as developmentally oriented contexts that support adult and leadership development. First, I provide an overview of how constructive-developmental theory informs this model as well as my thinking about how to support adult learning and development in our contemporary world. I then provide a detailed discussion of constructive-developmental theory, with particular emphasis on how understanding and attending to adults' different ways of knowing can enable us to build professional learning environments that serve as rich and dynamic contexts that support adult growth, leadership development, and capacity building to meet the complex challenges we face. I also dive deeper into the origins of the holding environment concept and further explain how this model extends that idea by acknowledging the importance of supporting growth at both the individual and group levels.

Then, to clarify the value of this new developmental awareness, I discuss a few examples of effective, developmentally oriented learning experiences and what they have meant to aspiring and practicing leaders in professional learning initiatives I have facilitated. I also share some of the main obstacles to creating growth-enhancing environments as identified by teachers, assistant principals, math/literacy and instructional coaches, professional developers, district leaders, and university professors who have graciously participated in research aimed at illuminating how they nurture contexts that support adult and leadership development.

I end chapter 1 by offering takeaways, an application exercise, and reflective questions to help you engage with the ideas presented. I hope they will help you in your efforts to support development in your educational milieu.

## Chapter 2, The Inner Circle: Core Elements of Learning Environments for Leadership Development

This chapter focuses on the heart of the model, or what I call the *core elements*: care, respect, trust, collaboration, and intentionality. These are the elements I consider essential to shaping professional learning environments that support adult and leadership development; accordingly, they are presented in the innermost growth ring of figure I.1. And although I describe these core elements as distinct entities at the heart of my model for leadership development, I also invite you to consider them, collectively, as expressions of self that spark the series of concentric circles depicted in figure I.1.

In this chapter, I discuss each core element in this innermost circle and offer examples to illustrate its importance and connection to leadership development. As the model illustrates, care, respect, trust, collaboration, and intentionality are connected or intertwined and thus located within the same growth ring. They are the fundamental elements a leader must embody in order to make learning environments of all kinds come to life.

Finally, at the heart of this innermost ring, you see a central dot. Each of us has a personal central dot, or a *core essence of self*. As I'll discuss, for me this innermost self is informed by my background (personal and professional), my family and other important relationships, the holding environments I've experienced, the power and promise of constructive-developmental theory, my education and experiences in schools, and the honor of having experiences of learning from, with, and alongside leaders.

## Chapter 3, Senses and Strategies: Putting the Core Elements into Practice

This chapter explains how the core elements situated at the heart of the model (i.e., the innermost ring) are manifested and expressed in professional learning enterprises that I facilitate to support growth. As you can see in the second ring from the center of this model, the ways in which they are manifested or expressed are largely sensory in nature: *listening* with presence, which has been proven to be a developmental support; using *language* thoughtfully by asking questions and offering feedback (both verbal and written) that supports growth; *seeing* with sensitivity, or attending to your own intuition about the emotional tone people give off; *building relationships* through listening, using language, and seeing through a developmental lens, which raises up what I call the "treasure of paid attention," or the gift of attending to the individual; and, finally, *modeling,* which involves teaching with transparency and responsiveness.

## Chapter 4, Shaping the Vision: Using Space and Structure in Professional Learning

In this chapter, you will learn about practical and concrete strategies for conceptualizing and planning professional learning opportunities that support adult and leadership development. In this, the second-outermost ring of the model, I offer five important aspects of designing workshops, classes, professional development sessions, and learning initiatives of all kinds that support growth. In particular, we will explore how we can work to *create a safe space* in teaching, learning, and professional development environments; the importance of caring for the *logistics* of professional learning environments; the vital importance of *planning* (before, during, and after facilitating learning opportunities of all kinds); the intentionality behind the *design* of effective leadership development initiatives; and examples of the four *pillar practices* in action to illustrate how you might invite adults to work together to support their own and each other's growth during professional learning.

## Chapter 5, Nuances: Little Things That Make a Big Difference

This chapter describes the nuances that make up the detail work of facilitating professional learning initiatives to support growth, as identified in the outermost ring of the model. These are things leaders can do in the room and in the moment that add flavor and life to the other practices, components, and elements I describe in the inner rings of this model. Here, in the outermost ring, we are reminded that the little things do count in tremendous ways.

As you know, there are many, many nuances that shape professional learning opportunities. Here, though, we will focus on five larger categories of nuance that are very important for supporting growth and leadership development across all contexts: *planes of listening*, or the different ways we can hold our bodies and our ears to convey attention and respect; *welcoming questions and discussion*, or the fact that how we respond to participant contributions during professional learning opportunities speaks volumes about our stance as leaders and facilitators; *extending personal connections*, or being mindful of the power and importance of seizing opportunities to connect with individuals in larger group sessions; *pacing and transparency*, or caring for the details of time and timing; and *refilling and reflecting*, or finding time in the moment as a facilitator to check in with participants and yourself to best meet a group's needs. As components of the outermost growth ring, these nuances pull through threads from the center and weave the model together in important ways. In this chapter, I discuss all of these categories, and related examples, in detail.

### Chapter 6, Coming Full Circle: Refilling the Self to Sustain and Support Others

How can professional learning environments that support growth be sustained over time? What can schools, districts, university education leadership programs, and *you* do to support and strengthen this work? In this chapter, I address these questions by recognizing that *refilling oneself* through self-development and self-renewal is critical to building and sustaining effective learning environments that support adult and leadership development over time.

In this chapter, you will learn more about the vital importance of refilling ourselves—of creating environments for self-development and self-renewal. We will focus on why it's important to find or create holding environments for oneself, and what strategies can be employed to do so. I also offer suggestions for ways that schools, districts, and school systems can help support and sustain the important and essential work of building human capacity. The examples presented in this chapter all involve refilling—securing opportunities for personal support, development, and renewal. By way of preview, a very important aspect of working to support our own growth and development is that, ironically, *we cannot do this alone.* In other words, one big takeaway from this chapter is the power and promise of growing oneself *through and in the company of others.* As you will see, many of the strategies offered for growing oneself highlight the importance of having a reflective partner, critical friend, or group of colleagues to assist in growing. This is essential, I think, because collaboration and dialogue (engaging in meaningful, deep conversations with other people) make up one of the most important holding environments you can carve out for yourself. I also talk about how I do this for myself.

### CLOSING THOUGHTS AND WISHES FOR YOUR READING JOURNEY

In the end, we are all designers of learning in our work and care. While this book is written primarily for leaders (as broadly defined in this chapter) and those who teach aspiring and practicing leaders, the ideas and practices it presents transcend context. Ultimately, this new model is really about how to shape environments that support growth in professional and personal relationships. Since the ideas and practices in this book apply to all who serve in schools and all of us as human beings, and since they draw from a variety of knowledge domains (e.g., adult learning, developmental theory, leadership practice, leadership preparation, and organizational collaboration), I hope that a wide audience will find the ideas and practices helpful, useful, and valuable.

From my point of view—and based on what I have learned over more than twenty years of working with, and learning from and with, adults in personal and professional relationships in myriad settings, and especially with practicing and aspiring leaders—learning environments that support growth are necessary not just in professional educational settings, but in life. We need to join together—hands, hearts, and minds—in order to help each other grow. Doing so will enable us to live life more fully, to become what we are capable of becoming, to thrive and do our best work in service to children and youth and to each other. We cannot do this important work alone. We need each other. Together, we can shape the places in which we lead, teach, learn, and live as powerful contexts for growth. Again, supporting adult development *is* the task of leadership. It is also an essential component of supporting leadership *development*. And none of us can do this alone. This is the premise of this book and the foundation of my new model for leadership development. I hope, with all my heart, that this work provides some helpful and useful ideas and practices for creating learning initiatives that support growth and capacity building in your context. Finally, I would love to learn from your wisdom and feedback, and so I also hope you will share your additional ideas.

# CHAPTER 1

# Feeling "Held"

## *Constructive-Developmental Theory and Adult Growth*

*The thing always happens that you really believe in;
and the belief in a thing makes it happen.*

—FRANK LLOYD WRIGHT

In this chapter, you will learn about the theoretical underpinnings of my new, learning-oriented model for leadership development, with particular emphasis on constructive-developmental theory. Throughout, I offer these ideas as I do when actively teaching professionals who facilitate leadership programs for educators—that is, as invitations for you to consider trying out a constructive-developmental lens. As I say in my workshops and classes, no single lens, theory, or framework helps us understand every aspect of life and growth, but it is my hope that you find this particular lens— which intimately informs my thinking about creating professional learning environments that support adult and leadership development—useful in your own important work. For the same reasons, this chapter is also an invitation to consider your own conceptions of growth in adulthood, and how it happens. What does it look like? How do we support it? How do we help our leaders grow? What are good leadership and good teaching?

I begin this chapter with an overview of constructive-developmental theory since it is the primary lens that informs my thinking about how to shape learning environments that support growth. In particular, I emphasize the importance of understanding adults' different *ways of knowing* (that is, the ways we interpret and respond to the world around us). As you will see, understanding and attending to these ways of knowing can enable us to create learning environments that serve as dynamic contexts for supporting adult growth, leadership development, and capacity building to meet the complex challenges of being an educator and leader in today's world. Shaping learning contexts that support adult growth will equip us all to better meet the implicit and explicit demands of leadership, teaching, learning, and life.

Next, I further detail the origins of the holding environment concept, and my extension of it, by sharing *why* holding environments are relevant for professional and personal development at both the individual and group levels, forms of growth I believe to be intertwined when it comes to leadership development in education. For instance, I discuss a few examples of how participants in my workshops and seminars have experienced growth-enhancing learning environments, and I also share an example of a powerful holding environment from my own experience.

Finally, I discuss some of the main obstacles to creating developmental learning contexts that have been identified by education leaders who have graciously participated in my research about adult learning and leadership development. They also talk about how they have used in practice some of the ideas you'll read about in this book. In ending this chapter, I offer tips and takeaways, an application exercise, and reflective questions to help you engage with the ideas presented. I hope they will help you in your efforts to support development in your educational milieu.

## A LOOK THROUGH THE LENS OF CONSTRUCTIVE-DEVELOPMENTAL THEORY

Perhaps more than any other single theory, constructive-developmental theory has had a profound influence on how I think about creating learning environments that support growth for others and for myself. For instance, as mentioned in the introduction, this theory directly informs my learning-oriented model of school leadership, which is composed of four pillar practices that support adult development in schools and other organizations through collaboration: teaming, providing leadership roles, collegial inquiry, and mentoring. As you will learn later in this book, I also employ these developmentally oriented practices when designing professional learning environments that support adult and leadership development. Along these same lines, there are several "big ideas" at the core of constructive-developmental theory: that as adults we make meaning in different ways, that we need both support and challenges to grow, and that when working to support growth we need to calibrate the nature of our leadership to the developmental orientation of those with whom we are working. These ideas can help you support adult growth and leadership development in your own practice in ways that are suited to adults' particular needs.

Although in this chapter we will invest care and attention into understanding central principles of constructive-developmental theory, I want to make clear that I understand that this is only one lens for considering adult development. No single theory can explain all things related to leadership, life, and living. In fact, William Graves Perry Jr., who was a beloved developmental psychologist at Harvard University, reminded us that we need at least three theories to understand ourselves, other people, and the relationship between the two because each theory, framework, or lens has both strengths and limitations.[1] It is important to consider how one way of thinking might fit, or not fit, with others. Nevertheless, I have found, as have many of the inspiring educators I work with, that a developmental perspective offers a promising and growth-enhancing lens through which to view one's own practice and experience and the practice of others, and it also helps us better understand how we can shape learning opportunities that support growth. I hope that you find it of value too, and that you will accept my invitation to "rent" constructive-developmental theory as you consider how, if at all, you may want to integrate it into your own noble practice and efforts to support leadership development.

## Origins of the Theory

> *Man's search for meaning is the primary motivation in his life and not a "secondary rationalization" of instinctual drives.*
>
> —Victor Frankl

A constructive-developmental approach to understanding growth and how to support development has evolved from more than forty years of research.[2] Robert Kegan's constructive-developmental theory is one such lens in this family of theories. Kegan's theory enables us to understand how we, as human beings, *make meaning*. This concept of meaning making, the activity of it, its evolution over our lifespan, and the idea and hope that we can grow throughout our lives provided we have developmentally appropriate supports and challenges are all at the heart of this promising theory. In addition, Kegan's theory helps us to be mindful of what I call *developmental diversity*, in combination with the other forms of diversity (e.g., race, ethnicity, class, gender, religion, sexuality) that educators strive to address.

Kegan's theory, like others in the constructive-developmental family of theories, is a neo-Piagetian approach to understanding and supporting adult development. By this, I mean that Kegan and other theorists have adapted many of the central principles of Jean Piaget's theory of children's cognitive development to serve as the foundation for constructive-developmental theory. While Piaget's theory focused on children's cognitive development, Kegan's theory applies to development across the lifespan. It addresses the cognitive line of development *in addition to* the affective (emotional), interpersonal (the way the self relates to other people), and intrapersonal (the way the self relates to itself) lines of development. In other words, constructive-developmental theory focuses on a person as an active meaning maker with respect to cognitive, affective, interpersonal, and intrapersonal (internal) experiences and how these aspects of experience intersect. In so doing, this theory helps us to consider how to shape environments that can support development and enables us to better understand others and ourselves.

More specifically, this theory offers hopeful principles about how to support growth and leadership development in adults who have different ways of understanding and experiencing the world. It helps us to understand how aspiring and practicing leaders—like all adults, including ourselves—will make sense of issues related to adaptive challenges, authority, responsibility, ambiguity, complexity, and the kinds of holding environments that might best support their leadership development.

There is great value and hope, I think, in understanding that as adults, we are never "done," but rather can continue to learn and grow in how we think, feel, and relate to others and ourselves throughout our lives—provided that we are offered developmentally appropriate supports and challenges to help us do so. Ultimately, constructive-developmental theory is both helpful and hopeful, for it allows us to understand the types of holding environments and conditions that can facilitate growth, and it also reminds us that we are all capable of growing bigger selves.

See exhibit 1.1 to complete a brief exercise that will help you reflect on your current conceptions of growth and development in adulthood.

### Roots and Branches: Appreciating the Connections Between Meaning Making and Actions

As its focus, then, constructive-developmental theory emphasizes the qualitatively different ways in which we, as human beings, make sense of our own experiences and the world, and it emphasizes that all people can continue to grow, learn, and develop throughout their lives. In terms of leadership and leadership development, it also helps us to understand that we can intentionally and caringly create developmentally oriented learning

EXHIBIT 1.1

**PAUSE FOR REFLECTION**

### What Are Your Conceptions of Growth and Development in Adulthood?

I have learned that educators find it very helpful to have a space where they can focus on what supporting adult development means to them. In light of that, it might be useful to consider your own understanding of growth and development in adulthood. What are your conceptions of such growth? How do you think it happens? What conditions need to exist, from your perspective, to support adult growth? How would you depict it?

Over the years, the school leaders I've had the honor of working with have shared many of *their* ideas about adult growth and development, including the following:

- It involves self-work and reflection.
- It often takes a "back seat" to the growth and development of children.
- It may be impacted by age, race, gender, culture, or environment.
- It can be affected by one's level of comfort (or discomfort).
- "Sometimes you take ownership of adult development and seek it out, and sometimes it happens to you through unexpected life experiences."
- "We tend to be more patient with the growth and development of children than with adults; in [our] work with children, we think about their physical and cognitive development as they grow, but we don't take this into account [with adults]—we expect them to be fully developed people."
- "[As adults we grow] when we fall down. We try to look for [the] nearest chair and [when] we try it out, people then [start] suggesting other chairs. Eventually we start looking for better chairs."
- "If our conception of growth is linear, it sets us up for disappointment. It's the upward spiral that's the growth [that] gets us [from] one place to another."

opportunities that support the processes of growth for aspiring and practicing leaders, the adults in their care, and ourselves.

Relatedly, this theory can help us look beyond surface behaviors—of our colleagues, the adults around us, and ourselves—to our ways of making meaning of experiences since these inform our actions. When we look at a majestic tree, for example, it is easy to observe the outward changes in its leaves and branches. Yet it is the tree's underlying root system that impacts and directs its life. Likewise, an understanding of constructive-developmental theory can help us dig beneath the surface to understand the "roots" of our own and others' thinking, feeling, and being, and can consequently help us determine how to best support and challenge growth for individuals and groups.

An example of the power of this construct might be useful here. When working with and learning from leaders in various settings where I introduce ideas and practices for supporting development and strive to shape the learning environment to support growth, I usually begin by inviting participants to share their biggest hope for what they want to learn in the workshop or university class. One commonly expressed hope is "to help adults who are resistant to change be more accepting of it."

A developmental perspective can help us better understand and reframe resistant behaviors in others and in ourselves. As is the case with any leadership role, school leaders sometimes express frustration when confronting what they often refer to as "foot dragging," or resistance in the face of new initiatives or endeavors. While of course there are many reasons for resistance, and it can often signal a need to re-evaluate our own actions or expectations, it is important to consider whether or not resistance might be developmental in nature.

For example, when an educator says, "I will not," it is possible that what he or she really means and is trying to communicate is "I cannot." As educators around the world have shared, in classrooms we regularly recognize resistance as a sign of challenge or distress for children, yet we rarely give adults the same benefit of the doubt. We are wisely trained to differentiate our instruction and accommodate student needs, yet we often and simultaneously expect a one-size-fits-all model to work for adults' professional learning. Constructive-developmental theory helps us understand the complexities of adult development, of leading professional learning and working to build internal capacity. It illuminates the fact that adults with *different* ways of knowing will need *different* supports and challenges in order to grow and thrive generally and in professional learning environments more specifically. Reframing resistance from a developmental perspective can help us enhance the learning experiences we create for those we serve.

## Investigative Opportunity: Starting Where We Are

Before we dive deeper into the key principles of constructive-developmental theory, including the ways of knowing that are most common in adulthood, I would like to invite you to engage in an investigative opportunity. This is an activity that I often use to open my classes and workshops, as it involves considering the various kinds of supports different educators find helpful. In exhibit 1.2, you will find four vignettes, snapshots that capture four aspiring principals' thinking about and experiences of a longer-term

## EXHIBIT 1.2

### Investigative opportunity

*In the following vignettes, four aspiring principals respond to two questions about their experience in a longer-term professional learning seminar. This seminar had several session meetings over the course of one year.* **What do you notice about each aspiring leader's experiences of the learning initiative?**

**JAMIE** *What parts of the professional learning seminar, if any, were most helpful to you in your work? What parts, if any, were unhelpful?*

Well, I think what helped me the most was the instructor's feedback during each session. It just felt really helpful because she encouraged me and made me believe that I had it in me to be a good principal—that I could do a good job. Just feeling her confidence and support gave me such a boost, even now. I really needed that. I was actually starting to wonder if being a principal was the right thing for me, but this seminar series helped me to remember my own potential!

It's kind of like I want to make my instructor proud, and do some of the inspiring things she did in our sessions in my *own* leadership, but I also learned in the seminar that it's okay if I'm still learning. The instructor was really understanding in that way. I mean, whenever I answered a question in front of the group, which wasn't always easy for me, the instructor helped me by pointing out the parts I'd gotten right, even though sometimes she helped me to see other things I hadn't thought of yet, but in a nice way. She's a really great teacher in that way as well, so it helps to learn, and I trust her.

She makes me feel like at least I'm learning something from her and it's helping me. I feel like some instructors would have handled the seminar very differently, and I don't think it would have been as effective. For instance, if the instructor called me out on my mistakes in front of everyone and couldn't see me for who I really was, I don't think I would have learned as much. And I probably would feel like, "What am I doing here? Is this really a good place for me? Am I even good enough to be a principal?" I can't stand those kinds of cutthroat environments.

That being said, there were things about these seminars that weren't always easy. Like I said, it was really hard for me to speak up when we were talking as a whole group, because I was nervous to share my ideas and there were some strong personalities in the room, if you know what I mean. One time, one of my fellow seminar attendees jumped in when I was talking and just went on and on about how I was wrong, and I felt so bad and embarrassed. I don't like to feel like I'm disappointing people or messing up—but who does? Also, a lot of times during the seminars, the instructor would ask me, "Jamie, how do you think you did with those new strategies?" I'd prefer that she let me know what I'm doing well and where I need to improve. She knows. And sometimes when I ask her a question about what she thinks about something I did or something I don't quite understand, she asks me, "What do you think, Jamie?" I'm not sure how I'm supposed to answer. I mean, she's the instructor—I want her to help *me* get better. The other day, she asked me if I now saw myself as a leader since I accepted a new role at school. I wasn't really sure why she asked me this. I said, "Do you see me as a leader? If you see me as a leader, I see me as a leader."

*(continues)*

**EXHIBIT 1.2** (*continued*)

**CASEY**  *What parts of the professional learning seminar, if any, were most helpful to you in your work? What parts, if any, were unhelpful?*

This seminar series was *very* helpful to me. In particular, it was extremely helpful that the instructor provided very practical strategies for me to use when I become a principal. I feel like I have a clear plan now, and that makes a big difference. When we did activities, she always told me what I did right and what I did wrong, and that's what I need to get better. I really appreciate that kind of straightforward feedback, because it helps me to understand exactly what I need to do to be an effective leader and principal and to do this job right.

Sometimes in classes and workshops we spend too much time talking about our feelings or hypothetical situations, so it was refreshing to come away with some answers and not just more questions. Like, in my planning assignment, the instructor helped me to come up with a list of rules—kind of like a checklist—that I can use to guide my conversations with my teachers as a principal. You can believe I'll do my best to follow them when I find a principal position, too, because I know it will ultimately help the kids in my school learn and do very well. So that was great. I really liked that part of the seminar. Oh, and the instructor also helped me to compile a list of phrases you can say to someone who's arguing with you, like a parent or teacher. Sometimes people ask you for special favors when you're a principal, and I think it will help a lot to have the words ready to go if someone asks me to do something that makes me uncomfortable.

One other thing that was really helpful in the seminar was the way the instructor outlined everything she expected of us as we were going into activities. I like that. I don't like to get things wrong, so her clear directions and seeing everything written out on the poster paper helped a lot. I always knew exactly what I was supposed to be doing!

The one thing that confused me was that she made us do freewrites at the start and end of each seminar. She asked, "What do you think went well today? What could be improved? How do you *feel* about today's learnings? Just take a minute and write down what you're thinking." I don't think that was helpful. I already know what I'm thinking, so why do I need to write it down? Plus, she didn't even look at what I wrote. Why write it, I thought. She said, "It's just for you!" What would help me more is just hearing more about what I did correctly and what was wrong. That's why we're paying the big bucks, right? I need to learn how to be a principal and get it right. That's what would really help me even more.

**SKY**  *What parts of the professional learning seminar, if any, were most helpful to you in your work? What parts, if any, were unhelpful?*

I have to say that these seminars were really helpful. The instructor really encouraged us—and from what I've heard, this is the kind of experience she likes to create—to let us have space to think for ourselves. She really helped us to reflect deeply on the kind of leaders we'd like to become, and I feel like I was given the space I needed to sharpen my own vision. I feel like it was important to the instructor to let us find our own ways, and she really respected my opinion whenever I had something to share.

Now, I've had different experiences with professional development that didn't go nearly as well. You might even call them a waste of time if you were feeling ungenerous. But sometimes instructors just want you to do everything like

**EXHIBIT 1.2** (*continued*)

*they* would do it themselves, and they don't seem to notice or care about the expertise I bring, too. Now that's frustrating. I mean, that can work okay when I don't know what to do, like when we're starting a specific activity or assignment, but for questions about values and beliefs? I don't know.

Leadership is such a personal endeavor, I think, and I already have a lot of ideas about what works and what doesn't. I really appreciate that the instructor in this seminar made room for me to talk about my ideas with her and my classmates, and the whole process of conversation and debate was honestly invigorating! I know that the instructor thinks I am competent, and I think she sees a lot of potential in me as a future principal. That felt good—I won't lie. It makes me feel like I have an ally in my aspirations.

Of course, she has a lot of expert ideas, too, and I've learned a lot from what she's shared. In fact, I feel like the best parts of what we learned were just better ways of expressing and thinking about things that were already rolling around in the back of my mind. Now I have a kind of language and framework to use for talking and thinking about leadership and my goals for the future.

I guess the parts of the seminars that were hardest for me were when some of my classmates seemed to get frustrated when I critiqued what they were saying. I mean, it wasn't personal or anything, I was just trying to help the group move to the best way of thinking about things—so I'm not sure why they took it so badly. Sometimes people are oversensitive, I think, so that was hard at times. But, on the other hand, I liked that I could speak up when the instructor shared something that didn't quite work for me. I thought she'd want to know, and I thought it would help the group. Just because she's the instructor, I'm not going to stop questioning or letting her know what I think!

**LANE**   *What parts of the professional learning seminar, if any, were most helpful to you in your work? What parts, if any, were unhelpful?*

Honestly, I have to say that what was most helpful about these seminars was the way that the instructor was genuinely working to improve the overall quality of our leadership and of education in general. You could tell that she used to be a teacher and that she cares deeply about schools and kids. Even though she was officially the leader of the seminars, she invited all of us into conversation and honored the fact that we're in the position of learners right now. I really admired that.

Thinking about leadership together and learning from the kinds of complex conversations we were able to have in this seminar allows us to learn about each other and to deepen our relationships as colleagues and human beings. Given the complexity of all we will be facing as principals, it helps so much to engage in these kinds of explorations together to learn more about how different people hope and plan to approach this work.

While I sometimes challenged the instructor's ideas and practices—or invited her to explore some of the paradoxes within what she was sharing and the way leaders at higher levels in the system think about overarching systemic issues, especially around some of the current mandates and accountability measures in education today—I understand where she's coming from. Still, I think that if we could become a little more open to questions, explorations, and experiments that look beyond measurable outcomes, it might better serve students, teachers, and schools. Sometimes when I brought this up, people perceived it as a criticism that

*(continues)*

**EXHIBIT 1.2** (*continued*)

they needed to defend *against* rather than a perspective, an idea, a possibility that I was offering as a way to help us—I mean all of us in the seminar, including the instructor—to look beyond what we are currently doing and the situation we're in and toward a different way of envisioning the future, our future leadership and practice, in order to best serve students.

I do appreciate the fear, loss, ambiguity, difficulty, and uncertainty associated with letting go—and moving from the way we do things right now—and often the way we've always done them. I just think that if we could really come together and collectively explore these kinds of questions and possibilities more openly, more thoughtfully, and more critically with a true learning stance, we could all benefit tremendously, experiment more thoughtfully, improve our practice, and increase test scores. It's just this kind of collective and authentic inquiry into criticism and possibilities for change that would make our leadership—my colleagues' and mine—more effective, promising, and richer. It could also help our schools to become even more robust learning places for all of us, both now and in the future.

professional learning seminar (i.e., several sessions over the course of a year). As you read, please take note of anything that stands out for you about each respondent's experiences of the professional learning seminars. You may want to underline phrases or jot down notes in the margins. What do you notice about each person's experience of the seminars and its instructor? In what ways does each aspiring leader feel the seminar series is helpful? What do they categorize as not helpful?

After you learn more about constructive-developmental theory, I will invite you to revisit these vignettes toward the end of the chapter in the "Application Exercise" section in order to apply your new or more enhanced knowledge of constructive-developmental theory as it relates to helping us shape relationships and contexts for growth.

## Key Principles of Constructive-Developmental Theory

*We don't see things as they are; we see things as we are.*

—Anaïs Nin

As we gear up to explore the big ideas of this theory, it might be helpful to know that when most people, myself included, first learn about it, we naturally try to figure out "where we are" along the developmental continuum so that we can consider what kinds of supports and challenges might help us to grow. Many leaders also tend to think about the adults with whom they learn, work, live, and love when considering these ideas. In both cases, what's also important is to consider the ways in which you might provide both yourself and others the types of supports that will allow you to move forward and grow together.

That being said, when considering Kegan's constructive-developmental theory, which attends to the structure and the process of an individual's meaning-making system, it is important to understand that the theory is based on three big ideas. While many theories are constructive in nature, and others are developmental in nature, one of many special and important tenants of this theory is that it is *both constructive and developmental.* Accordingly, the three foundational ideas of constructive-developmental theory are:

- *Constructivism,* or the belief that we, as human beings, actively construct and make meaning of our lives, our experiences, and our realities with respect to cognitive, emotional, intrapersonal (the self's relationship to itself), and interpersonal (the self's relationship to others) pathways of development. In other words, constructivism has to do with how we take things in and put things together in order to make sense of them.
- *Developmentalism,* or the understanding that the way that we make meaning of our experiences and construct reality can become more complex and develop throughout our lives provided that we have holding environments that offer developmentally appropriate supports and challenges. In other words, given the right conditions, we can continue to grow throughout our lives.
- *The subject-object relationship,* which concerns the way in which we distinguish between those parts of ourselves that we are aware of and can manage and control (what we hold as "object") and those parts that we are not aware of, do not yet have a perspective on, cannot be responsible for, and are "run by" (or "subject to"). Put another way, this relationship centers on what we have in perspective (i.e., what we hold as "object" and can control) and what we are embedded in and do not have in perspective (i.e., what we are "subject to" and identified with, and cannot really control).

These three big ideas shed light on the developmental principles that can inform how we create environments supportive of growth and leadership development, because practicing and aspiring leaders, like all adults, will orient to learning, growing, leading, and living in qualitatively different ways. To help leaders grow, we must understand and embrace this at the outset.

*The Subject-Object Balance: Self and Other, Subject and Object*

Growth, according to Kegan, is a process of increasingly internalizing and differentiating between what constitutes self and what constitutes the other. In other words, it is a process of constant compromise or renegotiation of what is self and what is other.[3] Kegan refers to this as a renegotiation of the *subject-object balance*, upon which, he asserts, one's way of knowing pivots. The self "is" what it is subject to; *it is run by it*, and it cannot see it or be responsible for it. On the other hand, the self "has" what it can take as object; it can be responsible for it, manage it, and control it. Put simply, we cannot take a perspective on what we are *subject to* because we are *identified* with it; it is not separate from our selves. In contrast, that which we hold as *object*, we can reflect on, manage, and control. What we hold as object does not run us; *we have it*. As we grow in the developmental sense, we build greater internal capacities for perspective taking; our way of knowing—our system of organizing reality—also grows and becomes more complex. Eventually, we may grow from one way of knowing to the next. When this happens, the self is able to reflect on what it was earlier subject to and hold it as object. As you might imagine, increasing our internal capacities and developing greater understandings of self and other are key to effective leadership today. For example, if a leader is primarily concerned with being accepted and liked by valued others but needs to make an important decision that is in opposition to what those valued others want—and that, from his or her view, will threaten that relationship (put it at risk)—the leader will feel internally torn and try to make a decision that does not offend them. The same is true when a leader needs to offer critical feedback to valued others.

Another way to think about this is to realize that the theory centers on *perspective taking*. It is powerful, I believe, to remember that the *way* we look at things—our perspective—influences what we are able to see and how we understand *what* we see. For example, I was once on an evening flight on the Fourth of July. The pilot announced, "Those of you on the left side of the plane should look out the window. Macy's is having its fireworks display." I was fortunate enough to be on that side of the plane, so I looked out the window and realized immediately that I had never seen fireworks from above. Suddenly, I was looking down at colors and lights that I'd seen only from the ground. Needless to say, I had a qualitatively different experience. I saw them differently. This example, I would argue, is not unlike a leader growing a larger perspective when experiencing shifts in his or her way of knowing.

Of course, in leadership just as in airplanes, context has a very powerful influence on one's perspective and development. One's environment can either help or hinder development, so it is fundamentally important to consider how our schools, school systems, university classrooms, and personal leadership could better facilitate adult development by understanding how we create learning opportunities that nurture growth and development. In my experience, all people want to grow and learn, and when teachers and other adults in schools feel supported in this way, everyone benefits. I find it hopeful that growth can continue throughout our lives, provided that we benefit from developmentally appropriate supports and challenges, and that we find learning environments and relationships that will support this kind of internal capacity building.

### Ways of Knowing

A person's *way of knowing* is the lens through which all experience is filtered; it enables an individual to interpret life actively, as it dictates how learning, teaching, leading, and all life experiences will be taken in, managed, and understood. It is the window through which we see the world, others, and ourselves. Table 1.1 summarizes the essential characteristics of four different ways of knowing in adulthood, each of which will be described in more detail shortly.

Understanding that we, as adults, have qualitatively different ways of knowing can help us to shape learning environments that acknowledge and support this essential aspect of who we are. Typically, a person's way of knowing is stable and consistent for a period of time and reflects a coherent system of logic or meaning-making system. In other words, people generally demonstrate the same way of knowing within different roles and across different contexts (e.g., work, family, friendship) since our natural tendency as human beings is to strive for internal consistency and coherence of self across contexts and relationships. Over time, however, as we grow and learn from appropriate supports and challenges, our way of knowing can evolve from a less complex system into a new, more complex meaning-making schema. As we grow as adults and leaders, we gradually begin to demonstrate capacities associated with more complex ways of knowing.

However, I want to share a few very important things about this point and the theory in general. First, research has shown that under rare conditions (e.g., psychological or physical abuse), development can be uneven, and a person can make meaning with a different way of knowing in one domain of life.[4] There are costs associated with this kind of unevenness.

**TABLE 1.1**

Most common ways of knowing in adulthood according to Kegan's constructive-developmental theory

| Way of knowing[1] | Orientation of self | Underlying thought structure[2] | Defining orientation of self | Preoccupying concerns | Guiding questions for self |
|---|---|---|---|---|---|
| Instrumental/ Imperial | Rule-oriented self | S: One's own needs, interests, wishes, and desires (usually concrete needs).<br><br>O: One's impulses and perceptions (views). | Orients to self-interests, purposes, and concrete needs. | • Depends on following the rules.<br>• Wants to do things the "right" way; behave in the "right way."<br>• Is most concerned with concrete consequences.<br>• Decisions are based on what the self will acquire and on following the rules.<br>• Other people are experienced as either helpers or obstacles to meeting one's own concrete needs.<br>• Person does not yet have the capacity for abstract thinking in the psychological sense or for generalizing from one context to another. | • "Will I get punished?"<br>• "How can I avoid getting caught if I do something wrong?"<br>• "How can I get the things I want and need?<br>• "What's in it for me?" |
| Socializing/ Interpersonal | Other-focused self | S: The interpersonal (relational), mutuality (felt by each; shared).<br><br>O: Needs, interests, desire, and wishes. | Orients to valued others' (external authorities' or loved ones') expectations, values, and opinions about the self and his or her work and thinking. | • Depends on external authority for values and judgments about self.<br>• Acceptance, approval from important others, and affiliation are of primary importance.<br>• Self is defined by important others' judgments.<br>• Self orients to inner states.<br>• Self feels responsible for others' feelings and holds others responsible for own feelings. | • "Will you (valued other/ authority) still like/love/ value me?"<br>• "Will you (valued other/ authority) approve of me?"<br>• "Will you (valued other/ authority) still think I am a good person?" |

| Way of knowing[1] | Orientation of self | Underlying thought structure[2] | Defining orientation of self | Preoccupying concerns | Guiding questions for self |
|---|---|---|---|---|---|
| Self-authoring/ Institutional | Reflective self | S: Authorship, one's internal government, identity, psychic administration, ideology (system of beliefs).<br><br>O: The interpersonal, mutuality. | Orients to self's values (internal authority) and the smooth running of one's own internal system. | • Self generates and replies to one's own internal values and standards.<br>• Criticism is evaluated according to internal standards.<br>• Ultimate concern is with one's own competence and performance.<br>• Self can balance contradictory feelings simultaneously.<br>• Conflict is viewed as a natural part of life, work, and leadership and enhances one's own and others' perspectives to achieve larger organizational and systemic goals. | • "Am I maintaining my own personal integrity, achieving my goals, and being guided by my ideals and values?"<br>• "Am I competent?"<br>• "Am I living, working, and loving to the best of my ability and potential?" |
| Self-transforming/ Interindividual | Interconnecting self | S: Interindividuality, interpenetrability of self-systems.<br><br>O: Authorship, identity, self government, psychic administration, ideology (system of beliefs). | Orients to multiple self-systems; open to learning from other people; wants to grow and improve different aspects of self—engages constantly in process of discernment about self. | • Is committed to self-exploration.<br>• Engaging with conflict is an opportunity to let others inform and shape thinking.<br>• Conflict is viewed as natural to life and enhances thinking.<br>• Can own one's part in conflict and wants to explore it with others.<br>• Is able to understand and manage tremendous complexity.<br>• Is substantively less invested in own identity and more open to others' perspectives.<br>• Constantly judges and questions how self-system works and seeks to improve it. | • "How can other people's thinking help me to enhance my own?"<br>• "How can I seek out information and opinions from others to help me modify my own ways of understanding?" |

*Source:* Adapted from Drago-Severson, 2009.

[1] My terms for the ways of knowing are listed first, followed by the term used by Kegan (1982).

[2] S refers to "subject," what a person is identified with and run by (cannot take a perspective on or control); O refers to "object," what a person can reflect on, be responsible for, and take perspective on.

Second, context matters. In some contexts, conditions are ripe for supporting us, in which case we can bring our biggest selves to them. Put more simply, some contexts enable us to not only bring our most complex selves, but also to demonstrate emerging developmental capacities that are not yet fully developed in us.

Let's consider an example that illuminates the importance of context. During college, when I was back home in the Bronx for summer vacation, I saved up enough money from working in several jobs to purchase a car. I had always wanted a Volkswagen Beetle. One morning, two of my brothers, John and Paul, told me that they'd found one in "good condition" out on Long Island that was within my price range. I was elated and bought the car. The problem was that it was a stick shift, and I knew only how to drive an automatic.

One rainy morning soon after, my mom woke me up and offered to help me learn to drive my car. "Of course!" I exclaimed. I had seen my brother operate stick-shift gears over the years, so I had a sense of the rhythm and motion of driving this kind of car. But I had never actually done it myself. Still, I *had seen others driving stick shifts* and had an image of what that looked like in mind. My mom drove the car to a nearby parking lot next to a set of baseball fields. Since it was drizzling, no one was there. The space was flat and empty, so it felt perfect to me.

My mom started by showing me what she was doing as she shifted gears and talked me through the process. After a while, it was my turn. While the ride was a little jolting at first, and I stalled out several times, soon I had the hang of it. I could start the car, drive for a while, and stop and go without stalling. What a feeling that was! I still remember.

A few days later, I got the courage to drive my car, rather than ride my bike, to my job at my father's pediatric office in another part of the Bronx. To get there, I needed to drive up a very steep road (seventy-degree angle) with not one, but three, traffic lights. I made it smoothly through the first two green lights, glad that I didn't have to test my new skills on such a steep and busy slope, and I remember praying that I would also make it through the third light at the top of the hill, the steepest part. When *of course* the light turned red at the top of that very busy street, my stomach sank in fear that I wouldn't be able to get my car moving again without rolling backward down the hill.

Well, under these stressful conditions, with trucks and buses surrounding me, horns beeping, and folks needing me to move, I froze. The capacity I could demonstrate in the parking lot was not well enough developed for me to exercise it at the red light. *The context mattered.* I eventually maneuvered my way out of the situation (with less grace and ease than I would have liked), but I share this story because it reminds us that context does matter. In some contexts—for leaders just as drivers—we thrive and can demonstrate the capacities we have and those we are developing. In others, it's more difficult. This story also highlights the importance of the conditions we seek to create in terms of shaping learning environments for others. What kinds of conditions serve to support adult and leadership development? How can we best create the conditions that will allow us to support those in our care, and their emerging capacities? I hope this chapter and book offer a useful map to one approach for this important work.

Another very important point to remember about constructive-developmental theory is that although, like other stage theories, it is hierarchical in nature, that does not mean that one way of knowing is necessarily better than another, unless the implicit and explicit demands of the environment, including our work-related responsibilities, call for higher-level capacities than we currently have. You may find it helpful to consider this in terms of the compatibility—what I call *goodness of fit*—between our way of knowing (our developmental capacities, which direct our competencies and how we demonstrate them) and the implicit and explicit demands or expectations placed on us in our work and personal life. Importantly, scholar David McCallum, like others, has found that in periods of extreme stress, some adults tend to "fall back," or temporarily demonstrate less complex ways of knowing. This kind of temporary falling back has also been noted in workplaces.[5]

Last, and related to the concept of goodness of fit, it is essential to note that certain kinds of positions—including leadership posts—do require the ability to demonstrate more complex developmental capacities spontaneously. For example, leaders must be able to understand other adults' points of view while simultaneously holding onto their own perspectives.[6] They must, in other words, be able to listen to, learn from, and take in feedback from valued others without being overwhelmed by it, and they must be willing, when necessary and appropriate, to take a stand for their visions and beliefs.

Using this theory as a guide to shaping more robust learning environments and leadership development opportunities can help us to better understand our own and other people's developmental strengths and limitations—what I call *growing edges*—and can also help adults and leaders grow into the complex capacities they need to do their work even better. We'll revisit the concepts of goodness of fit and growing edges later in this chapter, but now we'll explore the four ways of knowing common in adulthood.

***The instrumental way of knowing*** Adults who make meaning with an instrumental way of knowing have what I often describe as a "rule-bound self." Instrumental knowers orient toward "the rules," as the rules help them understand how to carry out their responsibilities in the "right" way, whether working as a leader, solving problems with colleagues on teams, or helping students with homework. Leaders who make meaning in this way have an "I will do to you what you do to me" orientation.

An instrumental knower is subject to and defined by—or run by—his or her own concrete needs, desires, and purposes. In other words, an instrumental knower cannot take a perspective on his or her needs, wishes, desires, and interests. However, the person has the developmental capacity to control, manage, take a perspective on, and be responsible for impulses since they can be held as object. While instrumental knowers understand that other people have feelings, needs, preferences, and beliefs, they do not yet have the internal capacity to fully integrate others' perspectives into their own. For this reason, instrumental knowers often experience other people as either helpers or obstacles to getting their own concrete needs met. In addition, these adults lack the internal capacity for abstract psychological thinking or making generalizations from one context to another. People with this way of knowing organize, interpret, and make sense of their experiences through the following lenses:

- Attributes, events, and sequences (I am a good leader; I like football)
- Observable actions and behaviors (good employees and good leaders follow rules and policies, work hard, do things the "right" way, act in the "right" way, set the "right" goals, and if they accomplish goals they will get some concrete reward)
- One's own point of view, needs, interests, and preferences (tell me exactly what I need to do to achieve my goals; if I do this in my job, I will have a better chance of getting a raise or a promotion; how can I get the things I want and need and if I do something wrong, how can I avoid being punished?)

While adults with this way of knowing will orient toward having their own concrete needs and goals met, they are not narcissistic and can be intelligent, kindhearted, and service-oriented.[7] It is important to understand that instrumental knowers demonstrate their competencies and care in very concrete ways and feel most comfortable when authorities (e.g., coaches, supervisors) offer explicit support, step-by-step directions, and directives. In terms of working to offer developmental challenges (stretching) to help leaders with this way of knowing grow, it can be powerful to offer them opportunities to learn about and consider multiple perspectives that help them to stretch their thinking over time. Inviting an instrumental knower to participate in the pillar practice of teaming, for example, is both a developmental support and challenge that can, over time, facilitate growth. More specifically, it is especially important to set ground rules (norms) as a support for instrumental knowers working on a team. Having boundaries around what the team will discuss, limiting how long meetings will last, and setting concrete goals is very important for the team to feel safe and productive, and establishes a good holding environment for growing because an instrumental knower values and needs rules.

Also, when inviting an instrumental knower to take on a new leadership role (another pillar practice), it is important to consider what *kinds* of roles might offer developmentally appropriate supports and challenges. Table 1.2 presents different kinds of supports and developmental challenges that can be infused into the four pillar practices (i.e., teaming, inviting adults to assume leadership roles, collegial inquiry, and mentoring/developmental coaching) so that they can serve as robust holding environments for adults with this way of knowing.

***The socializing way of knowing***  Leaders who make meaning primarily with a socializing way of knowing have grown to develop greater internal capacities for reflection and perspective taking. In fact, socializing knowers have the internal capacity to think abstractly in the psychological sense (i.e., they can think about their own thinking). In addition, these leaders can reflect on their own and other people's behaviors.

Socializing knowers have developed the internal capacity to make generalizations from one context to another. For example, a leader can transfer learnings from one context (e.g., working with a leadership cabinet) to another (e.g., working with the school council). Also, they have the developmental capacity to identify with and internalize the feelings of others (i.e., they are no longer run by their own desires and needs). However, they are not yet able to hold their relationships as object, and are consequently run by them. In other words, leaders with this way of knowing have a very difficult time disagreeing with those they value and with managing conflict. It tears them apart, since they *need* others' approval in order to cohere internally. They cannot reflect on their relationships and prioritize them since they are identified with and subject to their relationships with those who are most important to them (e.g., a

**TABLE 1.2**

**Supports and challenges that can be infused into the pillar practices to promote growth in adults with different ways of knowing**

| Pillar practice[1] | Instrumental knowers | Socializing knowers | Self-authoring knowers | Self-transforming knowers |
|---|---|---|---|---|
| **Teaming**<br>Examples:<br>• PLCs (professional learning communities)<br>• Grade-level teams<br>• Instructional leadership teams<br>• Leadership cabinets | **Supports:**<br>• Establish clear and explicit guidelines and norms for engaging in dialogue.<br>• Set concrete goals.<br>• Provide step-by-step procedures and deliverable dates.<br><br>**Challenges (stretching):**<br>• Offer opportunities for consideration of multiple perspectives.<br>• Invite engagement in tasks requiring abstract thinking.<br>• Supply multiple options as solutions rather than one "right" way. | **Supports:**<br>• Reinforce the value of contributions and perspectives.<br>• Offer opportunities to share in pairs or small groups.<br>• Provide guidance from experts or authority figures.<br><br>**Challenges (stretching):**<br>• Encourage voicing of own ideas and perspectives.<br>• Invite knower into lead role, broadening perspective and generating value in supportive context.<br>• Frame conflict as part of relationships and teamwork. | **Supports:**<br>• Offer opportunities for creating and designing options and proposals that allow for demonstrations of expertise and competencies.<br>• Provide space to analyze or critique presented proposals.<br>• Promote dialogue to explore the merits and complexity of team goals.<br><br>**Challenges (stretching):**<br>• Encourage critique of one's own value and belief system and the recognition of self as process driven.<br>• Pose questions about potential value of conflicting or opposing ideas and ideologies.<br>• Emphasize the socio-emotional dimensions of teamwork. | **Supports:**<br>• Offer opportunities for deep inquiry and self-expression.<br>• Collaborate with diverse perspectives.<br>• Promote dynamic and adaptive team structures.<br><br>**Challenges (stretching):**<br>• Expose learner to multiple points of view.<br>• Challenge learner to cope with and manage hierarchy.<br>• Encourage learner to identify beyond the team with authorities. |

| Pillar practice[1] | Instrumental knowers | Socializing knowers | Self-authoring knowers | Self-transforming knowers |
|---|---|---|---|---|
| **Collegial inquiry**<br><br>Examples:<br><br>• Faculty meetings<br>• Conflict resolution<br>• Walkthroughs | **Supports:**<br>• Establish concrete goals, rationale for needs, and examples of practice.<br>• Provide detailed instructions, advice, skill expectations, and information.<br>• Offer clear steps for engaging in dialogue.<br>• Frame colleagues as resources.<br><br>**Challenges (stretching):**<br>• Encourage dialogue and exploration of multiple perspectives.<br>• Create opportunities for generalization and transferability of broad, abstract ideas.<br>• Engage knowers in situations and problem solving requiring abstract thinking. | **Supports:**<br>• Establish group norms.<br>• Offer opportunities to voice and explore perspectives in pairs or small groups before sharing with larger groups or supervisors.<br>• Provide opportunities to meet the expectations of valued others.<br>• Ensure acceptance of colleagues to support risk taking.<br><br>**Challenges (stretching):**<br>• Support the voicing of knower's own perspective as expert and leader, regardless of judgment and approval of others.<br>• Encourage conflict tolerance and the development of individual beliefs and values. | **Supports:**<br>• Offer opportunities for demonstrating expertise and competencies and for critiquing proposals, designs, and initiatives.<br>• Create spaces for dialogue, conflict engagement, and sharing of perspectives.<br>• Emphasize becoming more competent and extending own options to achieve self-determined goals.<br><br>**Challenges (stretching):**<br>• Emphasize the importance of tolerance and openness during debate.<br>• Encourage sincere consideration of opposing viewpoints.<br>• Challenge knower to question own belief system. | **Supports:**<br>• Provide clear rationale for engaging in inquiry.<br>• Articulate a shared sense of strategic vision.<br>• Provide ample freedom and resources.<br>• Include conflict in the collegial inquiry context.<br><br>**Challenges (stretching):**<br>• Challenge this knower to remain committed when the sense of purpose is unclear.<br>• Challenge learner not to take over and rush the process.<br>• Coach learner to be sensitive to the feelings of those who do not have the same capacity (e.g., for conflict). |

*(continues)*

**TABLE 1.2** (*continued*)

| Pillar practice[1] | Instrumental knowers | Socializing knowers | Self-authoring knowers | Self-transforming knowers |
|---|---|---|---|---|
| **Mentoring**<br>Examples:<br>• Mentoring new faculty<br>• Mentoring new principals<br>• Coaching aspiring principals<br>• Mentoring assistant principals and teacher leaders<br>• Coaching teachers (e.g., math and/or literary)<br>• Instructional coaching | **Supports:**<br>• Clearly state purposes and objectives for mentoring relationship.<br>• Offer expertise and advice as well as best practices.<br>• Share reasoning behind perspectives.<br><br>**Challenges (stretching):**<br>• Encourage movement beyond "correct" solutions.<br>• Facilitate abstract discussion and consideration of others' needs/perspectives. | **Supports:**<br>• Explicitly acknowledge and confirm beliefs and perspectives.<br>• Suggest "best" solutions to complex problems.<br>• Ensure mentee feels known, cared for, and accepted as a person.<br><br>**Challenges (stretching):**<br>• Encourage mentee to recognize and establish own values and standards, and to tolerate conflict without feeling threatened.<br>• Encourage mentee to examine held loyalties and to separate feelings from the feelings of others. | **Supports:**<br>• Create space to demonstrate own competencies, critique own work, and move forward with self-determined goals.<br>• Offer opportunities to learn about diverse perspectives and points of view.<br>• Accept and express approval of mentee's independence and self-governing capabilities.<br><br>**Challenges (stretching):**<br>• Engage in dialogue and offer additional goals, viewpoints, and problem-solving alternatives for contemplation.<br>• Challenge mentee to let go of investment in own understanding and ideology. | **Supports:**<br>• Create space within relationship to explore own creativity and to express it openly.<br>• Encourage experimentation.<br>• Promote a peerlike experience based on mutual sharing.<br><br>**Challenges (stretching):**<br>• Support knowers through their own intense and/or disorienting feelings and emotions.<br>• Offer support in learner's becoming more "permeable" to the feedback of others.<br>• Challenge mentee to appreciate importance of learning from others, regardless of others' ways of knowing. |

| Pillar practice[1] | Instrumental knowers | Socializing knowers | Self-authoring knowers | Self-transforming knowers |
|---|---|---|---|---|
| **Providing leadership roles**<br><br>Examples:<br><br>• Faculty-led staff developments<br>• Principal for a Day<br>• Conference presentations<br>• Leadership in teams<br>• Teacher-leader of grade level or vertical team | **Supports:**<br>• Offer concrete goals and rewards, share rationale behind actions, and offer concrete feedback.<br>• Provide guidance in terms of due dates, rules, deliverables and process.<br>• Model leadership and explicitly make thinking transparent.<br><br>**Challenges (stretching):**<br>• Encourage consideration of alternative ways to achieve goals (beyond the "right" way) and others' perspectives.<br>• Challenge knower to build confidence and trust in self-worth.<br>• Provide opportunities for abstract thinking and the management of less concrete goals. | **Supports:**<br>• Explicitly acknowledge contributions.<br>• Validate and recognize risk taking and achievements.<br>• Provide opportunities to share perspectives with authority figures before sharing with those being led.<br><br>**Challenges (stretching):**<br>• Encourage individual to turn toward self for generating values, goals, and judgment.<br>• Introduce conflict and support as mentee works through it.<br>• Challenge knower to autonomously create procedures and standards for evaluating own leadership. | **Supports:**<br>• Offer opportunities to demonstrate competencies, design initiatives, learn about diverse points of view, and contribute to developing mission and/or vision.<br>• Scaffold decision making through dialogue.<br>• Make time for discussion of complexities and generation of personal goals.<br><br>**Challenges (stretching):**<br>• Utilize questioning to encourage knower to conceive of the potential value and connection between perspectives, alternative proposals, and problem-solving strategies in direct opposition to knower's own.<br>• Challenge knower to recognize and develop awareness of the relative and created nature of own leadership goals and ideas. | **Supports:**<br>• Promote a culture of collegiality within the team, group, or organization.<br>• Provide room to use imagination to explore new ideas and/or possibilities.<br><br>**Challenges (stretching):**<br>• Challenge knower to take authority when appropriate, even when knower might be unsure about doing so.<br>• Assist as knower navigates complex responsibilities that require quick decisions.<br>• Provide guidance on strategies for delegating responsibility. |

*Source:* Adapted from Drago-Severson, 2009.

[1] This table includes only a limited number of examples of pillar practice implementation. Please refer to the text for more examples.

coach, a supervisor, a principal) or to their closely held ideas (e.g., religious or political ideologies, societal expectations).

For this reason, I refer to adults with this way of knowing as having a self that is *co-constructed*. Or, as one school principal put it after learning about this way of knowing, "it's like 'you are my mirror' if a person is a socializing knower." Another school principal, who participated in a series of workshops with all educators in her district last year, approached me privately after we had discussed the different ways of knowing during our second gathering. She said, "I remember when I first became a principal and I was a socializing knower. I didn't know what to do. Every night I would go home and cry to my husband because I wasn't sure I could continue in this role. It was so painful to have people mad, angry, and upset with me."

As this heartfelt example illustrates, the expectations of valued authorities and important others *run* or *compose* an adult who has this way of knowing. In fact, those expectations and judgments become a socializing knower's own expectations and judgments for self. In other words, if I am a socializing knower, and you, as my principal or supervisor or treasured loved one, think I am doing a good job in my leadership or teaching, then I think the same about myself. Conversely, negative judgments and evaluations can feel devastating to adults who make meaning in this way. Interpersonal conflict at work, at home, or in any cherished relationship is experienced as a threat to the self's very essence. Thus, socializing knowers avoid conflict because it is a risk to the relationship and to the coherence of their very selves. As you might imagine, in terms of leadership preparation, it is important to help aspiring or practicing leaders who make meaning primarily with this way of knowing grow to understand that conflict can be productive and essential—if not inevitable—when working to lead and support other adults or a school community.

As table 1.2 indicates, there are ways to support the growth of socializing knowers and to help them build internal capacity over time. For example, to support these adults' growth, you might pose questions in goal setting meetings and/or mentoring relationships to help them develop, voice, and draw upon more of their own thinking. This will encourage these leaders to develop their own internal authority rather than adopting others' solutions and ideas, which will support their growth over time.

Considering appropriate developmental supports and challenges is also important when inviting a socializing knower to participate in a leadership role—say, as a team leader. Who, for example, might be able to think out loud with the new leader about the experience of the role? Its complexities? How he or she is feeling about it? This dialogue, as you know, can support growth and leadership development. You'll find additional ideas for customizing the four pillar practices to support and challenge adults with a socializing way of knowing in table 1.2 and throughout this book.

***The self-authoring way of knowing***   Adults who make meaning primarily with a self-authoring way of knowing have developed the internal capacity to have a perspective on their relationships and society's expectations. In other words, they are no longer run by or subject to these. Instead, they have the capacity to hold out, consider, prioritize, and reflect on external perspectives, and decide for themselves what to do or believe. Their own internally generated values and standards guide them, their thinking, their actions, and their being in the world. I consider these knowers as having a *reflective self* because they have grown from being *composed of*, or *made up by*, their relationships to being able to regulate and prioritize them. Self-authoring knowers can control their feelings, actions, and emotions and are able to discuss their internal states.

Adults with this way of knowing can identify with abstract values, principles, and long-term purposes. For them, competence, achievement, and responsibility are vital concerns. Self-authoring knowers take responsibility for their values and philosophy, and can hold opposing feelings simultaneously without feeling threatened or torn apart by them. However, self-authoring knowers are limited by—in other words, vulnerable around—critiquing their self-system. For example, they do not have the internal capacity to take perspective on their own value system and autonomy. Demonstrating competency and achieving personal goals, in accordance with their own internal standards, is of utmost importance to them. For them, it is a challenge to consider perspectives that conflict, in diametrically opposing ways, with their own.

Put another way, leaders with this way of knowing cannot take perspective on their self-system because it is embedded in their ideals and principles. Consider, for example, a leader who cannot fully take in feedback because he or she is so firmly entrenched in a particular understanding, value, or commitment. While this firmness of vision can be a leadership strength, it can also blind self-authoring leaders to new and promising possibilities. Accordingly, encouraging leaders with this way of knowing to reflect on and consider alternatives can support their growth and development, and help them open up to opposing viewpoints over time.

As noted previously, table 1.2 presents different kinds of supports and developmental challenges that can be infused into the pillar practices so that they can serve as robust holding environments for adults with this way of knowing. Offering these supports and challenges can help self-authoring knowers grow to better manage the challenges and demands of working, leading, teaching, and living.

*The self-transforming way of knowing* Given the complexity and ambiguity of contemporary life, research suggests that an increasing number of adults are growing to make meaning beyond the self-authoring way of knowing. Adults with a self-transforming way of knowing, for instance, have the developmental capacity to take perspective on their self-systems and identities, and can hold out their own beliefs and values for critique in order to challenge themselves and grow. Moreover, these leaders recognize that their own perspectives and beings are incomplete without others, so in ways different than socializing knowers, they seek out others' ideas and close companionship. Rather than define identity, however, as they do for socializing knowers, relationships and interconnectedness serve as important *aims* for self-transforming adults. In the same way, self-transforming knowers orient to conflict or extremes in position by exploring the relationships between perspectives, and can enjoy the freedom to express the self and let others do the same.

Adults who have grown to make meaning with a self-transforming way of knowing have the developmental capacity to take perspective on—and they have a meta-awareness of—their self-authorship, their identity, and their ideology. For self-transforming knowers, the self-system is constantly available; they are constantly discerning it, judging it, and working to grow and enhance it. Adults who make meaning in this way have a deep appreciation and lively passion for questioning how one's self-system works. They have the capacity and deep desire to explore and examine issues from multiple points of view and, most important, to work to understand how seemingly opposing perspectives overlap. They thrive on this.

Another core characteristic of self-transforming knowers is that they orient to contradiction, inconsistency, and paradox in ways that no longer threaten their self-system. These become recognizable and appreciated by the self-transforming knower. They are conversant with the relationship between what might seem like diametrically opposing perspectives and self-systems instead of feeling the need to choose between them. Rather than prioritizing the protection of their self-system, self-transforming knowers are open to learning from relationships *between* self-systems. In addition, self-transforming knowers experience a new sense of freedom to express the self and let others be themselves. And they yearn to understand their role in conflict.

In comparison, self-authoring knowers might work to hold oh-so-tightly to their perspectives and the smooth running of their own internal systems that they may be more oriented toward changing others than themselves. Self-transforming knowers, on the other hand, want deeply to be changed by others; they thirst for this kind of growth. They have sophisticated strategic capacities. For them, decisions are based on the common good for schools and families (a generational perspective), society, and within societal organizations.

As table 1.1 shows, self-transforming knowers make sense of the self as emerging and growing constantly. They are committed to self-exploration and growth. They experience other points of view as opportunities to shape their own thinking and grow from them. Self-transforming knowers thrive on involvement with multiple, diverse communities in which they can learn from diverse perspectives. To best support these leaders' growth, you might find it helpful to offer the supports and developmental challenges listed in table 1.2.

## Growth as a Process: Remembering Goodness of Fit

Now that we've explored the four ways of knowing with which adults make meaning, it is important to remember that development is different than intelligence (as measured by IQ), and to understand that individuals with any way of knowing can be caring, but may express and feel care in different ways depending on how they make meaning of their experiences. As mentioned earlier, it is likewise important to note that "higher" in the constructive-developmental hierarchy isn't necessarily better. What "counts" in developmental terms is the *goodness of fit*, or the match between our capacities and the demands of our professional and personal environments. That being said, research suggests that leadership today requires at least some self-authoring qualities, and attending to adult development in our professional learning and leadership can help build such capacity within our schools, school systems, and selves over time.

It is also important to understand that surface behaviors are not always indicative of our primary way of knowing. When entering a new workplace, for instance, a teacher might concern herself primarily with the rules, policies, and procedures of that particular environment, which is a very instrumental learning orientation but *different from having an instrumental way of knowing*. Needing to understand these fundamental expectations does not necessarily indicate that this teacher makes meaning with an instrumental way of knowing. It is logical and necessary for us to orient ourselves to a new environment, just as it is natural to want to be liked. We have all been in situations that demand certain behaviors—like playing nice with a challenging boss or following a directive that we may not agree with—but when we consciously understand these behavioral decisions and consciously choose them, we are no longer run by them.

### The Significance of Ways of Knowing to Leadership Development and Practice

Ways of knowing are important because they help us understand that adults who make meaning differently also experience their work and colleagues differently. They also help us understand that we must offer various kinds of supports and challenges in order to support the development (internal capacity building) of aspiring and practicing leaders. Doing so will help leaders to manage the complexity and ambiguity inherent in leading today, and to be better able to handle and grow from conflict and from giving and receiving feedback.

As you may already suspect, others' ways of knowing will influence what they expect of and need from you as a leader, facilitator, mentor, and colleague. Your understanding of ways of knowing will enable you to offer the kinds of supports and challenges that will help others to grow and that will create the most productive and positive working and learning environments.

## USING CONSTRUCTIVE-DEVELOPMENTAL THEORY TO SHAPE HOLDING ENVIRONMENTS

*You never know what it feels like to feel and be well held until you feel it.*

—Aspiring school principal

As mentioned in the introduction, the term *holding environment* was originally coined by D. W. Winnicott in 1965 to shed light on the qualitatively different types of care, or "holding," an infant needs for healthy development in early life.[8] Such environments, according to Winnicott, need to be responsive to the child's changing needs as he or she grows out of infancy. For instance, a baby who is learning to walk needs a lot of spotting and support to take those first steps. Gradually, however, as the child grows more confident and capable, parents or caretakers need to step back and allow the child to walk independently. After this milestone is reached, support *looks and feels different for both the child and the adult*. Importantly, Robert Kegan extended this truth to a human being's entire lifespan.[9] As you know, Kegan's theory centers on creating the conditions to foster adult growth throughout the lifespan by offering supports and challenges that are developmentally appropriate to the *different ways in which we each make sense of our experiences* (i.e., ways of knowing). Similar to the conditions provided to facilitate a child's growth, holding environments, as Kegan describes them, offer developmentally appropriate supports and challenges to *adults* who make sense of their experiences in different ways and have unique developmental needs and preferences.

To be most effective, a holding environment—which can form within a relationship, a series of relationships, an organization, a team, a family, or almost any group—must serve three important functions. First, it must "hold well" by recognizing and confirming who a person is and meeting that person where he or she is (in terms of meaning making and developmental needs) without urgently pushing for change. In other words, this space must accept individuals for who they are and how they are making meaning. This is most important. Second, and only when a person is ready, it must also "let go" in order to challenge, stretch, or encourage that person to grow beyond his or her current meaning-making system. Facilitating this "letting go" is like standing at the edges of someone's thinking and feeling, and gently stretching. Third, robust holding environments must remain in place as the person grows into new ways of knowing, so that relationships can be re-formed in supportive and affirmative ways.[10]

Notably, the most effective holding environments provide individuals with high support and high challenge in order to encourage growth. However, as we will learn in more detail in the following sections and throughout this book, effective support and challenge will mean different things for different individuals. For example, a supervisory relationship that feels supportive and empowering to one teacher, because of the scope and depth of feedback provided by the supervisor, might feel overwhelming and uncomfortable to another. Like good teaching and learning relationships, holding environments that support adult growth require a keen awareness of and appreciation for individual needs and differences, and a willingness to honor and see those in our care for who they are and who they are becoming.

While my work in creating professional learning environments that support growth incorporates some of these ideas, as well as the fundamental principles of Kegan's theory, I extend Kegan's work by focusing on how to simultaneously create these supportive environments for individuals *and groups* in a variety of professional learning contexts, K–12 schools, university leadership preparation programs and classrooms, and professional learning opportunities offered in schools and school districts. Very intentionally, I work to create holding environments in my work with educators, and I invite adults to experience the very practices and processes that shape these growth-enhancing environments while they are learning about them so that they can nurture similar contexts for those in their care.

I consider a holding environment, in this larger sense, to be a context in which adults feel well held psychologically, supported and challenged developmentally, understood in terms of how they make sense of their work and the world, and accepted and honored for who they are. In other words, these are learning contexts in which adults feel known, cared for, listened to, and safe, and in which they are met "where they are" and feel comfortable taking the risks needed to grow. As you will see, professional learning initiatives that support growth are made up of different kinds of holding environments—for individuals and groups—and they also serve in and of themselves as larger, encompassing holding environments that are greater than the sum of their parts. At both the micro and macro levels, the kinds of learning environments presented in my new model are both filled with and created by the elements and conditions that support adult development, which you will learn about in greater detail in the chapters that follow. In these environments, whether they are professional learning experiences created within schools or districts, or university leadership preparation programs and classrooms, adults learn about *and* experience the conditions needed for supporting their growth and leadership development.

## Real-World Examples: Feeling Well Held as Learning, Growing Leaders

I have learned through my experiences and research that once adults have had the kinds of powerful experiences I've described, they can better shape effective learning environments for other adults in their care, as well as themselves. (You will learn more about caring for self-development in chapter 6.) In other words, when you, as a leader or facilitator, create the conditions needed for developmental growth, the participants in your workshop or seminar will be better able to shape similar contexts for others and for themselves, an ability that is vital in today's complex educational world. As I've learned from my two decades of experience learning from practitioners, and as I emphasized in the introduction, supporting adult development *is* the task of leadership. Leadership development *is* adult development. This kind of learning and growth can help us to build our internal capacities and assist in helping others grow in order to better manage the complex challenges we collectively face today. Remember from the introduction that by *internal capacities*, I mean increases in our cognitive, affective (emotional), intrapersonal (self to self), and interpersonal (self to other) abilities that enable us to better mange the complexities of leading, teaching, learning, and living.

Of course, it is critical that those participating in learning-oriented professional development initiatives experience them as such. I can have the best intentions in creating these spaces, but, in the end, what really matters is how participants receive—or experience—the learning opportunity and the processes and practices that create it. Leaders and educators (including principals, assistant principals, teachers, coaches, improvement leaders, district leaders, and aspiring principals in university leadership preparation programs) who have participated in the learning experiences I've offered in education leadership programs, workshops in schools and districts, and longer-term developmental leadership academies have shared that they *do* experience these contexts as powerful supports for growth. I have learned this both through evaluations and from longitudinal research I've conducted with two colleagues.[11]

In this longitudinal research, my colleagues and I surveyed and interviewed leaders who had successfully completed a course I taught in 2003, 2004, and 2005 at Harvard's Graduate School of Education. The course, called Leadership for Transformational Learning (LTL), was based on constructive-developmental theory and the pillar practices for growth derived from my research. We wanted to learn from the leaders how, if at all, they were employing practices in their schools that they had learned in these courses six, seven, and eight years ago. What stood out for them in terms of their experience in the class? What, if any, ideas from theories and practices discussed and experienced in the course were they employing today in their work?

We learned that these graduate students, who are now school leaders and education leadership university professors, remembered the class as a holding environment, and that they were using the processes and implementing the practices they learned about and were employed there to better support the adults they are now privileged to serve. They felt well supported and "safe" in what they referred to as the "trusting environment" of the course, and many of them said that they felt they were able to grow from experiencing the class and can now better assist in supporting the growth of adults with whom they work.

Jed Lippard, who is now Head of Prospect Hill Academy, a large K–12 charter school in Cambridge, Massachusetts, said the following when asked about how he uses practices learned in the LTL course he completed in 2004: "So much of what we do [at my school now] is just exactly what [LTL] was about, which is for a moment in time, having a group of people hold the dilemma or hold the issue or the question or the challenge or the struggle of one person in a way that really moves the thinking forward. That's what we do."

Matt Aborn, who was a teacher when enrolled in LTL in 2003 and is now lower-school division head of a school on Long Island, New York, explained how he remembered and appreciated the ways in which the instructor—me, in this case—was able "to build space" and demonstrate the importance of "valuing people" (meeting them where they are) and how he works to do the very same thing in his work with adults in his school to support their growth. As Matt shared:

> One [thing I appreciated] is that a lot of the time, at the beginning of each class, Ellie would offer us a time as a class to knowledge-build around the reading that was new or [around] pertinent ideas, and she would generally lead a discussion, and the discussion would involve people sharing, and she would write down the thoughts . . . each thing that somebody had shared . . . on the board. I really liked that. And . . . I use that as a tool sometimes in my own chamber meetings [at my school]. I think what I liked the most about it, though, was that Ellie . . . in the process of doing that, really validated and connected everything that was shared, and as the class progressed from a time when we were all just getting to know each other to . . . the end of the year, we started becoming very comfortable with each other. And I would associate that [with] Ellie's ability to build space in our class . . . And I think that in my own work, I look for opportunities like that, where I can spend time valuing each individual that is with me and connecting their ideas in a way that is really essential to moving us forward.

Others recalled that LTL and the "nonthreatening" and "nonjudgmental" space created within it made them "feel safe to take risks," "elevated," and "well held," as the aspiring principal whose words opened this section explained. One student shared that the experience she had in the LTL class "changed the shape of her relationships" and helped her "to grow," and that she now works to create that kind of "space" for the teachers she serves.

Another very powerful and profound example comes to mind about how adults experience these kinds of developmental learning environments. Autumn, a former principal of twenty-six years who now supports other leaders' development in New York City, was in her sixties when I met her this past spring. She was participating in a series of workshops that I had the honor of facilitating. We all met for five hours on three different days spread over a three-month period. This workshop series was offered as a "leadership academy" to thirty members of one cluster of leaders in New York City (clusters are like regions or districts).

In addition to the cluster's CEO and Assistant CEO, the workshop participants included coaches, principals, assistant principals, teacher leaders, professional developers, and other leaders in the cluster. They all had responsibilities of supporting other adults' development in schools. Autumn, who is currently responsible for supporting the development of principals, assistant principals, and teacher leaders in her cluster, shared the following insight during the last moments of our third workshop together:

> *I came to these learning seminars [workshops] thinking that I would learn how to be a better supporter of adults in my work . . . [and] I did learn a lot about all of that . . . But, what surprised me, a lot [emphasis hers], is what I learned about myself, my husband, and my family. During the first meeting [you said] that you wanted this [workshop] to be "personally and professional meaningful for us." I just didn't think then that it would be—I mean, personally helpful. Wow. It's hard to explain how much this work has helped me in my personal life. I learned that my husband has a different way of knowing than I do. And it made me realize why he says the things he does, feels the way he does, why I respond to him the way I do, and why we argue about certain things. I used to think he wasn't really listening and sometimes, that he didn't really care. Now I have a much deeper understanding of how I make meaning of myself— what that means to me, why I respond to him the way I do, and, I think, why he responds to me the way he does. I've learned so much—and it's been personally helpful. This was a surprise to me.*

Like Autumn, and many of the other aspiring and practicing leaders I've had the honor of learning with and from, I too have learned a lot about myself and those closest to me through this work. This learning has had a profound influence on who I am both as a person and as a leader of adult learning. It's not an easy task to describe the precise nature, or texture, of an effective holding environment, or how one's personal journey as an individual bubbles over and influences the work we do and can do in our professional lives, but I would like to share one particular example of how a very personal holding environment has both supported and challenged me to grow my inner capacities over the years. As I've mentioned, personal development is professional development, and I hope this example helps illustrate how much I *live and breathe* what I'm describing about the importance of holding environments for our lives and leadership development.

The example, in case you're wondering, is about my husband. Soon after entering graduate school close to twenty-five years ago, I had the blessing and tremendous life-changing gift of meeting David Severson, a fellow graduate school student whom I would eventually marry. When we first met, I found myself admiring so many of David's qualities. He was warm, generous, thoughtful, caring, a great listener, and a kind, sensitive human being. One other quality he possessed was that he always seemed to have, what I called then, a deep courage. David was able to somehow share with us, his fellow students, his thinking and feelings in a way that impressed me and others as authentic, caring, honest, and sincere. We trusted him. While I watched David interact with others and with me, I remember thinking how much I wanted to develop this ability in myself.

What I mean is that, at that time in my own development, it was very hard for me to disagree with others. I worried that my relationships with them would be damaged in important ways if I disagreed or engaged in anything that remotely resembled conflict. I was at that time a socializing knower. I would often try to share my opinions in ways that would not cause anyone to be upset or disappointed with me.

As David and I grew our relationship, I found myself developing new capacities and competencies. Yet, how did David help me realize this growth? While it is difficult to describe all the dimensions of this very significant holding environment, I will try to share some of its central characteristics.

One important aspect of the space I shared with David was that I felt so very closely *listened to* by him. Even when talking on the phone, I could hear and sense David listening to me—paying attention to every word and idea I shared with him. It wasn't just that, though. I found myself feeling very safe and comfortable sharing with David my way of making sense of experiences, the questions I had about work and life, and what I understood as my own growing edges. I felt okay and accepted in sharing with David my fears and anxieties about what might happen if I said or did something that might disappoint people I loved or whose positive opinion I valued and needed. In his attentive listening, his thoughtful questioning, and his acceptance and lack of judgmentalism about what I was saying, David offered a space in which I could feel safe to articulate my thoughts and test my ideas, feeling simultaneously encouraged and respectfully challenged. He asked questions that caused me to consider alternative perspectives and ways in which other people might react to me, my thinking, and my professional practices. He helped me to see and understand that it takes a certain courage to be authentic and genuine in relationships, both personal and professional. I needed to first figure out my own thinking and feelings in this safe context, and then call on my courage so that I could share what I was really thinking and genuinely feeling at any time.

The holding environment that David seemed to create naturally for me became one in which I felt safe and supported in testing new and growing capacities *to be myself*, to develop *my own voice*, to *create my own values*. David was impressively patient with me, and I learned a great deal from the way that he behaved. This experience of getting to know and understand my self and to learn from David, his modeling, and his questions, and to grow from being in this holding environment, seemed to help me to see a new way *of being* in the world and to gradually test out this new way of *being*. I found myself taking risks to explore and learn from alternative perspectives and stances held by other people.

Importantly, David seemed to support me and my thinking even when my view differed from his on a particular issue. I felt heard, understood, and cared for. We could disagree and our relationship was still strong. (I hope and expect that I have also offered the same kind of space for learning and growth and development to David over the ensuing years. He assures me that I have.) It was very soon after meeting and coming to know this sensitive and wonderful man who would become my husband that I began to demonstrate new capacities, capabilities, and competencies in other relationships and settings of my personal and professional life. I was experiencing growth and development, a process that continues to this day and writing.

The holding environment that David offered in support of my growth changed my life to the point of making possible the contributions that I now make available to so many other people. I use all that I learn in service to the creation of these kinds of environments for others. It is also my hope to be helpful to others as they create opportunities for growth and development in their own contexts for people with whom they have privilege to work and live and love.

## A Word About Obstacles

As we will discuss in great detail in the next chapters, any teaching, learning, and professional development initiative (e.g., a workshop, seminar, classroom, retreat) can become a holding environment if infused with developmental principles and practices—that is, if the environment becomes one that supports learning and facilitates growth and development. As we will continue to explore throughout this book, creating learning initiatives that support the growth and development of aspiring and practicing leaders, like all adults, can yield rewards personal and professional, individual and collective. Indeed, experiencing ideas, practices, and structures that support growth *while one is learning about them* is a promising new approach to leadership development, and one that infuses the model we are about to explore. Still, as you might imagine, supporting adult and leadership development is hard but important work. For leaders in schools, just as leaders of professional learning, growth is not without its challenges.

Over the years, for instance, I have learned from educators who have participated in my courses, seminars, and leadership academies that after leaving these contexts, they seek to find and create similar holding environments to support their continued growth and learning. I have also learned through my longitudinal research that leaders who have learned about and experienced developmental practices in my courses sometimes encounter obstacles in the midst of their successes when working to support adult and leadership development in their schools.[12] While painful, they shared, these obstacles simultaneously make this kind of leadership work more challenging and more essential.

For example, Sarah, who successfully completed my LTL course in 2003, has told me that she yearns for a holding environment in her current role as an assistant professor in order to grow and improve her teaching and leadership in support of aspiring and practicing educational leaders. Likewise, Jackie, who also completed the course in 2003, and who now serves as adjunct professor at a college as well as an English tutor for high school and university students, shared that what she misses most and wants deeply in her work today are holding environments in the form of "trusting relationships" with other adults, so that she can learn and grow from "ongoing contexts for conversation." The obstacle, she explained, is that she and others have "over-full lives," and very little time to set aside for this kind of mutual holding.

There are other obstacles that leaders have shared as they work to create these kinds of effective environments for others and for themselves. I have learned about these from educators who have enrolled in courses I've had the honor of teaching or workshops I have facilitated. These obstacles include difficulties with (a) accepting innovation and/or change, (b) developing mutual, professional connections and relationships with other adults that would serve as holding environments for growth, (c) gaining credibility with adults and authority figures in their work contexts in order to support adult development when they themselves are young and do not have many years of teaching and leadership experience, (d) developing trusting relationships, (e) working to alter deeply ingrained cultural norms and practices, (f) the nature of adult growth (i.e., it is a long-term process), and (g) lacking a shared vision in communities for leadership in support of adult development.

Some leaders also cited what they perceived as limited or absent administrative support as an obstacle constraining their growth, their leadership, and their opportunities to shape learning enviornments that support adult development. In spite of these obstacles, leaders reported that they were able to develop strategies for creating holding environments in their workplaces and are implementing practices for supporting adult growth and leadership development. You will learn more about how to do this in schools and professional learning contexts of all kinds throughout the chapters that follow. And, in the final chapter, you will learn more about strategies for supporting your own growth, which is a key ingredient of sustaining effective holding environments. In short, the specific ideas, strategies, structures, and practices that I describe throughout this book will help you to support adult and leadership development in your own contexts, lead with developmental mindfulness, and both anticipate and overcome the obstacles and challenges that will arise in your noble and important work in care of others.

## TAKING STOCK, PAUSING, AND STEPPING FORWARD

In this chapter, we looked closely at the big ideas and principles of *constructive-developmental theory*, which informs the foundations of my new learning-oriented model of leadership development. As we explored, understanding the qualitatively different ways adults make sense of teaching, leading, learning, and living is essential when working to shape learning environments that truly support adult growth and leadership development. Understanding *ways of knowing* allows us to effectively differentiate the supports and challenges we offer adults in professional learning opportunities. We've learned that caring for *developmental diversity* in this way involves meeting adults "where they are" in a developmental sense, both individually and collectively, and represents both the task and the promise of a developmental approach to leadership and leadership development.

Likewise, in this chapter we dove deeper into the concept of a *holding environment* and its expanded role in this book's model for creating professional learning initiatives that support adult growth. We heard from leaders who experienced these kinds of professional holding environments in my university courses, workshops, and seminars, and I also offered a very personal example of how effective holding environments can help support growth at both the personal and professional levels. As I've emphasized, the two are intertwined and fundamentally important to our approaches to leadership, learning, and life, and have implications as well for how we are able to support others and how we face the challenges inherent to leading for adult development.

In fact, in the next chapter, we begin again at this personal level, because effectively shaping professional learning opportunities for others involves drawing from and extending our most deeply held values and beliefs. Before focusing in on the innermost ring of my new model for leadership development, however, I invite you next to review the key takeaways from this chapter, consider a series of reflective questions about what we've just explored together, and revisit the opening vignettes (about the four aspiring principals' experiences of their seminars) in the concluding application exercise. I hope you find these helpful.

## TAKEAWAYS

While knowledge of constructive-developmental theory and ways of knowing has a number of important implications, the following are key to leaders who want to facilitate adult learning in their own teaching environments (e.g., university courses, professional development initiatives, workshops, and seminars) and also in the environments their students and participants will go on to create in *their* teaching and leading contexts. In other words, when designing and facilitating professional learning initiatives that support growth, it is important to remember that:

- ✦ Adults can grow throughout their lives, and the best holding environments offer *both* supports and challenges.
- ✦ Approaching leadership development from a developmental perspective can help us to build individual and organizational leadership and internal capacity.
- ✦ Understanding the principles of constructive-developmental theory can inform leadership orientation and practice in powerful ways and can help us to consider *developmental diversity* when crafting environments for growth.

✦ School leaders and university professors can benefit from employing developmental perspectives as we consider how to build internal capacity and meet adaptive challenges because adults will experience leadership and learning opportunities in different ways.

✦ Being mindful of the need to differentiate supports and challenges for adults in order to help them grow can improve conditions for building growth-enhancing cultures in schools and university classrooms.

✦ Developmental diversity can inform our visions for capacity building. Adults with different ways of knowing need different supports and challenges to grow.

✦ Consideration of the *goodness of fit* between one's expectations, whether implicit or explicit, and adults' capacities to meet them will help us shape more effective contexts for growth.

✦ Adults will orient to leadership, authority, teamwork, and life in qualitatively different ways, and we must intentionally attend to this developmental diversity when working and learning with, for, from, and alongside others.

✦ Understanding ways of knowing, the importance of differentiating supports and challenges, and the essential need to create robust holding environments gives us ideas for *how to build capacity and support development* and a common language for *naming, talking, and thinking* about growth, development, and capacity building. This enables us to help and better understand others, our organizations, and ourselves.

✦ Creating holding environments wherein adults feel *well held* for who they are and respected can support their leadership development and growth and, in turn, can inspire them to create genuine growing environments for others.

✦ Growing our own capacities can enable us to better support the development of both children and adults.

## REFLECTIVE QUESTIONS

Please take a moment to consider these questions, which can be used for independent reflection and collective dialogue. They are offered to help you and your colleagues consider and make sense of the ideas discussed in this chapter and how, if at all, you might employ some of them in your noble practice of shaping opportunities for growth. I encourage you to reflect privately first (by either freewriting or freethinking) about these questions before sharing your reflections with a colleague or engaging in group conversation.

1. What are three of your biggest hopes for your learning in reading this book?
2. What are two of the more powerful insights or connections you have had after reading this chapter?
3. What are some of your burning, sizzling, and/or simmering questions at this time? (You might want to discuss these with your colleagues. See exhibit 1.3.)

---

### APPLICATION EXERCISE: REVISITING THE VIGNETTES

---

As I have shared, intentionally caring for adult development and leadership development by shaping environments for growth can make all the difference. Before considering the core elements of this model of leadership development in the chapter that follows, and in light of what you've learned from reading this chapter, I invite you to revisit the vignettes we examined earlier in exhibit 1.2 (p. 25). This is an opportunity to apply your new learnings about constructive-developmental theory, ways of knowing, and crafting holding environments to support development. Please consider marking data (words, phrases) from Jamie, Casey, Sky, and Lane's responses that help you to understand the primary way with which each makes meaning of his or her experience in the professional learning seminars. The following questions are offered to guide you in your reading: (1) With which ways of knowing do each of these aspiring principals seem to be making meaning? What leads you to think this? Is there anything else you would like to further explore about what they have expressed in these vignettes in order to understand their way of knowing more fully? (2) How do you think their ways of knowing influence their perceptions of the seminar? (3) If you were the instructor in service to their growth, what kinds of supports or challenges might you offer to help them grow? In other words, how would you work to create a holding environment for each person's growth and development?

**EXHIBIT 1.3**

## Leaders' questions after learning about the ideas presented in chapter 1

Recently, I asked eighty aspiring principals who were participating in a summer leadership course to share their burning, sizzling, and simmering questions immediately after they learned about constructive-developmental theory. I invited them to write down their questions on color-coded paper (i.e., bright pink for burning, orange for sizzling, and pastel yellow for simmering), and to select the color that best represented the kind of question they had at that time. The questions shared by this cohort of students were very similar to those offered by prior cohorts of graduate students and practitioner school leaders with whom I have had the honor of learning. Here, I offer examples of some of these questions to help you in your conversations with colleagues.

### Burning questions

- Can you help someone grow into a different way of knowing if you have not reached that way of knowing?
- I'm struggling with learning that principals, and the position of principal, requires that a person be able to demonstrate self-authoring capacities—spontaneously. I am split between self-authoring and socializing, and I see my use of socializing as a way to keep those around me on my side and not aggravate them. How can you ensure that as a self-authoring leader you're being supportive and positive to your teachers as well?
- Can I move others or myself from one way of knowing to another? If so, how is this possible?

### Sizzling questions

- Is it recommended or ever helpful to have staff members understand [ways of knowing] in order to help them in their work as well as understand our students or families?
- If you create a holding environment (safe and supportive), what do you do if teachers don't want to be challenged? (Challenge them?)
- What's next for self-transforming learners? How will they continue to develop their own learning?
- How does one effectively determine an adult learner's current way of knowing and growing edge?

### Simmering questions

- How might you differentiate your teaching, leading, mentoring, and coaching to best attend to people with different ways of knowing?
- What kind of leadership roles do you think might be helpful to hold instrumental knowers well and lead them toward their growing edge? What kind of leadership roles do you think might be helpful to hold socializing knowers well and lead them toward their growing edge? What kind of leadership roles do you think might be helpful to hold self-authoring knowers well and lead them toward their growing edge?

# CHAPTER 2

## The Inner Circle

*Core Elements of Learning Environments
for Leadership Development*

> *Authenticity is the alignment of head, mouth, heart,
> and feet—thinking, saying, feeling, and doing the same
> thing—consistently. This builds trust, and followers
> love leaders they can trust.*

> —LANCE SECRETAN

As leaders and educators who have the honor of teaching both aspiring and practicing leaders, we all bring our own values, and the essential elements of who we are, to the work of supporting adult growth and leadership development. In this chapter, I share what I believe to be the elements that are universal to this development: care, respect, trust, collaboration, and intentionality. As you see in figure 2.1, at the center of this inner circle of core elements is a dot, which, as I mentioned in the introduction, is our self—who we are—and which has a great deal of influence on how we create spaces in which others can grow. I'll say more about the importance of this dot—the self—in this chapter in addition to introducing the five core elements.

Although I describe these *core elements* as distinct entities at the heart of the model, I invite you to consider them, collectively, as the origin of a series of concentric circles (as depicted in figure I.1 in the introduction). While the concentric circles in this model appear to be distinct, they are also interrelated, connected, and continuous in intimate and important ways, like the rings of growth in a tree. As noted in the

**FIGURE 2.1**

**The central dot: the self, which influences how we create spaces where others can grow**

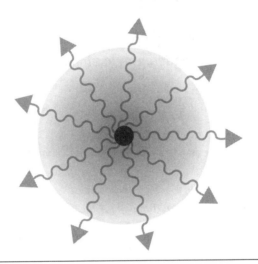

introduction, each chapter in this book focuses on key ideas from one concentric circle or ring of growth. Taken as a whole, the rings create the conditions that support adult growth and leadership development at both the individual and group levels in teaching, learning, and professional development environments.

In this chapter, I will first discuss the dot at the center of the innermost concentric circle. After that, you will be introduced to the five interconnected core elements in the innermost circle—care, respect, trust, collaboration, and intentionality—as illustrated in figure 2.2. I'll offer examples from my work with school leaders in different kinds of professional learning initiatives to illuminate how the core elements connect in important ways to create environments that support growth in interpersonal relationships and leadership development. These core elements, as you will see in later chapters, are also essential to supporting development in whole-group teaching, learning, and professional development environments. Put simply, these are the elements that I believe are vital—for myself and for others—to realizing a fully supportive environment for growth and learning.

**FIGURE 2.2**

### The innermost growth ring: the five core elements

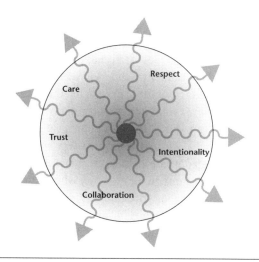

## THE CENTRAL DOT: THE CORE ESSENCE OF ONESELF

*Who you are is speaking so loudly that I can't hear what you're saying.*

—Ralph Waldo Emerson

At the heart of the innermost growth ring in this model, I have placed a central dot. Each of us has a personal central dot—the core essence of oneself. This dot represents the individual, who you are as a teacher, leader, coach, mentor, parent, and all of the roles you fill in your life. When reflecting on the pieces of my own central dot, I can see that my innermost self is informed and influenced by my background (personal and professional), family and other important relationships (e.g., friendships, mentoring relationships), spaces I've experienced that have supported my growth and contributed to my internal capacity (as described in the introduction), my understanding of the power and promise of constructive-developmental theory, my education and experiences in schools, and all I have learned from, with, and alongside practicing and aspiring leaders. My central dot influences the way I strive to create holding environments for others and for myself. In many ways, it influences all other components of this model.

My theory, point of view, and approach to creating professional learning opportunities that nurture leadership development and the growth of internal capacity are heavily and importantly influenced by constructive-developmental theory. For me, it is not just a lens I use when working with practicing and aspiring leaders; rather, it is a part of *how I see*—how I understand myself, the people around me, and the world. It is my basic theory of life and living in all domains of my personal, professional, and private life. As such, constructive-developmental theory is a big part of my "dot."

While I know that there is a lot of debate in education and psychology about the nature of *selfhood* (and I'm not engaging with that particular question here because I do not think it would be helpful to you or this discussion), I also know that who we are informs the way we shape opportunities for growth and leadership development in any teaching, learning, or professional development environment. In my case, who I am has informed the creation of this new, learning-oriented model for leadership development. As you might imagine, a person's dot (however one wants to conceptualize or define it) has important implications for the kinds of values and practices he or she prioritizes as a leader, teacher, or university professor. While constructive-developmental theory, care, respect, trust, collaboration, and intentionality are essential parts of this model of leadership development, they are not ingredients in a recipe that apply indiscriminately. Rather, how you wear them, hold them up and out, and model and embody them influences the way they work and are understood. Given that, arguably, one's self is a complex conglomeration of experiences, background, beliefs, values, and relationships, you might find it helpful to engage in the reflective opportunity presented at the end of this section to consider how your own values, beliefs, and influences inform your central dot, and your nonnegotiables about what it means to lead and support others.

Three other points that are important in relation to this dot, and to crafting professional learning environments that support growth and leadership development, should be stated explicitly. These may resonate with your own beliefs as well. First, I believe deeply that we need to be a *model* of what we believe in. Modeling and embodying one's approach to leadership development is vital to the task. What we say is important, but what we do is even more important, as Ralph Waldo Emerson's quotation at the opening of this section illuminates. What we do, I have learned, is what people pay attention to, whether one is a parent, a teacher, a team leader, a coach, an assistant principal, a university professor, or a leader of any kind. This is one of the most important reasons why the dot is in the center of the model and connected to the core elements. You cannot create environments where other people can grow unless they trust you.

Second, self-knowledge is vital. In other words, we must know who we are—we must know and be comfortable with ourselves in order to create effective growing opportunities for others. This is an ongoing process. The better we know ourselves, the better able we are to serve others and build holding environments and professional learning opportunities that support their growth and internal capacity building. Third, and related to the importance of knowing oneself, is *authenticity*—being genuine. You are authentic when your inner self aligns closely with your outer self, the self you present to others. I also want to point out that the capacity to know oneself and to be authentic is intimately connected to a person's way of knowing. For example, a person who makes meaning with a socializing way of knowing will make sense of and enact the idea of being authentic in a very different way than a self-authoring leader or teacher leader. Consequently, when crafting learning environments for adults with different ways of knowing, it's wise to consider what being authentic might mean to each individual. People can become more authentic and develop greater self-knowledge as they learn and grow as leaders and human beings.

Two examples might help to highlight how a person's central dot informs his or her approach to supporting others' growth. As noted in the introduction, each summer I enjoy the privilege of teaching a cohort of eighty to one hundred aspiring principals in the Summer Principals Academy (SPA) at Teachers College. These teacher leaders, coaches, assistant principals, professional learning specialists, curriculum directors, coordinators, and other kinds of leaders enroll in my intensive two-and-a-half-week core course, School Leadership for Adult Development, to learn about some of the same ideas you are reading in this book. During the first few days of class, and throughout our time together in this professional learning environment, one of the ideas I stress is the importance of "having the courage to be oneself" when working to support adult growth and leadership development. I also invite these current and aspiring leaders to pay careful attention to what I do and say in our class and let them know that it's all intentional. "Everything I do, everything the teaching team does for and with you, and all we do together is intentional and purposeful. We are working to model the very practices that support adult growth and leadership development in this class. This class is a space where you will not only learn theory and content but will also experience the very practices that we hope will support your growth. We do this because we feel this will help you to create these kinds of learning experiences and growth environments for others." Again and again I remind them, "It is very important to remember that you can create these holding environments for others' development. Who you are matters. Having the courage to be oneself in is vital to their creation." I have found that aspiring leaders hold this learning—*having the courage to be one-self*—close to their hearts. They rightly see it as being essential to supporting their own and others' growth and leadership development; knowing oneself and having the courage to be oneself—*to reveal oneself*—is indeed essential to creating professional learning environments that support growth.

Recently I facilitated a workshop at the annual conference of Learning Forward (formerly known as the National Staff Development Council), an international professional learning association for district leaders, principals, assistant principals, instructional coaches, teacher leaders, and education leadership professors interested in learning how to better support adult development and growth in their schools and districts. After learning about constructive-development theory, as discussed in chapter 1, and the importance of our central dot, participants noted the relevance and implications of these ideas for how they carry out their work as leaders and educators. One superintendent of a large urban district shared what he and colleagues at his table had discussed and realized during their break: "While there are many approaches to building schools and improving instruction and instructional leadership, understanding adult development, practices that support it, and how our own way of knowing influences how we lead, how coaches can coach, [and] how teachers teach and lead is really important. We were talking about that. All of this has really important implications for what we expect leaders to be able to do, for understanding how to support them, for who were hire, for how we support their growth and how they support other's development—and do their work."

To similarly reflect on what constitutes your own central dot and how it informs your approach to leadership development and growth, I invite you to please complete the brief exercise in exhibit 2.1.

EXHIBIT 2.1

## PAUSE FOR REFLECTION

### What Constitutes Your Own Personal Dot?

Perhaps you'd like to take a few moments here to think about the following question: what are the influences, values, and beliefs that inform your own central dot? It might also be helpful to consider your "nonnegotiables" for leadership and supporting growth. In other words, what things are most important to you as a leader, and what values and ideas do you want to enact and make visible in your leadership work with and for others?

## CARE

*I feel the capacity to care is the thing which gives life its deepest significance.*

—Pablo Casals

You will notice that care is a core element in the innermost growth ring. While each element is important in its own right, remember that none of the elements in this or any growth ring in the model works in isolation; rather, they are woven together and work synergistically to create holding environments that support growth and leadership development. Most basic is the fact that one needs to genuinely care for and *value* another's growth and development. Finding something to celebrate authentically and value in every person *is* caring and demonstrating care. When we focus on what's best for another person in terms of helping to build his or her internal capacities, we are demonstrating care.

### The Meaning of Care

There are two main parts to my definition of care: honestly valuing aspects of a person and focusing on that person's well-being. *Merriam-Webster* also defines *care* in two primary ways: "painstaking or watchful attention" and "regard coming from desire or esteem."[1] I cite the dictionary definition for this word, and for the other core elements within the growth rings, to draw a distinction between its commonly understood meaning and its usage when enacted and experienced in an environment that supports leadership development.

When you have a person's best interests in mind, that person becomes more willing to listen and learn when you share an insight. What you say makes a difference because the person knows that you care and trusts that you have his or her interests in mind and soul. When we genuinely and sincerely care about another person—his or her well-being, development, and growth—that person comes to matter to us in more and deeper ways. This kind of caring brings us more profoundly into the person's experience of life, living, leading, teaching, coaching, and growing. It's difficult to describe what this looks like, though I trust we all know what it *feels like* from both sides to care for another human being and to know that a person cares for us. Caring for the welfare of another human being is a gift and a privilege, and also a responsibility.

When I was a younger teacher, I would often share with my father situations I encountered in the classroom. He listened carefully and caringly about my experiences with students, and how much I wanted to help them. After I shared these often-painful stories, my dad would ask me, "Do you know the difference between you and so many other people?" When I had no answer, he said, "You care so much—[that's] what makes a difference and that's why you can make a difference." This was something he told me often, and something I came to believe as wisdom.

This example with my dad and the examples I am about to share illuminate the essence of care. In addition to acknowledging the dictionary definitions of care, it is important to emphasize the intimate connection between care and compassion. The meaning or etymology of *compassion* involves feeling together, or feeling with (i.e., *com*, meaning "with or together," and *passion*, meaning "feeling"). The following examples demonstrate the relationship between care, "feeling with," and creating holding environments that support adult growth, development, and leadership.

## Care in Action: Stories from Life and the Field

Before presenting examples from practice, I want to share a story that reminds me of how deeply we as human beings can care and "feel with" one another from very early in our lives. A friend shared a story about his twin boys, who were just beginning to walk. While walking, one of the twins, Owie, fell down and broke his arm. After the doctor put a cast on Owie's arm, Owie regressed to crawling because the cast affected his balance. After a day or so of watching his brother crawl rather than walk, Abe, Owie's twin, stopped walking and started to crawl alongside his brother. This image of crawling or walking alongside another—being *with* another—connects the meanings of care and compassion and the vital importance of each in shaping holding environments for growth.

So, you might wonder, how does this example relate to care for adults and to helping adults grow and develop as leaders? It highlights the importance of demonstrating care by *feeling with another*. The next example further connects *feeling with* to care and describes how we can support adult growth by valuing individuals for who they are, caring about their growth and development, and feeling with them.

### Care At the Individual Level

Some years ago I was working to mentor, coach, and support the growth of a very talented master's student who was brand new to our education leadership program. Kathy (not her real name) was in her first semester and expressed an interest to me in eventually becoming an education leadership professor. To help her acclimate to graduate study, and to introduce her to some of the responsibilities of the professorship, I invited her to work with me for the year in a work-study position. This, I knew, would give her a small taste of academic life, and would allow me to support her in multiple capacities. This new relationship began while I was on sabbatical, so I was not at the university during this semester. Still, throughout the first two months of the semester, I worked very hard in ways I thought were supportive to her to show my care, to feel with her, and to create spaces for her growth and leadership development. How did this work? What did these spaces look like?

Knowing that Kathy was new to our university, to our program, and to the intensity of graduate-level coursework, when working to support her growth and development as a leader, I did not want to overburden her with exact deadlines for our projects together. Instead, I would ask, "When do you think you can complete that task?" Importantly, I did not want to pressure her to join in any collaborative work or give drop-dead due dates for our assignments because I thought it would cause her anxiety, and also because I trusted that she would complete her work and send it along for my review when she was able. In addition, I worked to support Kathy in *growing her own interests* by inviting her—out of care—to select the writing and research projects she wanted to work on with me, based on her interests rather than mine. We communicated a lot by email during the first two months.

After nearly two months of working together, however, Kathy explained during one of our biweekly (every other week) phone meetings that she wanted me to specify "exact due dates for assignments," "exact times when things would be due," and "which projects [I] wanted [her] to help with" (rather than allowing her to choose based on *her* interests). As I listened to Kathy, I realized that while I was working to support her development and growth as a leader by feeling with her and doing what I thought was best for her growth, Kathy needed something quite different. Surprised, in some ways, that this was the first time she shared this with me, I also understood that she might have felt uncomfortable voicing this earlier in our mentoring relationship. After listening to both what she voiced and what she did not, I shared that what I was trying to do was care for her and feel with her as a first-semester master's student. I did not want to place even greater demands on her and her time; instead, I explained, I was coming from a place of care and respect for her and her growth. I understood, though, that in order to create a holding environment for her growth and development as a leader, I would have to address Kathy's needs for more structure, rules to follow, deadlines to guide her, and direction from me. And, importantly, I had the powerful realization during this call—after learning more from her about how she was making meaning of her experience—that, while I had been treating her as a self-authoring knower, she was more instrumental in her way of knowing. I appreciated her courage in voicing what she needed, and I subsequently adjusted my way of caring—of being and feeling with her—because I cared about her and wanted to support her development and growth.

How did this happen? What can we learn from this example? First, care means giving someone what he or she needs, which may not necessarily be what you want or expect to give. After learning more about Kathy, I was able to give her the kinds of supports that helped her best: exact times and dates for project delivery, direction as to what projects we would work on together, specific guidance on project tasks, models and examples of work she could emulate, and lots of feedback on submitted work. This helped her feel cared for and about, and helped her flourish in the space of our mentoring relationship.

As you move forward in your own important leadership work, I hope Kathy's story can serve as a reminder of the importance of expressing care in ways that fit an individual's specific needs and way of knowing. This type of caring, feeling and being with, is at the heart of holding environments for adults of all kinds, and it is also the foundation of creating effective professional learning opportunities that support adult and leadership development.

### Care At the Group Level

As mentioned earlier, each summer I have the gift of teaching eighty to one hundred aspiring principals. Many students comment—even years after experiencing my intensive School Leadership for Adult Development course—that one of their biggest takeaways is how much they valued my desire to structure the class as an environment where they felt cared about and supported in their growth and leadership development. Benefitting from this kind of experience, they explained, not only helped them to grow and feel cared about but also helped them to understand how to create such environments for other adults in their own schools and school systems.

For example, one aspiring leader, who self-identified as being quiet and "a little shy," sent me a note at the end of the course expressing her gratitude for the experience of being in the class. She began by sharing, "I did not want to go forward without telling you how much I appreciated this experience [the class]. I feel that I will be able to take what I have learned, and go on to have more meaningful personal and professional relationships." She continued, "What I also take away from this experience is your genuine desire for us to learn and grow, and the way in which you *respected and showed us care.*"

One specific demonstration of care that she deeply appreciated and referenced in her note was how I occasionally invited students during class to close their eyes and give a show of hands as to whether or not they understood or were able to complete the assigned readings for class that day. As I explained to the students, I did this out of my deep desire to meet them where they were in terms of delivering the content for the day and also given my understanding of the very hectic, demanding pace of the students' program. At times, I knew, these graduate students were working so hard that they barely had enough time to sleep. So, for this student and others, my simply acknowledging this fact was experienced as compassion and care. This is not to say that my expectations were not extremely high. On the contrary, I encouraged students to work very hard *for their own benefit*, and, when it seemed helpful or necessary, offered difficult but important feedback to the group about submitted work, deadlines, or other sensitive issues. For this student, however, the fact that I turned away from the class when offering this kind of constructive feedback and said, "I'm not looking at anyone" helped her feel safe. She continued, "This and your more subtle actions were a clear demonstration of your *care* [emphasis hers]. I look forward to using these techniques with my students!"

Recognizing, appreciating, and admiring individuals' experiences are key to creating caring, compassionate environments that facilitate growth. Indeed, celebrating another's gifts and prioritizing his or her well-being are powerful supports, and ones that are rich with meaning for adults on all sides. I am reminded, in closing, of a story my husband, David, shared with me about an experience he had teaching a first-semester university class. At the end of one semester, the students in his class let him know that they felt "lifted up and carried by his care." While at first, some felt lost or uncertain in their new doctoral program, the deep care that David demonstrated as they engaged in his course, and his transparent and felt commitment to their success, made all the difference. This is the kind of care I always try to impart to my students, and, as you know, the kind of effect you, too, can have in your work as a school leader.

# RESPECT

*As we grow as unique persons, we learn to respect the uniqueness of others.*

—Robert H. Schuller

*Every human being, of whatever origin, of whatever station, deserves respect. We must each respect other even as we respect ourselves.*

—U. Thant

Because care and respect can be so connected, it's not always easy to differentiate between them. But it's *possible* to respect someone—or someone's accomplishments—without necessarily caring about him or her, and vice versa. Respect is about seeing and acknowledging individuals' rights to *be who they are*, and care is finding *something meaningful and beautiful within those identities to value.* You might find it helpful to think about respect as one way of letting your care come through, or how you demonstrate it. Respect means *seeing and celebrating* individuals, their right to be who they are, and acknowledging their own unique life path. Before offering a little more about how respect is closely linked to our ways of knowing, the importance of attending to developmental diversity, and how both of these connect intimately to supporting adult and leadership development, I'd like to emphasize a few important points about respect.

First, there is *reciprocity* to respect. Respect is something we must give and receive. Earning and growing respect is a process, and as a leader you know that it is mutual and reciprocal, given by each side. We all know when we feel respected by another person, right? We also know what it feels like to be disrespected, or to sense a lack of respect. And, as a leader, you know how vital it is to be and feel respected in order to support others' growth and leadership development. You also know that showing respect to others helps you receive respect from them in return. This is vital to leadership and essential when thinking about how to create holding environments for supporting adult growth and leadership development. Building holding environments for growth that are infused with respect for individuals and groups enables others to create these kinds of experiences for the adults they are supporting as well.

Second, respect is about *recognition*—seeing someone in the psychological sense and paying attention to that person, to his or her uniqueness. *Merriam-Webster* defines *respect* in the following two ways: "high or special regard: esteem" and "the quality or state of being esteemed."[2] When you respect someone, that person feels listened to, heard, *seen*, and acknowledged for who he or she is. Respect is an intangible yet *felt* quality of a relationship, and a fundamental element of creating a holding environment for growth and leadership development.

Third, when you are facilitating professional learning initiatives, it is important to respect that adults have different preferences, needs, and developmental orientations. When presenting new material, I invite participants to "rent" the idea, as I did in chapter 1, rather than forcing them to adhere to it. As you will see later in this book, when inviting adults to reflect on ideas or questions, I always give them a choice to either *freewrite* (i.e., write in response to a question, prompt, or idea about whatever they're thinking and/or feeling without self-censorship) or to simply *freethink* (reflect on something in one's mind rather than write it out). Giving adults choices when leading adult learning is a simple practice; it is also a simple way to respect and honor them. School leaders in both K–12 systems and university settings have told me that being offered these kinds of invitations empowers them and helps them to feel respected.

Fourth, as you know, it's important to respect adults' knowledge and experience; this show of respect can open the way toward establishing a holding environment. A large percentage of the aspiring principals in the 2011 Summer Principals Academy mentioned earlier had some experience leading professional development as directors or coaches in schools and districts. When entering the Supporting Adult Development in Schools course, some of these leaders had the courage to voice their experience and their accomplishments in leading and supporting teachers. I thanked them for their courageous sharing, celebrated their presence, acknowledged their experience and expertise (as well as everyone else's) publicly and privately, and invited them to share with all of us. "We all have much to learn from you and each other," I assured them. The experience of being and feeling respected, they shared, enabled them to listen, learn, engage, and contribute more fully to the collective course experience during the semester. It was a genuine invitation for them to shine, to share their gifts and experiences and expertise, and to contribute in important ways that only they could.

Finally, in addition to recognizing an individual's expertise, preferences, and experiences, respect also includes honoring a person's way of putting the world together (or way of knowing) when creating an environment for supporting his or her growth and leadership development. More specifically, it's essential to meet the person where he or she is developmentally, and in other ways too. By "meet the person," I mean accepting, honoring, and valuing that person's way of knowing—*joining him or her* as you strive to understand how he or she makes meaning of and experiences the world. The examples that follow will help to illuminate the importance of meeting adults where they are and how doing so can support adult growth and leadership development.

## The Role of Respect in Growing to See Oneself as a Leader

One of the most important things I've learned about respect is that it is reciprocal: you need to give it to get it. As a school leader, you know that respect is fundamental to your ability to do your job. But how can you get or deepen respect? How do you show it to others?

### The Contagious Nature of Respect

Recently, I had the honor of working with a group of newly appointed coaches in Harlem, New York. They were already master teachers and were selected by the principal to serve as math and literacy coaches in their elementary school. Still, for many of them, the experience of formal leadership was new, and they were interested in growing themselves as well as helping their coachees to grow. Their coachees were teachers who worked in grades one through eight. The new coaches worked with these teachers individually and in grade-level teams.

I met with these newly appointed coaches once every three to four weeks during the academic year, for an hour at first, but later often for more than two hours. In addition to talking about their practice as coaches, and how they were acclimating themselves to this new position, we discussed questions such as: how might understanding adults' different ways of knowing be of help to them and enable them to better support the growth of the teachers they were coaching? How might they employ developmental ideas in their work with teachers to help them grow? How might employing the pillar practices of teaming, engaging in leadership roles, mentoring, and collegial inquiry (mentioned in the introduction and chapter 1) help them to support the growth of individual teachers and grade-level teams? How might these ideas help them understand what they, themselves, needed to grow and develop? We'd sit around a table in a classroom and have these sorts of deep discussions—which I often thought of as "kitchen table conversations."

In particular, I worked to shape these meetings as holding environments for the new coaches, who were striving and at times struggling to grow their identities as leaders. Many of them confided that they did not really see themselves as leaders, and feared the teachers in their schools didn't either. They wanted deeply to be of help, but didn't yet feel respected in their schools—a painful and challenging obstacle.

Powerfully, for this group of new coaches the experience of meeting and learning together seemed to help. By feeling respected—listened to, heard, supported, and acknowledged—they were inspired to bring and translate this feeling into their coaching work. Moreover, after learning about ways of knowing and the pillar practices for growth, they were better able to understand their own needs and orientations to the world, and to better differentiate supports and challenges that would be most valuable to the growth and learning of their coachees.

In both our kitchen table conversations and their work in schools, then, these new coaches came to see the great promise in a differentiated, developmentalized approach to supporting adult growth and leadership development. Not only did such an approach help them demonstrate respect for the grade-level teachers they were working with, but it also helped them tap into the reciprocal respect that grows from mutual and genuine relationships. One of these coaches, Francy, shared with me that the experience in the coaching group helped her "dramatically shift [her] orientation toward working with the teachers." As she courageously shared, Francy at first felt compelled to "deal with" challenging teachers as problems to be solved, as obstacles to be managed and ultimately fixed. Her new understanding of developmental theory, however, helped her to approach her new role as coach as an opportunity to "work with" and meet the teachers as individuals and human beings instead. In moving away from her more defensive, controlling stance and toward one that embraced connection, collaboration, and genuine reciprocity, Francy, like many of the other coaches, took a powerful step toward gaining the respect of teachers by demonstrating to them *first* that they were respected unequivocally.

For me, Francy's story, and that of all the coaches in the group, offers a powerful example of the contagious nature of respect. While I cared deeply for the coaches as individuals and wanted them to feel my profound respect for their inspiring work and professional journeys, we were able to create—together—an environment supportive of growth and leadership development that felt comfortable and respectful for each of us. Excited and encouraged by this kind of respect, the coaches aspired to re-create these nurturing contexts for their coachees. By approaching their work with the teachers in this respectful way, rather than as "problems" in need of fixing, the coaches were better able to see and develop the potential of living, growing human beings doing their very best to do difficult and very important work.

*The Reflective Power of Respect*

Another example about the power of respect involves Malka, a student in my 2006 offering of Leadership for Adult Development at Teachers College (TC), who was pursuing a master's degree in education leadership and barely twenty years old at the time. This course, like this book, centered on adult developmental theory and the four pillar practices, and how they apply to growth and leadership development. The daughter of an orthodox rabbi, Malka told me when we first met that she had attended private religious schools all her life and was struggling to find her way at TC. As she shared with me later, she found it difficult to adjust to the "unfamiliar world full of unfamiliar faces" at our very large university, and felt she did not fit in with her traditional black clothing and head covering. While she was committed to serving as a force for good in the world of religious education and wanted "to become a voice that was worthy of being heard" through her continued studies, she nonetheless felt disconnected, lost, and overlooked in her new environment. During her first fall semester, she explained later, "I barely spoke in class. What did I know about diversity, John Dewey, and No Child Left Behind? I felt that I did not have the skills, knowledge, and experience to gain anything substantial out of this experience . . . and when I compared myself to those around me, I [felt] lack[ing] in some very major ways. I thought I had nothing to give that would be understood or valued."

Of course, Malka was in fact already a voice "worthy of being heard." She was very wise, gifted, and absolutely full of light, but couldn't yet see this about herself. Given her glowing inner beauty as a person and educator, it is an incredible honor to me that she now credits some small part of her subsequent success to the respect she experienced in the holding environment of our class that spring. She told me, for instance, that because I *saw* her—and welcomed her for who she was—she was better able to see the possibility in herself. Inviting individuals to be themselves is perhaps the most important aspect of respect, and one that Malka carried forward in her own work as a teacher leader. In the class, she explained, she "learned that we are all different and our unique experiences only serve to help us better teach and understand others." This insight has inspired her to give back even more to others, especially teachers in her school. As she shared with me: "I have something to give now. I create holding environments for [teachers in my school]. I show them the respect you showed me. I feel like I create these places where adults can grow through respect and what you taught and did for me."

Recounting her experiences in an email she sent me years after the class, Malka also used a poetic image that I find quite powerful. She described the enduring effects of her experience in the course by saying that she was "still reflecting the light" I shined on her. Just as the coaches in Harlem were able to take up and carry forward the lived experience of feeling truly respected, Malka blossomed under the intangible but very real feeling of being well held and accepted as an individual. Respect is something you can actually feel—like the warmth of sunlight on your face. Yet, you can't really pin it down or hold it in your hands. While Malka experienced me as "giving her" this light, it is clear from her work with children, youth, and adults that she also understands now what I understood about her then—that her light already shone brightly from within. As she told me, "The beauty of being part of another person's growth is that you are not giving them anything that they did not already have, except the awareness that they have it all within themselves." In fundamental ways, then, the feeling of being respected filled her up—in the emotional and psychological sense—and enabled her to give back by shining her own light and creating holding environments for others.

## TRUST

*Trust is the highest form of human motivation. It brings out the very best in people. But it takes time and patience.*

—Stephen R. Covey

Trust is a bridge to building environments that support growth and leadership development, and, as Covey writes, it takes time to establish it and still more time to deepen it. Establishing and building trust happens when we are transparent in our thinking and feelings. Being transparent and open and vulnerable, while not always easy—especially in a leadership role—is vital to developing trusting relationships. Modeling these qualities, and living them, helps those we are trying to support in their growth and leadership development to trust us. Trust is fundamental to all relationships, to building true human connections and deepening compassion for others. And it is essential to supporting adult and leadership development at both the individual and group levels. As school leaders, you know that your community must trust you and have faith in you if you are to lead effectively.

*Merriam-Webster* defines *trust* as "assured reliance on the character, ability, strength, or truth of someone or something; one in which confidence is placed; dependence on something future or contingent: hope."[3] Before presenting examples of the relationship between establishing and deepening trust and creating professional learning environments that support growth and leadership development, I'd like to highlight a few points. These are probably things you already know, but my aim is to link them to supporting leadership development so that you can see how they are part of the fabric of the holding environments presented in the examples that follow.

First, every effort to create a holding environment or professional learning opportunity requires the establishment of trust between you and those who are looking to learn from you. And to establish trust, we must first show we are trustworthy. Those we are working to support need to *see* and *feel* that there's an alignment between what we say, what we do, who we are on the outside, and who we are on the inside. This is a precondition for establishing and then deepening trust. And, yes, it takes courage. As mentioned earlier, it requires the courage to be oneself, to be authentic, to be open, to admit mistakes, and to share vulnerabilities. When you do this, I have learned, it usually inspires others to do the same. Allowing others to see us as *we* are can inspire them to show themselves as *they* are and enable us to see them that way. Establishing trust in this way is essential when beginning to create the kinds of environments for growth and leadership development that need to be present in professional learning initiatives that support internal capacity building.

Second, once established, trust can be deepened through relationships. The upcoming example about Lena (not her real name), in particular, shows how this can happen. It also highlights the importance of how trust can be deepened through honest conversation and genuine care. In addition, it shows the necessity of confidence in the other as part of deepening trust. I've found if I begin my relationships with a trust in the other person, he or she grows to trust me over time. As noted earlier, deepening trust is a process that takes time.

Third, as you know, trust and safety go hand in hand and are both essential when you are building holding environments. Understanding from a developmental perspective that what constitutes safety in a relationship will mean different things to adults with different ways of knowing will help you when working to establish and deepen trust with learners. We saw in chapter 1 how our ways of knowing influence how we experience the world, our relationships, and professional development opportunities.

For example, it's important to remember that for instrumental knowers, safety might primarily mean that they can depend on you—the supervisor or leader—to follow and enforce rules, to abide by policies, and to explain exactly what they need to do to perform well. On the other hand, what makes a socializing knower feel safe in a relationship will mostly center on a leader's acceptance of and care for him or her as a person. Adults with this way of knowing orient to the human qualities of their leaders as well, wanting to know, for example: are they caring? Are they patient with me? Do they like me? Adults who make meaning with primarily a self-authoring way of knowing will feel safe in a relationship, for the most part, when they feel respected and valued for their competencies. They experience conflict and disagreement as paths toward better solutions and seek relationships in which they can disagree, demonstrate their competencies, critique ideas, and share and implement *their vision*, which is generated by their internal self-system. Self-transforming knowers, who know that their own internal system—and any inner system, for that matter—has limitations, will feel safe in relationships and experience trust in relationships when both partners can engage in honest dialogue about contradictions, paradoxes, and sticking points. While they will seek harmony in relationships with their leaders, they do have the capacity to mediate conflict among constituencies.

It's important to remember, then, that as we strive to create spaces for growth and leadership development that work for the entire group, we need to differentiate the ways in which we build and deepen trust with unique individuals. Next I share a few examples of how you, as a leader, can cultivate trusting relationships in the context of professional learning initiatives.

### Starting with the Small Things

Many leaders with whom I have the honor of working have told me that their approach to establishing trust is to "start with the small things." I do this too when working to establish trust and create holding environments for growth. As you'll read more about shortly, it is important to offer opportunities for adults in teaching and learning and professional development environments to get to know each other.

You might be wondering, why should you do this, and how can you do this? Inviting adults to share a little about themselves and/or to discuss ideas and nonpersonal issues at the start of a learning adventure helps adults—including you, as leader/facilitator—to get to know each other and to establish trust. This is a first step to building safe and trusting relationships in general and in professional learning environments in particular. Learning to talk to each other about "small things"—nonpersonal issues—and then working our way up to talking about things that matter more to us personally helps to create holding environments that support growth. It also, as school leaders have conveyed, makes large groups feel smaller and more intimate. Leaders appreciate being given the time and space to get to know each other, and have told me that it enables them to share deeper challenges and to be more open to sharing in these contexts.

For example, at the start of a professional development workshop, or team meeting, inviting participants to introduce themselves in dyads (one-on-one), triads, or small table groups and to share a little about who they are, their position, what they do, and something they'd like others to know about them can be an effective way to begin building trust. When inviting adults to share what they've discussed in small groups with a larger group, I ask for volunteers to share "whatever you feel comfortable sharing."

Starting with the small, nonthreatening things helps to build holding environments and eventually leads to deeper trust and more personal sharing when engaging in deeper conversations in relation to leadership or project work. This process takes time. These "small things" serve as stepping-stones for creating contexts where adults are more willing to take risks and to share, for example, personal dilemmas of practice, challenges in leadership, difficulties with offering feedback to peers, or how they experience conflict with supervisors. This process creates a setting that allows for deeper and more connected conversations, and it can help leaders to feel safe disagreeing and engaging in conflict rather than shying away from it.

## Working with a Team

Recently, I witnessed another powerful example of the importance of establishing and deepening trust when supporting growth and leadership development. I was leading and facilitating a series of developmental workshops that made up a "developmental leadership institute" for aspiring and practicing school leaders (principals, assistant principals, teacher leaders, coaches, diversity specialists, and district leaders). A team of five volunteers (mostly teachers and graduate students who were interested in leading learning-oriented professional development) helped me lead and facilitate the institute's plenary, workshops, and breakout sessions. We were fortunate to have many leaders—about one hundred—participating in the institute. To make this a successful and meaningful experience for participants, one in which they would not only learn content but also *experience* it, my team and I had to do a lot of behind-the-scenes planning and preparation before, during, and after each day of the institute. One such task included commenting on participants' reflective writing assignments, which they submitted before the institute began so that we, the teaching team, could learn a little about their backgrounds and experiences and the big takeaways they were expecting as a result of participating in the institute. While most of the volunteers on the team had experience working with me in different contexts, I invited a new member, whom I'll call Lena, to join the team because we were expecting such a large turnout. I also knew that Lena was very interested in learning more about creating environments that would help adults grow. I wanted to help her and thought it would be a meaningful experience for her.

A superstar former graduate student in education leadership who went above and beyond in everything she did—including her graduate studies, research, and work in K–12 schools and systems—Lena had my full confidence, and I was excited and delighted about bringing her on board. I knew that she would be a gift to our team and to the leaders we would be working with. However, despite offering Lena what I thought were appropriate supports, guidance, and feedback on her contributions in this new role, I felt something was "off." Lena's feedback to participants about their written prework assignments didn't always feel supportive in a developmental sense. And I was especially surprised when she diverged from the team's agreed-upon norms about our email communications to institute participants. For instance, to model the ideal of teamwork, we had agreed to sign off emails using everyone's name—no matter who was the actual sender. In addition, while each of us sent personalized communications to a designated group of leaders who would be institute participants, we drafted the main text of the emails together to ensure that participants would feel treated and supported (*held*) in similar ways. Lena, however, sent out a round of emails to participants that diverged *completely* from the script. And, since she signed *only* her name at the end, they seemed to be *only* from her.

Concerned about what I could have done better to help Lena succeed on the team, what might have gone wrong for Lena on her end, and what these slips might unintentionally communicate to the aspiring leaders in Lena's group, I asked her if we could schedule a time to talk. It was important to have an honest conversation and to determine how Lena was understanding our work.

The conversation, as you might imagine, was difficult yet caring. After establishing that Lena was all right, I felt it was important to talk with her about her "lone wolf" emails—for her own sake, the sake of the team, and for the institute participants. As soon as I broached the subject, though, Lena became nervous and upset. "I understand if you need to fire me," she explained, "I was just trying to do a good job." Taking this kind of initiative, she helped me understand, was usually welcomed in her other work contexts, and she had just hoped very much to "show up" impressively in this new role as well.

Touched by Lena's honesty and the trust she demonstrated in me by making herself so vulnerable and sharing so transparently, I understood much better and was happy to move forward. "All we talked about was offered to you with love," I told her—and I meant it. Lena, I knew, and as I always believed, was a gift for the institute, and I wanted her volunteer experience to likewise be a gift, and a growing opportunity for her as well. But trust played an even bigger role in this story yet.

For Lena, the knowledge that I was not going to "fire" her—that she could make mistakes and still be welcomed and valued as an important part of the team—was utterly transformative. She explained that she was used to the high-stakes, high-pressure world of K–12 schools, where teachers and administrators often feel increasingly at risk of losing their jobs. The genuine safety of the team's holding environment, however, allowed Lena to step back from the competitive, aggressive stance with which she first approached the work. Free to learn, grow, and *be with* the volunteer team and participants without trying to prove herself, she ended up a shining star on the institute team. The trust we established and deepened through honest conversation and genuine care ran both ways and blossomed in the institute sessions.

## Ways to Build Trust

In closing this section, I'd like to highlight a common problem and challenge that leaders in both K–12 schools and university contexts talk a lot about in relation to trust. Whether you are a principal, assistant principal, teacher leader, team leader, coach, or any educator serving in a supervisory capacity, it's tough to be *both* an evaluator and a critical friend who offers support for improving instruction and practice. In other words, wanting to offer support in order to be of best help to someone while simultaneously having an evaluative responsibility for that person is challenging. The following example is one you might find helpful when confronting this issue yourself, and one that may resonate with your own experiences and/or those of educators with whom you collaborate.

Recently, I was facilitating a learning seminar for K–12 teacher leaders, coaches, principals, and assistant principals about many of the ideas discussed in this book. Toward the end of the first day, when participants were about to begin designing action plans to implement ideas from the seminar in their unique contexts, an instructional coach, Bob, shared his dilemma. As a coach, he facilitates *learning walks* in his high school with groups of teachers. (A learning walk is when a group of teachers and their coach, assistant principal, or principal observe practice together. They gather evidence and engage in dialogue about their observations with a goal of learning from each other to improve instructional practice.) "I've been noticing," he explained, "that when we're on learning walks, the teachers are not really telling me and their colleagues the truth about the kinds of things they need help with in order to improve their practice." He continued, "Instead . . . it's like they overprepare to make everything seem like it's going well in their classrooms rather than ask for the help they need . . . I am not sure what to do."

Deeply appreciative of this complex challenge and inspired by his courage, I thanked Bob for his honest sharing and then inquired, "Why do you think they are doing that?" He immediately responded, "They are afraid because I am *also* evaluating them." We talked for a while about how difficult it is to wear two hats. Participants agreed emphatically. I asked if Bob had established norms with the group of teachers for creating safe and productive holding environments during learning walks and developed confidentiality agreements, and if he had shared with them how difficult it can be for him to fulfill two roles, one supportive and the other evaluative. He hadn't. To help him as he worked to establish and deepen trust within these teacher groups, I suggested that he 1) develop norms with the teacher groups and talk with them to make confidentiality agreements to establish trust and safety, 2) collaboratively develop a protocol that would guide each learning walk (e.g., a protocol could include focused questions about what each teacher would like help with during observations, guidelines for offering feedback), and 3) make clear to teachers when he is wearing his evaluative hat and when he is wearing his more collegial one. These techniques can help with establishing and deepening trust both at the individual and group level, which in turn will serve to create safer, more trusting spaces that support adult growth and leadership development.

## COLLABORATION

*The strength of the team is each individual member. The strength of each member is the team.*

—Phil Jackson

When the New York Jets were playing the New England Patriots in the January 2010 playoffs, something the Jets' head coach, Rex Ryan, shared at the start of the fourth quarter struck me. "I have a lot of very talented people on my team," he explained. "The key is placing them in the best place so that they can share their talents and shine." His comment reminds me of how I think about real collaboration and creating holding environments for growth and leadership development. When collaborating, it is important to recognize the different kinds of gifts each person brings, to create contexts where individuals can both shine and grow from collaboration, and to be intentional about offering appropriate supports and challenges. Doing so creates the conditions that make it possible for people to work together to contribute in important and meaningful ways to their shared goal and to supporting each other's growth and leadership development.

*Merriam-Webster* defines *collaboration* in two ways: "to work jointly with others or together especially in an intellectual endeavor" and "to cooperate with an agency or instrumentality with which one is not immediately connected."[4] Both of these involve connectivity and engagement with others.

As you will see, true collaboration is powerful and essential to building environments for growth and leadership development. It's about engaging, having connected conversations, and making connections as we work *together* to accomplish goals, improve leadership, and support growth and leadership development. I strive to build opportunities for collaboration when nurturing holding environments for aspiring and practicing leaders, and when working in any professional learning initiative. But what is true collaboration? And how can we create opportunities for adults to collaborate meaningfully and with developmental intentions? In this section, I discuss collaboration and include examples of the ways in which I collaborate with others and of situations in which groups of adults collaborate to support growth and leadership development.

Collaboration is a value I hold. I try to promote it in the groups and teams I work with and employ it in my individual work. Collaboration must value autonomy and interdependence. It's more than simply getting the work done; it is about *how* the work gets done. When building environments for growth and leadership development, we must consider how to enhance the ways in which we collaborate in order to create a context for growth. As I mentioned in the introduction, all educators face adaptive challenges, and we must help aspiring and practicing leaders grow their internal capacities to meet these challenges. Given that fact, we need other people, and we need to enhance how we collaborate in order to grow ourselves and to strengthen schools, districts, teaching and learning environments, and professional development environments for practicing and aspiring leaders. Collaborating is more than the sharing of ideas (though that is important); it is also creating contexts in which we can grow and develop greater internal capacities from working and learning together. A wise mentor of mine taught me long ago that one of the fundamental rules of good teaching and leadership practice is "Don't do it all alone—and don't work in isolation." For me, this wisdom underscores the power of collaboration and the ways in which it can be a structure for supporting growth and leadership development.

Next, I highlight a few key points about collaboration from a developmental perspective. After that, I provide two examples from my own experience of collaboration that will, I hope, help you to engage in real collaboration in your own work and life.

## A Developmental Perspective on Collaboration

First, approaching collaboration from a developmental perspective means leading *with* and *for* others, with concern for their growth and leadership development at heart. All voices are valued and cherished. Collaboration is not a top-down enterprise. Second, to build holding environments for growth, it is important to meet a person where he or she is in terms of the person's way of knowing. Third, collaboration is not always easy, though it's certainly worthwhile. Fourth, yes, I realize you might be thinking about how collaborating with others can elongate project or team work time. That's true: collaboration typically takes more time than doing things alone. But it also makes for richer learning contexts, more robust opportunities for individual growth and leadership development, and better pathways for building community and increasing our collective capacities to improve learning. I go out of my way to work with others and to bring people together, and, as you know, it's important for all school leaders to do this, modeling the goal of productive collaboration for others. Fifth, there are many things we can do, big and small, to enhance contexts for collaboration so that they become environments for supporting growth and leadership development. One that I find very helpful is "checking in and checking out," which I discuss in detail shortly.

So, while collaboration does require greater investments of time and energy up front, I think you will find that the returns are worth it. Investing in collaboration with developmental intentions in any professional learning environment is of great value to all involved. I hope the examples that follow will not only illuminate the close connection between building safe, trusting, and respectful holding environments for growth and engaging in true collaboration, but will also demonstrate how collaboration can catalyze group members' desire to work with and for each other.

## Practices That Enhance Collaboration

There are ways that we can transform the process of "working together" or alongside each other into one of true collaboration. What follows are two very effective practices, *checking in and checking out* and *taking time for a reflective pause*, that I've found to not only enhance collaboration but also to create and nurture safe, trusting, and respectful environments that support growth.

### Checking In and Checking Out

A simple yet very powerful practice I often use to support and enhance genuine collaboration—which goes beyond cooperation for the sake of expediency or necessity, and involves truly embracing the value and unique gifts diverse individuals bring to a team—is what I call "checking in and checking out." Put simply, this practice involves prioritizing time at the beginning and end of meetings to allow the team or group to share how they're thinking or feeling about the work, lingering questions, and life in general. While some people who are unfamiliar with this practice initially express worry about "wasting time" on such concerns given the urgency of their work and the demands on their time, the act of checking in and checking out quickly creates a sacred, caring space that actually enhances the work and the possibilities of true collaboration.

I employ this practice in many contexts: university courses, team meetings, leadership team meetings in districts, professional development courses in schools, and leadership academies I design for leaders at all levels. Of course, the protocols (i.e., the questions raised and addressed when checking in and out) that I design vary depending on context, duration of time together, and my assessment of group needs. Here, I share one particular example of how checking in and checking out helped my instructional team of eight people develop a caring, collaborative, developmental holding environment while preparing for and teaching nearly one hundred students in the Summer Principals Academy (described earlier and in chapter 1).

As team leader, and the person who invited each team member to join, I had the honor and privilege of knowing each member and the unique gifts he or she would bring to the team, but many of the team members had not met before our work together, and we needed to collectively accomplish a great deal before class even began. This teaching team was composed of graduate students, practicing principals and assistant principals, and doctoral students I was mentoring. Our prework (i.e., what we needed to do before the class began) included caring for students' very personal writing assignments by offering developmental feedback on their papers, uploading all of the course materials into the learning management system, ordering books and supplies for the course, and creating and organizing handouts. In other words, as is true of the teams you may lead, there was much important work to do to prepare for the class, and we all needed to be on the same page regarding logistics and to get to know as much as we could about the students by discussing their work together.

At the outset, however, the team members were spread out across the country and attending to many different responsibilities as teachers, principals, and graduate students in education leadership, so we did a lot of prework team building and planning over the phone. Checking in and checking out was an essential part of that process. This practice allowed us to get to know each other better and more deeply, and to develop a true esteem and respect for each other that made both the prework and the in-class work much more manageable and meaningful. Taking the time to listen and to share our thinking on course preassignments, as well as aspects of our personal and professional lives, as we embarked on this intensive journey together helped us shape the team as a holding environment for each of us, just as we were working to support the growth of our SPA students carefully and well. By intentionally setting aside the time to ask, for example, "How are you today?" "How are you feeling about what we discussed on the call?" and "How are you feeling about the work you are doing in the course?" we were able to gel as a real team before we ever even met in person. Like feeling cared about and respected, feeling known supports deeper levels of collaboration, which in turn makes the meaningful work of supporting adult development that much more of a gift.

What we gained from the feelings of mutual esteem and the collaboration that developed during our prework as a teaching team shined through in our work with students throughout the class. As one student shared on our last day of class, our teamwork helped illuminate the possibilities of genuinely working together with others toward a common goal: "Thank you for pushing our learning and for helping us grow. I am amazed by what the teaching team has done; I'm grateful to have witnessed such unconditional love and respect and am certain it is the reason for my growth. I have hope and faith that a holding environment can be fostered when sincere and amazing people initiate . . . I will never forget this experience."

### Taking Time for a Reflective Pause

Real collaboration, as you know, can help with building collaborative climates within systems, organizations, groups, teams, and individuals and is connected to cultivating environments in which trust and care are palpable. While it is not always easy to truly work together, adults need to be able to share what they are really thinking and feeling—even if it's hard for them to engage in conflict and disagreement—because in such honesty lies great possibility and benefit to the team.

As a final example of a collaborative practice, I offer my recent experience of facilitating a series of three all-day professional learning initiatives for almost one hundred faculty and administrators at a school in a Boston suburb. One afternoon, after creating action plans related to the developmental ideas we're exploring in this book, the teams shared their work with the large group. Just before we ended our time together, we engaged in a *reflective pause*. This was an opportunity for these leaders to reflect on the day and to share any insights or questions they had. A teacher—let's call her Sandy—who had been teaching high school science for more than twenty years at this school, shared the following as her closing reflection: "I learn from different perspectives. I value them. I respect them. It's not always comfortable for me to collaborate, especially when sometimes someone's perspective is so sharply different from my own. I find it hard to take it in. But I do learn from them and honor them. Collaboration enables me to learn and grow."

Sandy's sharing points to important lessons that I have emphasized in this section, including the value of being clear and honest when working to establish true collaboration—that is, the importance, challenge, and promising potential of genuinely engaging in work with other dedicated adults. Providing honest, authentic, clear feedback; listening deeply to both concerns and needs for support; balancing each individual's request for growth with compassion, understanding, and care for his or her strengths and needs; acknowledging leaders' own needs for growth; and above all, forging deeper relationships, one-on-one and with the group as a whole, all rest at the heart of collaborative enterprises. Engaging in all of these aspects of real collaboration can help you establish groups, teams, and schools as holding environments that strongly support growth and leadership development, both individually and collectively.

To help you reflect on your own conception of collaboration and on how you might apply it in support of your own and others' growth and development, I invite you to please complete the brief exercise in exhibit 2.2.

EXHIBIT 2.2

**PAUSE FOR REFLECTION**

### What Does Collaboration Mean to You?

Perhaps you'd like to take a few moments here to think about the following questions in light of what you've learned from reading this chapter.

How does what you've learned about collaboration help you with your own leadership, especially in relation to creating and sustaining true collaboration? What ideas, if any, might you incorporate into your own collaborative work to support leaders' growth?

## INTENTIONALITY

*Change is inevitable, growth is intentional.*

—Colin Wilson

Intentionality is another core element that informs how I think about building and sustaining professional learning environments that support growth. One way in which *Merriam-Webster* defines intentionality is "done by intention or design."[5] Intentionality in our context, then, means being purposeful about how we craft—*design*—contexts and attending to developmental and other forms of diversity. It also connects to the goal of *purposefully* bringing people together in ways that support their learning. In addition, developmental intentionality connects intimately to bridging theory and practice and shaping growth-oriented learning opportunities. In these kinds of learning enterprises, as you know, the big idea is not only to teach content but also to create an atmosphere in which participants *experience* the very practices they are learning about. The creation of holding environments (in teams, in classrooms, in professional development sessions, in groups) does not happen accidentally; it is intentional. And it centers on purposefully caring for developmental diversity as well as the experiences of the adults in the room. In other words, it involves thinking carefully about every aspect of the work, from the smallest detail to the largest, and designing environments that match through and through.

Put simply, intentionality is closely related to how we:

- Work to establish a safe, trusting, and respectful holding environment
- Acknowledge, honor, and respect each other's learning styles, experiences, ways of knowing, and expertise
- Work to incorporate a variety of supports and challenges within these contexts to meet the needs of adults with diverse of ways of knowing

Being intentional is very important when creating professional learning environments in which adults feel cared about and well held, and it is also vital in building and deepening trust and a sense of community. For instance, intentionality is intertwined with developing respect for and honoring commonality (what we have and hold in common) and differences (visible and invisible). In other words, being intentional about *explicitly* acknowledging what we have and hold in common and naming and embracing our differences—and seeing both as strengths and gifts—nurtures safe, trusting, and respectful holding environments in which adults feel free to take risks and grow. In addition, carving out space to deliberately discuss these can support growth in all of us, regardless of our way of knowing. This is true from a developmental perspective as well as more generally.

Intentionality is closely related to modeling (which you will learn more about in chapter 3). For example, in a recent research project, two colleagues and I sought to understand how leaders who had participated in one of my graduate courses on leadership for adult development five to seven years earlier were applying their learning now, in actual practice.[6] The leaders commented on the power of the course's developmental intentionality—in terms of its design and their experience in it—and how it helped them to be intentional in shaping holding environments for others in their own work contexts. They explained that *experiencing* the value placed on adult development and practices that support it *as they were learning* about them carried over to the work they were doing now. They shared that it was not just the way the course was designed that helped them learn, but also the interactions they had with the teachers and their colleagues in the course that were meaningful and supportive of their growth.

As they learned, and as you will learn more throughout this book, every aspect of the course design, assignments, and activities was *intentional* in nature, and aimed at supporting students' growth. In other words, it included structures, practices, processes, and facilitation that were informed by constructive-developmental theory. I strove to be mindful of developmental diversity in my facilitation, ways of listening, questioning, and feedback, which in turn helped these leaders experience what it feels like to be in an environment that rests on this kind of intentionality and caring mindfulness. Approaching your own leadership work similarly can make a tremendous difference. As one student, an aspiring leader, recently shared with me after taking a semester-long version of my class, understanding the value of being intentional is indeed an important takeaway, and a promising stance to carry forward: "During every step of the way (even before the class met for the first time), I felt like I was provided an adequate level of challenge and support. My hope is to bottle this feeling about the holding environment offered to me and be intentional in trying to provide it to others."

A strategy I employ in all teaching, learning, and professional development settings, intentionality encompasses many things, including sending welcoming emails before first meetings, paying careful attention to the kinds of comments offered on papers and in person, deliberately modeling the practices that nurture and support growth, and creating an atmosphere of trust that gives adults opportunities to get to know one another. At its very heart, though, and no matter what its form, intentionality is about doing everything in your power to create the kinds of environments that allow people to grow—to feel respected, safe, and cared about and for. It means being mindful about all of your actions as leader and facilitator and having a deep concern for how these actions will be received and understood.

## Using Time Intentionally

The following two simple examples of an intentional use of time demonstrate how intentionality can help transform groups and individuals. The first involves the creation of "Tea Time" by a woman named Barbara who was the chair of a science department in a large Boston high school. She created Tea Time after she participated in a leadership academy I facilitated that focused on supporting adult development through leadership. Recognizing the need for greater community in her department, Barbara set out to find a way to help her teachers come together more regularly, and get to know each other better as colleagues and individuals. Barbara worried that her department, which consisted of fifteen teachers, rarely had opportunities to communicate. There were monthly faculty meetings, of course, but otherwise the teachers hardly saw each other. They were spread out across the school, with classrooms on different floors, and were kept very busy by the pace of the school day and their many responsibilities.

Determined to address this lack of shared time, Barbara intentionally carved out fifteen minutes of every day for the full department to meet. During Tea Time, the teachers shared updates—sometimes work related, sometimes not—and began to discuss things that really mattered in their instructional practice and their lives. By checking in and out in this way, and intentionally creating a sacred and separate time to do this, Barbara and the teachers in her department rediscovered each other, and eventually even sought out more opportunities to meet and collaborate.

The second example involves Chris, a teacher leader at an urban charter school who also participated in the leadership academy and embraced the idea of using time and space more intentionally. At his school, teachers would spend the hour between the end of classes and the beginning of their faculty meeting walking off-campus to get coffee, individually or in small groups. Hoping, like Barbara, to help all of the teachers find more time to connect and collaborate, Chris asked the school administrators if they would be willing to supply coffee in a designated room at the school before the faculty meeting. They agreed, and the teachers naturally congregated at the school's new "coffee bar," which gave them more casual opportunities for community building and collaboration. In this example, simply designating a few resources—a coffee maker, filters, and coffee—with the intention of creating a connective space made a big difference for the teachers and ultimately for their students.

## Intentionality as Investment

Being intentional about creating environments that support adult and leadership development *is an investment of time, care, love, and energy.* Yes, it does take time in the planning, in the actual learning event itself, and after the event occurs, but it is time well spent. When I think about being intentional, and what adults have valued about my being intentional when working to support their learning and development, there are a few additional important ideas that come to mind:

- The importance of considering growth as a *process* that can occur in teaching, learning, and professional development contexts provided that we are intentional about creating holding environments for adult and leadership development.

- The importance of recognizing that constructive-developmental theory can inform the ways in which we intentionally care for building contexts for others and for ourselves at both the individual and group/school level.
- Learning about theory and practices supportive of adult development while *actually experiencing and engaging in these practices* can help adults to understand the value of creating holding environments for others, as well as how to create them.

Being intentional is also related to additional practices that you can employ to support growth and leadership development. In chapter 5, you will learn more about the nuances of the space and our actions within them.

So, while here I have emphasized the importance of these *core values* in my new, learning-oriented model for leadership development, in the next chapter I invite you to consider how implementing components of the second growth ring—namely, listening, seeing, modeling, building relationships, and using language—can help you intentionally support adult and leadership development in your own noble leadership work.

## TAKEAWAYS

Looking back at the core elements discussed in this chapter, you can see that they are all related to intentionally creating holding environments for growth and leadership development in order to support meaningful professional learning. Intentionality is the core element that helps bring to bear all of the others: care, respect, trust, and collaboration. Deliberately and caringly prioritizing these elements and making them apparent in your leadership work—no matter the context—is key to creating safe, nurturing, growth-enhancing environments that support growth and leadership development. The following are this chapter's key takeaways:

+ At the heart of the innermost growth ring in this model, I have placed a central dot. Each of us has a personal central dot—the core essence of oneself. This dot represents the individual, who you are as a teacher, leader, coach, mentor, parent, and all of the roles you fill in your life. Our central dot influences the way we strive to create holding environments for others and for ourselves. In many ways, it influences all other components of this model.

+ Most basic in creating holding environments is that one really needs to genuinely *care for* and value another's growth and development. Finding something to celebrate authentically and value in every person *is* caring and demonstrating care. There are two main parts to my definition of care: honestly valuing aspects of a person and focusing on that person's well-being.

+ *Respect* is about seeing and acknowledging individuals' rights to *be who they are*, whereas care is finding *something meaningful and beautiful within those identities to value*. Respect means *seeing and celebrating* individuals, their right to be who they are, and acknowledging their own unique life path.

+ *Trust* is a bridge to building environments that support adult and leadership development. It takes time to establish trust and even more time to deepen it. Establishing and building trust happens when we are transparent in our thinking and feelings, which is vital to developing trusting relationships. Trust is fundamental to human connection, human relationships (both interpersonal and group), and human compassion. As school leaders, you also know that your community must trust you and have faith in you if you are to lead effectively.

+ *Collaboration* is powerful and essential to building holding environments for growth and leadership development. It's about engaging, having connected conversations, and making connections as we work *together* to accomplish goals, improve leadership, and support growth and leadership development. Collaboration must value autonomy and interdependence. It's more than simply getting the work done; it is about *how* the work gets done. When leading professional learning initiatives that support adult and leadership development, we must consider how to enhance the ways in which we collaborate in order to create a holding environment.

+ *Intentionality*, the last core element we learned about in this chapter, informs building and sustaining growth-enhancing professional learning opportunities. Intentionality means being purposeful about crafting holding environments that attend to developmental and other forms of diversity. It also connects to the goal of *purposefully* bringing people together in ways that support their learning. In addition, developmental intentionality connects intimately to bridging theory and practice and shaping the contexts and conditions for growth.

## REFLECTIVE QUESTIONS

1. What are three important ideas that stand out to you after reading this chapter? Why? How, if at all, might you incorporate these ideas into your leadership practice of supporting adult growth and leadership development?
2. How, if at all, do the core elements discussed here resonate with your own experiences of building contexts for growth and leadership development?
3. What, if anything, do you feel is missing from the central growth ring? What additional core values would you add?
4. Which of the practices that we learned about here might you incorporate into your own work?

# CHAPTER 3

## Senses and Strategies

*Putting the Core Elements into Practice*

*We make a living by what we get, but we make a life by what we give.*

—SIR WINSTON CHURCHILL

In chapter 2, I described how the core elements of care, respect, trust, collaboration, and intentionality inform my new model for learning-oriented leadership development. Of course, when you are crafting professional learning initiatives to support adult learning and growth, it is critical to *authentically* align your beliefs with your practice. It's one thing to say that the core elements are important. It is another thing to actually "walk the walk" and to align your core values with the expression of those elements in practice. This alignment of values and behavior is the glue that holds successful professional learning initiatives together. In other words, how we listen, how we use language, how we go about building relationships, how we model, what we model, how we perceive the emotional tone in the room, and how we see and attend to learners' needs all matter. You know how children and adolescents can usually immediately *sense* from your presence and what you say and do whether they can trust you, whether they can share honestly with you, and whether they want to learn from your teaching and leadership? Well, it's very similar with adult learners and leaders. They use *their senses* to make these determinations. And, as shapers of contexts for growth and leadership development, we need to use ours as well.

In this chapter, you will learn about *how* the core elements situated at the heart of the model (i.e., the innermost growth ring) are manifested and expressed in professional learning environments that support adult and leadership development. As you see in figure 3.1, I've now added a second growth ring to the one presented in chapter 2.

There are five ways in which these core values are manifested or expressed—that is, put into practice—and they are largely sensory in nature. They include:

- *Listening with presence.* This means listening sensitively to understand another person's experience, not just listening to what is said but also to the meaning it holds for the person.
- *Using language thoughtfully.* This includes paying careful attention to the words you use, and how you frame your teaching and facilitation (through asking questions and offering verbal and written feedback that nurtures the development of a holding environment).
- *Seeing with sensitivity.* This means attending to your own intuition about the emotional tone that people give off.

**FIGURE 3.1**

**The second growth ring: the five ways in which the core values are manifested**

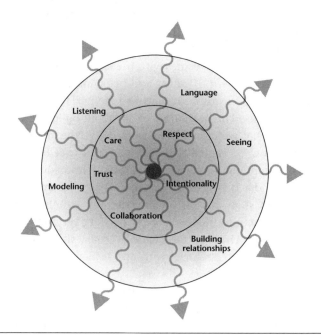

- *Building relationships.* This includes offering human connections through storytelling, listening, using language, and seeing through a developmental lens, which concerns what I call the *treasure of paid attention*, or the gift of attending to the individual.
- *Modeling.* This involves teaching with transparency and responsiveness.

*Merriam-Webster* defines *sense* in some of the following ways: "conscious awareness or rationality," "a particular sensation or kind or quality of sensation," and "capacity for effective application of the powers of the mind as a basis for action or response."[1] Having a "conscious awareness" of the ways we *listen* (a sense); how we notice and *see* (another sense) learners and what's happening in any teaching, learning, and professional development environment; and what we are modeling in our use of language can help us to *act* and *be responsive* to learners in ways that transform professional development initiatives into environments that support adult growth and leadership.

## LISTENING

Listening is essential to meeting a person where he or she is, and is intimately connected to each of the core elements (care, respect, trust, collaboration, and intentionality). Listening, for instance, is perhaps the first and best way we let others know that they matter to us, that their views have merit and value, and that we are "with" them psychologically and developmentally. Listening in a developmental sense has to do with joining the person in his or her meaning making. Research, too, has shown that the quality of our listening *is* a developmental support. Truly listening to understand others and to stand *with them as they are*, without urgently pushing for their growth or change, can make all the difference. This means that listening sensitively, or *listening with presence*, can support both the adults that we work with and our own leadership. Listening with presence can help us to understand how individuals make sense of their experience (i.e., way of knowing) and in turn can help us to provide the appropriate supports and challenges that are needed to support their growth (internal capacity building).

### Listening with Presence

I consider it a privilege to listen with presence to another person, whether engaging in a one-on-one conversation or with a large group of leaders in a professional development environment. One way that *Merriam-Webster* defines *listen* is "to hear something with thoughtful attention: give consideration."[2] Giving our "consideration" and "thoughtful attention" are also ways in which we listen *with presence*.

Sometimes, as a person is speaking about his or her experience, you realize that it is the very first time that the individual is discovering something about him- or herself, or that the experience is of deep personal importance. Listening carefully and caringly can help us to be fully present and to be of use to others as they courageously let us into the ways in which they make meaning in life. Witnessing this moment is a gift. By being present as we listen to others, we can better support their growth and leadership development. We can do this one-on-one, and we can do this in teaching, learning, and professional development environments. It is important to be mindful of *how* the individuals to whom we are listening receive or experience our listening and the supports and challenges we offer to support their growth and leadership development.

When facilitating professional learning initiatives, I often share the following example to illustrate how we can tell when another person is listening to us even over the phone. When my husband, David, and I talk on the phone, I feel that he listens deeply and caringly to what I am saying and to what I'm not. I cannot see him, but I can *feel* his thoughtful attention and care. His listening with presence is palpable; he gives his *undivided attention*. Without even seeing him, I know he is listening and, what's more, *listening without judgment*—and it is a gift I cherish. Listening in this way connects back to the core elements in the innermost growth ring, especially to demonstrating care, respect, intentionality, and deepening trust.

With these important ideas in mind, next I'll describe the different ways in which I listen when learning with and from educators and leaders of all kinds in my workshops, university courses, and any teaching, learning, or professional development initiatives I'm facilitating. After that, we'll consider specific examples that highlight some of the more important aspects of listening with presence as we work to create holding environments at both the individual and group levels. My big hope is that you find these ideas, practices, and examples helpful in your own work.

## Ways of Listening

The following are ways I listen to individuals and groups when building holding environments and facilitating professional learning. In addition to being ways of listening, they are also *forms of action* that can make a difference in terms of helping someone to know and feel that you are listening with presence, thoughtful attention, and consideration. Engaging in these practices demonstrates care and respect, supports development, and establishes and deepens trust:

- Giving your undivided attention to the person.
- Listening without judgment.
- Paraphrasing (restating and sometimes rewording) what a person has said; this lets people know you are hearing them, you are with them, and you are listening. It also helps them hear what they said, which can be especially helpful when it appears that they are in the process of trying to make sense of how they think and feel in that very moment.
- Listening for emotion behind and in words and responding to what is both spoken and unspoken.
- Listening and allowing for *silence*—not responding right away can give a person some needed time to pause, gather thoughts, and reflect.
- Checking to see if you understand what the person is saying. In doing this, you might find it helpful to ask clarifying questions (e.g., "I hear you mention $X$; can you say a little more about what you meant by that?" "Can you help me understand a little more about what $X$ means to you?" "When you mentioned $Y$, I wasn't sure of the context and when and how that happened?" "A few minutes ago, you shared $Z$ . . . it sounded important to you; can we go back to that?"). It can also help to simply check in (e.g., "Would it be okay if we paused for a moment? I just want to make sure I understand. I think you are saying . . . " "What I am hearing you say is that . . . is that what you mean?" "You seem like you are upset/angry/disappointed about $X$ . . . you must have felt $Y$?").
- Working to connect what the person is saying and feeling to the larger *context* of his or her life and experience (if you have the gift of knowing it).
- Letting the person know you are with him or her (e.g., "I'm with you" or "I'm following").

When we are truly listening, the other person can feel it, even if we don't say a word for a while. We can also listen on different levels. For example, we can listen intently for:

- *Feelings (emotions and affect)*. What is your intuition telling you about the other person's feelings? What are you feeling as you're listening to him or her?
- *Thoughts and ideas*. What seems most important to the person? What stands out to you as you listen? What lessons/puzzles/dilemmas is the

person sharing? How is he or she making sense of them? What seems most important to her or him? What is hardest about the situation being shared? What's at stake? What, if anything, is at risk? Did the person share what he or she was thinking and feeling with those involved in the situation? If not, why not? How did the person come to know what he or she knows?

- *Actions/behaviors.* What happened? What did the person do?

Making time and space to listen with developmental intentions and in the aforementioned ways can help a person to feel well held in the psychological sense. Our questions and presence can also help individuals learn to consider alternatives and challenge them in a developmental sense to grow as leaders. One thing that leaders I've worked with and learned from have found very helpful is the power of sharing what they *truly* feel and think with others, especially when in difficult situations. (You'll read more about this in the upcoming section on language.)

Listening is a core skill to consider when building holding environments and when facilitating professional learning initiatives. Life is more full when we listen deeply to other people—and, in so doing, we create opportunities for growth. Truly listening is also a precious gift we can give, because it is not always easy to make the time and space to be there for another person, especially in the midst of competing pressures and demands. School leaders I've worked with have shared that they really valued the experience of being truly heard, and that it has helped them to listen more effectively to those in their care.

## The Importance of Listening: Stories from the Field

You might find it helpful to learn from what other schools leaders have shared about the importance of listening in the ways just described. As you may recall, I have had the honor of working with and learning from school leaders in facilitating developmental leadership academies. Like other kinds of experiences I lead, these academies are ongoing sessions that have dual purposes: they not only teach content and practices for supporting adult growth and leadership development but also create environments in which the leaders themselves experience the very conditions and practices that support internal capacity building.

*Example 1: Really Listening to Someone is Hard and Important Work*

I recently facilitated one such academy for thirty teacher leaders, school principals, assistant principals, and specialists who came from five different public and charter schools in the Boston area. We met four times during the course of an academic year (Friday evenings and all day Saturday) to learn about adult developmental theory and the pillar practices for growth (these were introduced in prior chapters and will be discussed in more detail later) and how they can support internal capacity building. After our first weekend seminar together in October, we reconvened in December. As we began the Friday night session, I invited participants to voluntarily share "the one small action step" they'd implemented since our previous time together. I did this to check in on how things were going with their developmental leadership work and to give them an opportunity to share and celebrate. First, they privately reflected by either freewriting or free-thinking, and next they had a chance to share with a partner or two. After that I asked, "Does anyone have something they'd feel comfortable sharing with all of us?"

One teacher leader courageously offered the following about how she had been practicing listening after experiencing our first seminar together in October: "I've been working on listening for two months—ever since the last time we met . . . I mean *really* [emphasis hers] listening to my colleagues and to my friends and family. Listening to what the person is *really* saying. I've been focusing on *them*, their words, trying to understand *their* meaning. It's been very powerful, and it's really hard work." Listening deeply and working to understand another person was very important, she realized, and a skill she wanted to develop and continue working on. Searching to understand both the words and the emotion behind the words was something she found valuable, noting, "it is making such a difference."

*Example 2: Listening Carefully and Naming What You're Hearing*
During the Friday evening seminar of our last weekend session, held in April, another teacher leader shared what he had noticed me doing and found to be a powerful way of listening during our prior seminars: I had *named* what I was hearing. In doing so, I was trying to be transparent in my effort to support growth.

In his opening reflections about the developmental work he had been engaging in since our previous time together in February, he offered the following about how he had been practicing an important way of listening to others: "Naming things has been very helpful and it ties back into the idea of listening and reflecting back what people are saying to you."

Another participant in the academy, a director of learning and development at a charter school, shared her reflection in the post-session survey: "Several people mentioned the 'pair sharing' [sharing privately with one other participant] to me tonight, and that it was so helpful not only to have someone else's perspective . . . [but] also to *know that someone else is listening."*

These examples highlight the power of listening with presence. I hope you find them helpful in your own leadership practice and in your work building holding environments for growth and leadership development.

## USING THE POWER OF LANGUAGE

*Whatever words we utter should be chosen with care, for people will hear them and be influenced by them for good or ill.*

—Buddha

Using language thoughtfully and with developmental intentions—including paying careful attention to the words we use and how we frame our teaching and facilitation—is very important in general, and in particular when we're considering how to shape professional learning environments that support adult and leadership development. We not only shape these contexts in relation to what we *do* but also in relation to what we *say*.

*Merriam-Webster* defines language in some of the following ways: "words, their pronunciation, and the methods of combining them used and understood by a community" and the "form or manner of verbal expression; *specifically*: style."[3] In this section of the chapter, you will learn more about how we can use language intentionally, including the sounds we make (e.g., "mmm-hmm" in response to a reflection or insight); the words we use; the ways in which language reflects our ideas, beliefs, and efforts to support internal capacity building; and how we can frame our questions and feedback to support development. You'll also learn from examples of how the intentional use of language works in professional development contexts and how some leaders experience its power to support growth and leadership development. Indeed, language is an important shaper of holding environments at every level. For another important perspective on the power of language, you'll find it useful to read *How the Way We Talk Can Change the Way We Work*.[4]

### Voicing Appreciation and Making Spaces for It

First, I have found that *voicing appreciation* for leaders' questions, comments, and insights in any teaching, learning, and professional development environment is one essential way to begin and sustain developmentally oriented professional learning. It can be as simple as saying, "Thank you for sharing that," or "I appreciate your question." When I say this, I *mean* it—and it is a form of language that I employ very intentionally. Although I've had leaders initially tell me that they are "not used to being thanked" and sometimes find gratitude "hard to take in," two of the comments that proliferate in evaluations and reflective surveys are that leaders a) *really* appreciate being appreciated, and b) find it so supportive of their growth and learning that they have adopted the practice of voicing appreciation in their own leadership contexts.

One additional and helpful practice that you might want to remember when facilitating professional learning initiatives is making space for voicing "appreciations" at the close of each session in the spirit of *ending well*. When I do this, I don't demand that leaders say anything, but rather I create the space and invite them to "pass or play" their turn (meaning that it's completely voluntary) to share with the group something they found themselves appreciating or valuing about our time together. I tell them, "It is *your* space," meaning they are free to share about someone specifically, about our group as a whole, about their experiences that day, or not at all. Making space for this kind of collective sharing helps to nurture growth and leadership development. As one of my students shared in an end-of-course survey, appreciations are contagious and transformative: "Thank you all [members of the teaching team]! It really has been a great experience, and I was extremely skeptical at first and sarcastic about all the appreciations [you expressed during the first few days of the course]. Thank you [for] being persistent and teaching me so much. Thank you for sharing your appreciations. It was humbling to see all of the amazing [teaching] team leaders expressing gratitude."

## Using Questions as Developmental Supports

Second, using language intentionally in the way we ask questions and offer feedback, both verbal and written, during professional learning can support growth and leadership development. In listening with developmental intentionality (e.g., one might ask clarifying questions or mirror back what was heard) and using appropriate developmental questioning and feedback, we are standing at the edges of someone's thinking in order to support growth and advance meaning making.

Since questioning and feedback are related in many ways, I'll discuss both here. There's great power in *how* we frame questions and feedback. Offering developmental feedback usually involves asking questions or proposing alternatives (e.g., "Have you considered what might have happened if you . . . ?"). As you know, questioning is a part of how we use language, and it is especially important when seeking to support adult growth and leadership development; our questions can spur growth, just as our feedback can. In general, we can use questioning as a developmental support and challenge. Questions can help individuals consider new and alternative perspectives, focus on how they were feeling during a difficult moment (feelings and thinking are intimately connected), and assess how they are feeling and thinking in the moment. Questions can help people to imagine what might have happened *if* they had shared what they were *actually* thinking and feeling in a difficult conversation, conflict, or confrontation with a supervisor or good friend, for example. As professional learning facilitators, we can use questions to help us *stand with* and *stand by* a person and also to *stand at the edges* of his or her thinking and feeling in order to support growth, internal capacity building, and leadership development. As you know from the previous chapters, it's important to consider people's ways of knowing when offering questions and feedback. For more information about ways of knowing and the types of questions that support growth, you might want to revisit chapter 1 or read *Leading Adult Learning.*[5]

I've also found it *very* important to pause silently after asking developmentally oriented questions and offering feedback (both verbal and written). Leaders often comment on how rarely they are given this kind of space—what we usually refer to as *wait time.*

An additional word about offering comments and questions: one thing that is crucial, especially from a developmental sense, is balancing the supportive and challenging questions and comments. As discussed in chapter 1, when facilitating professional learning we need to offer both high support and high challenge. The same is true of offering comments and questions on leaders' work. Leaders have told me that this has really helped them to make room for their own growth. They can "take in" the developmentally oriented questions (high challenge) more fully when they also feel appreciated for sharing their experiences (high support).

Next, I'll offer a few examples of the kinds of questions I normally ask when working to support adult growth and leadership development, whether I am physically with leaders in a workshop or seminar or offering written comments on leaders' work. Many of these questions can be helpful when you are working to support leaders' development as they are struggling through difficult moments in leadership (e.g., negotiations with supervisors, conflicts with educators, resistance, challenges with colleagues). You can also employ them when leaders are working through troubling and painful experiences they have had with other adults, when leading teams, or when coaching others in how to give feedback to colleagues. For example, one common core difficulty that teachers, principals, and assistant principals have shared with me is the challenge of helping other adults to provide developmentally oriented feedback on a teacher's instructional practice after classroom observations. Moreover, growing comfortable with sharing feedback—especially sensitive or critical feedback—is an enormous and common challenge for leaders at all levels. And so, my hope is that these developmental questions will be useful to you when helping others grow.

For instance, when offering written feedback on education leadership graduate students' papers—especially papers in which they share personal experiences about a challenging time in their leadership—I've found that these kinds of questions can help them to sort through their thinking and feeling at the time and in the present, to examine how they were making meaning (their way of knowing) during the event, and to move a little further in their own development:

- Did you share what you were thinking and feeling with the person involved at the time? (This could include sharing honest feedback about instructional practice, a team conflict, a breach of norms or promises, or leadership actions that were unhelpful or even hurtful, etc.)
- If so, how did you feel? How do you think the person felt about what you shared?
- If not, do you know why you decided not to share what you were really thinking and feeling? What do you think might have happened if you had shared what you were really thinking and feeling? What would be the worst, scariest, or hardest part of sharing your innermost thoughts and feelings?
- If you had shared your feelings and thoughts with the person, what do you think might have happened? How do you think he/she would have reacted? What might he/she have said and/or done?
- What might have happened had you told the person how events and experiences with him/her made you feel?

Of course, when we ask these kinds of questions and offer feedback, it's important to consider ways of knowing and context. So many leaders have shared that they have found this developmentally oriented questioning and feedback valuable; it has grounded them, built their awareness, and enhanced their growth by allowing them to consider different ways of thinking and feeling—and eventually to test them out.

## What We Say Matters: Shaping Holding Environments

There's another way in which we can use language to fill the room and those in it as we shape holding environments and build meaningful, developmentally oriented professional learning opportunities. For example, you might remember that in chapter 1, I "invited" you to "rent" the theory discussed there, using intentional language to underscore this book's approach and to recognize—and respect—that your own theories or beliefs may differ. Inviting educators and leaders to rent ideas, expressing appreciation for their hard work, thanking them for their contributions and insights during meeting times, inviting them to share "only what [they] feel comfortable sharing," encouraging them to "select what [they] find most meaningful to work on," reminding them that your feedback "is offered in the spirit of being helpful to [them]," and emphasizing that we (the team facilitating) "are here to be of best help to [them]," can shape contexts where adults feel appreciated, valued, met where they are in terms of meaning making, respected, trusted, valued, and well held.

## Managing Difficult Discussions

Leaders often ask about one very challenging and common issue that arises in their own practice and with the individuals they are helping to grow as leaders—namely, having difficult conversations. You will read more about this topic in the next chapter, when we discuss mentoring, but it might be helpful to share a few things now that relate to framing these kinds of conversations. Leaders have found these techniques helpful in coaching, mentoring, team leading, and strengthening both collegial and interpersonal relationships, and I hope you do too.

Of course, how we frame difficult conversations connects to our ways of knowing in terms of understanding what's at risk for a leader in sharing honestly. For instance, leaders with a socializing way of knowing can have difficulties broaching hard or painful conversations with colleagues because, for these leaders, valued others' approval is of the utmost importance. In other words, engaging in conflict feels extremely uncomfortable to leaders with this way of knowing, and is experienced as a threat to the very fabric of their selves and their interpersonal relationships. These leaders will need support, encouragement, and modeling in order to engage in difficult conversations over time, as well as reminders that conflict can help foster deeper discussions and that relationships can stay intact and even grow stronger through conflict. On the other hand, leaders with a self-authoring way of knowing often approach conflict and difficult conversations as natural parts of leadership and collaboration that can lead to more effective processes and outcomes. These leaders feel supported when they have opportunities to share their internally generated perspectives, even when they are opposed to valued colleagues' viewpoints. Still, for these leaders, understanding that not all adults experience conflict in this way can help them frame difficult conversations with colleagues in ways that are both supportive and challenging from a developmental perspective. With all these points in mind, it can be helpful to start difficult conversations in the following ways (and only if you truly feel this way, of course):

- "I'm really nervous about saying this . . ."
- "There's something I've been noticing about . . ."
- "This has been bothering me for a while now, so I wanted to share it with you and check in to see how you are feeling about . . ."
- "I feel like I need to share this with you because I respect you, and our relationship matters to me . . ."

Framing difficult conversations in this way can help to build holding environments for growth. It also helps with meeting a person where he or she is, deepening trust, and creating the conditions that support risk taking, growth, and learning.

During a university course I facilitated for aspiring principals a few summers ago, the teaching team and I employed certain phrases and ways of naming things that participants found very powerful. They asked if we could provide them with a list of such words and phrases to help them in their efforts to build similar environments in their schools and districts. In the hope that you'll find it useful in your own practice, I've supplied this list, as well as some additional phrases, in table 3.1.

### Finding Two Positives Before Offering Criticism

As described earlier, saying thank you—and meaning it—is an important way in which language shapes growth. A close cousin to expressing appreciation is balancing healthy criticism with an effort to see the "good" in ideas, proposals, initiatives, and perspectives. This, I think, is also true when offering feedback regardless of context and whether the feedback is verbal or written. One teacher leader from a developmental leadership academy I facilitated spoke about the power of this strategy, echoing a sentiment that other school leaders have expressed. During our fourth and last weekend seminar together, this teacher leader shared that she wished she could help her colleagues "get better at not killing an idea right away," and

**TABLE 3.1**

## Uses of intentional language in a developmentally oriented learning environment

| Used when | Language used |
|---|---|
| Considering a question; inviting leaders to freewrite or share in pairs; inviting leaders to consider something new or an alternative perspective. | I invite you to . . .<br>I'm wondering . . . |
| Offering a developmental challenge to one's thinking and feeling; offering an alternative to consider. | You might want to think about . . .<br>What would happen if . . . |
| Adding to a leader's sharing; offering an additional perspective. | I offer this up to you . . . |
| Adding to a comment; trying to explain rationale; explaining an assignment. | In case helpful . . . |
| Someone offers a question about material, content, process, etc. | Thank you for asking. |
| Giving adults a choice to share after engaging in dialogue in small groups or working on a project and not requiring them to share. | Pass or play. |
| Someone says something that moves and touches us. | What you just offered gives me goose bumps. |
| Listening with presence to a person who is sharing a personal experience or something he or she needs help with. | I am so with you. |
| Checking in with a group and sensing that they need a stretch or a break. | How's your energy? |
| Another way of talking about a person's development edge for growth and leadership development. | Growing edge.<br>Standing at the edges of thinking and feelings. |
| Checking in with a group to see if they had a chance to complete a reading or to take a temperature of a group to see if they are understanding what's been discussed. | I'm inviting you to close your eyes . . .<br>I'm not looking at anyone—and I'm just wondering . . .<br>Let's pause for a moment. I just want to take a temperature to see . . . |
| Signaling timing and time left for an activity. | Tick tock . . . Just to let you know, we have *x* minutes left.<br>Does anyone feel they need more time? |

**TABLE 3.1** (*continued*)

| Used when | Language used |
| --- | --- |
| Signaling work for the next day or next steps. | As a gentle reminder . . . <br> By way of previewing . . . |
| Opening a professional learning initiative or sending emails to participants. | Warmest greetings. |
| Explicitly voicing appreciation to groups by thanking them for coming—giving "a piece of your time." | I'd like to voice my appreciation. Thank you. |
| Signaling important ideas. | OK, this goes in 1,000-point red font with yellow highlight—Chicago or Impact font. |
| Expressing appreciation and gratitude and voicing respect. | It is an honor to be in your company! <br> It is so good to be with you. <br> You are a gift. |
| Sensing there's a need to stay where the group is currently. | Let's press the pause button for a minute. |
| Working to show respect and care and to build holding environments. | I look forward to learning with, alongside, and from you. |
| Summarizing the most important aspects of what will be discussed and what has been discussed. | I'm going to highlight the big ideas. |
| Offering the most important and concentrated ideas related to some aspect of material. | This is the Tang version. |

*Source:* Adapted from a collection of phrases compiled by a Summer Principals Academy (Teachers College, Columbia University) teaching team based on what instructor Ellie Drago-Severson said during class.

planned to say to them, "find two good things about an idea before you decide to disagree with it." She found this practice so powerful that she planned to adopt it herself and to introduce it to colleagues on her team so that they, too, could "experience [its] power."

## Moving from "I" to "We": Using Language to Model Collaboration

Another simple but very powerful example of how language can help to shape teams and groups as holding environments that support growth is moving from using *I* to using *we* when collaborating with others. As I have learned from educators and leaders, using the collective, inclusive pronoun *we* augments both the modeling and witnessing of true collaboration.

The use of *we* in both life and leadership speaks to a commitment to collaboration as a powerful enhancement to learning and growth. In working with my team of teaching fellows in the Summer Principals Academy, for instance, we intentionally strive to use *we* when speaking with students and when speaking to or about each other. We've learned, however, that becoming accustomed to speaking in the *we* voice instead of the *I* is not always easy.

You might be wondering why this is sometimes so difficult. I've found that in today's educational leadership work, speaking in the big voice of *I* is what we naturally do, likely because it demonstrates our competencies; it acknowledges the *I* as expert. I have learned, though, that if we as learners, leaders, and educators can adopt and truly live a *we* stance, it can help all of us to nurture true collaboration in the developmental sense, and to better serve adult learners and developing leaders regardless of context. In today's atmosphere, modeling and living with *we* in mind as we use language and take actions, and helping other adults to understand the power of *we*, signals that we value true collaboration and in turn helps grow internal capacities in aspiring and practicing leaders.

While modeling true collaboration through language and actions is harder in some ways—at least initially—than going it alone, it is more powerful and fruitful, especially in terms of building holding environments for growth and leadership development at both the individual and collective levels. Indeed, the use of *we* enhances growth on so many levels, and supports both team members and adult learners.

When I lead a course or program with one or more colleagues, participants say that being able to see collaboration in action—what it looks, feels, and sounds like—is one of the most powerful experiences of the course or program. As one student shared: "This has been an unbelievable experience. I feel privileged and lucky to be a part of this learning, to feel that I have grown so much in such a completely different way than I am used to growing in formal education. I feel privileged because I now feel part of this unique group of people who speak a different language and understand the world a little bit differently as a result." In this particular instance, by living collaboration openly and tangibly in the way we spoke as a teaching team, we modeled genuine teamwork for these learner leaders. They were able to *witness* and *experience it*, which helped them to better understand how to engage in collaboration and how to help others do the same.

In summary, speaking and being in the *we* mind-set is central to developing robust holding environments and supporting adult development, yet it's often experienced as such an unusual stance. I hope you find this approach to collaboration useful in your noble practice.

## SEEING WITH SENSITIVITY AND INTUITION

*Deep down we have the qualities of clarity, awareness, sensitivity, warmth and love, but, we have little idea at the outset just how deep and vast those qualities can be.*

—Anonymous

In this section, I discuss the importance of carefully watching and responding to the people in the room—of *seeing,* with sensitivity and intuition, the needs of individuals and groups. Seeing with sensitivity is similar to listening with presence, but instead of listening to what people are saying, asking, and telling you about their experiences, you are attending carefully and caringly to nonverbal cues: reading their body language, homing in on potential problems or questions, and noticing the need for a break or even a deeper dive into the material being discussed. In other words, when facilitating professional learning initiatives that support growth and leadership development, I try hard to be mindful and aware of the *emotional tone* given off by both individuals and the group as a whole, as such awareness connects fundamentally to the operationalization of the core elements discussed in chapter 2.

The *Merriam-Webster* definition of *see* includes a number of related, abstract concepts, such as "to come to know," "be aware of," or "perceive the meaning or importance of" something.[6] Seeing with sensitivity and intuition is also an abstract concept, hard to pin down and describe but nonetheless of vital importance when crafting and leading teaching, learning, and professional development environments to support adult growth and leadership development. Next, to help demonstrate the importance and power of this way of seeing, I offer concrete examples from my own practice and from the practice of an experienced school leader who shared with me the great significance of seeing and feeling the needs of his teachers when working to support their development.

### "With-It-Ness" Coupled with Responsiveness: Attending to Feelings, Needs, and Tone in Professional Learning Environments

Regardless of the context or the duration of my time with a group—from an afternoon workshop to multiyear engagements with principals, assistant principals, coaches, professional learning communities, or teacher leaders in schools, districts, or university courses—I work very hard to see and care for the needs of both the group and individuals at any given time by noticing reactions and following my "gut" feelings about how things are going. One of my students and a coteacher in my courses, Jessica Blum-DeStefano, refers to my way of seeing when facilitating university courses and workshops as "with-it-ness," and this description rather succinctly captures what I try to be and do when supporting adults' learning and leadership development. In case helpful to you and your own noble leadership, I offer the following strategies, which I have found useful when working to see with sensitivity and intuition as a facilitator (we will be learning more about these nuances in chapter 5 when we discuss the nuances of learning-oriented professional development initiatives):

- Noticing when someone seems uncertain or isn't feeling well—and then letting the person know you understand and care.
- Mingling in the room when small groups and individuals are at work on a task, and respectfully listening for questions, concerns, or potential contributions.
- Asking permission to join small groups in order to be of help and learn how individuals are doing and feeling.
- Taking the "temperature" of the room by asking about energy levels and understanding, and offering breaks when necessary.

When facilitating a group or supporting individuals in the psychological sense, it's often helpful to pause to figure out what they seem to need right now. Sometimes asking them directly works best. I call this *thinking out loud*, as it involves sensing something and then expressing it. For instance, I sometimes ask, "Right now, I'm sensing that you might need a stretch break—how many of you are feeling that way?" While this obviously gives you, as the facilitator, a moment to gather your thoughts and consider what might be the appropriate next step, it also is important because it gives a group a chance to think and reflect on what's been discussed. It also helps with deepening trust and respect (core elements we learned about in chapter 2) and with building relationships, as we'll discuss a little later in this chapter.

Seeing with sensitivity is equally important when you are working one-on-one. Sometimes, when you sense a feeling, issue, or question bubbling just beyond what you're able to directly hear or observe, this insight can play a key role in the types of supports and challenges you offer and the way you respond. Just as with listening, seeing between the words that you hear can allow you to support growth—in even bigger ways than people sometimes feel comfortable or capable of asking for.

### Seeing Others and Yourself: Recognizing the Importance of Developmental Diversity in Leadership

When we are in a leadership position, we need to be sensitive enough to realize how (or whether) our own expectations and approaches to feedback *meet* the developmental needs and capacities of the adults we serve. Leaders have shared with me that sometimes their initial plans do not meet the needs of the adults they are working to support, despite their best efforts and intentions, and they need to caringly and carefully adjust in order to be of better service and help. Similar to when a lovingly prepared lesson plan isn't going quite as expected with younger students, seeing the gap between what we had hoped for and where the students are—and how they are making meaning of our teaching—is important to effective leadership, because not everyone is comfortable speaking up to let us know that our strategies or structures are unclear or unhelpful to them.

Describing his own insights about this truth, Jed Lippard, the leader of Prospect Hill Academy—a large, urban charter school in Cambridge, Massachusetts—courageously shared with me his early struggles (almost ten years ago) with this very common leadership challenge. As a self-authoring knower and new principal then, Jed explained, his first inclination was to offer feedback in *just the way he would have wanted to get it himself.* Still, many of his teachers didn't seem to be "getting it" or responding as he hoped, and he quickly came to realize that he would need to differentiate his feedback in order to meet the teachers where they were, in terms of their ways of knowing, when offering them feedback to improve instructional practice. Because adults at different developmental places orient differently to authority figures and feedback on their performance, Jed's ability to *see* into this need, and to recognize the importance of offering qualitatively different kinds of feedback to support adults with different ways of knowing, enabled him to better help his teachers grow and build internal capacity. This in turn helped improve the learning and experiences of all school participants, including the students.

An analogy might help to reiterate the importance of meeting adults where they are in the developmental sense. Before someone is able to solve a quadratic equation, the person needs to understand what the $x$ represents. Or, before teaching someone to dive, we must first teach the person to swim. Jed had to learn *to see* that offering a socializing knower, for example, feedback that was more appropriate to supporting and challenging a self-authoring knower (like himself at the time) was not going to help the socializing knower grow. Feedback must be customized in ways that both meet individuals where they are and support growth by offering developmentally appropriate challenges.

## BUILDING RELATIONSHIPS:
## THE POWER OF MEANINGFUL CONNECTIONS

This section on building relationships, in its essence, really encompasses all you've been reading about thus far in this chapter and the preceding chapter on the core elements, and all that follows. From my point of view, and perhaps from yours, building relationships is at the heart of effectively supporting growth and leadership development in any teaching, learning, and/or professional development environment, and in any environment calling for human connection.

Meaningful relationships are needed for life and for supporting the development of any human being—for how can growth occur without connection? As a leader, you build your relationships based on sharing and trust, and demonstrate your humanity by offering personal stories and examples. By sharing parts of your own experiences, and listening carefully and caringly to those of others, you can elevate leadership to what I call the *treasure of paid attention*—the gift of lovingly attending to the individual and the group. Building relationships in a developmental sense draws from and intertwines everything we discuss in this book, and is of great importance to this learning-oriented model for leadership development.

Forming connections and attachments is essential to effective leadership today. In fact, it would not be an overstatement to say that leadership is all about relationships as a means of support for growth and development. As we've discussed before, listening, language, and seeing are all parts of relationship building. To shine a light on different aspects of this work, I've artificially teased them apart in this chapter to help clarify and make transparent the many components of supporting adult development as I see, value, and practice it. In this section, my intention is to highlight the strategies and practices most closely related to relationship building, although they draw from and expand on many of the other ideas we've been exploring in this book.

## Making Genuine Connections

While building relationships inarguably takes an investment of time and heart, how could we possibly accomplish our goals and support growth without them? Regardless of the context, I work to build relationships and also encourage those I work with to do the same. Establishing these personal connections is very important to both aspiring and practicing leaders.

From the moment I begin my work with an individual or a group, I strive to create and sustain connections through personal phone calls or welcoming emails, by saying hello to individuals, following up on personal sharing people have offered either in or out of class, and sometimes even sharing special gifts. Like listening with presence, using language thoughtfully, and seeing with sensitivity, building relationships requires intentional effort and purposeful interactions that honor and hold up the beauty of those we meet. The time and hard work are always worth the investment. As one of the leaders of the Summer Principals Academy reflected one summer after our class, "Relationships are the most important things when leading adult learning. *People must be held.*"

Next, I offer two examples to help illustrate the importance of genuine connection in leadership, as well as the type of intentionality needed to create and sustain growth-enhancing relationships.

### *Investing Time*

Each year, I have the honor of meeting with seasoned faculty in the mentoring/coaching program at Teachers College and their mentees, program participants who are new to the university. I facilitate a workshop close to the start of the year and then a second workshop near the halfway point. These gatherings last for about two hours, and in addition to teaching content, I hope—as I do in all the professional learning initiatives I facilitate— that I simultaneously offer a meaningful and growth-enhancing experience for the workshop participants (you'll read more about some ways to do this in chapter 4). One of the main purposes of these gatherings is to offer a space for discussing important questions and engaging in dialogue about the mentor/mentee relationship, and to learn more deeply about mentoring from a developmental perspective (through many of the ideas you're reading about in this book).

This past year, I was struck by something one of the mentor/mentee pairs said, which simultaneously highlighted the busyness of our lives and the importance of creating a sacred space and *time* to build relationships in order to support growth and leadership development. The mentor faculty member, who had been at the university for more than twenty years, shared about the mentee, "Even though our offices are right next to each other, we *never* have a chance to talk [about] our mentoring relationship, and to carve out time for it. We talk about work all the time, sometimes on the fly. Thank you for creating this time for us. I cannot explain how much it means."

Despite the mentor and mentee working literally side by side at the university, the workshop was the *only* space they were able to carve out for thinking and reflecting together about their mentoring relationship and things of importance to them beyond their work. This sad, true, and all-too-common reality exists regardless of context; I have heard similar stories from principals mentoring assistant principals, assistant principals mentoring teacher leaders, and teacher leaders mentoring or coaching teachers. For all of them, too, prioritizing time to build relationships in order to support growth and development became a cherished gift.

### Sharing Personal Stories and Ourselves as Leaders

Sharing a bit of who we are as leaders also really supports others' growth and learning. Just as I have done in this book, when I'm teaching and facilitating in any context, I share stories from my own life to illustrate important points, to help participants remember (in the truest sense—holding close to one's heart) key ideas, and also to make myself vulnerable, just as I ask those learning with me in sessions to do. Still, even knowing this, I am always moved when students ask for "more Ellie stories," or when they pick up on the importance of "being real," as other leaders term it. When reflecting on the biggest learning from my course, for instance, one student explained: "Being real . . . can inspire us all to be real and share with our staffs to better reach more adults in an appropriate manner, which in the end reaches and meets the needs of our children."

Another student, who took one of my university courses about supporting adult development many years ago, recently shared that the stories I told in class about my own family and life helped her to connect with me and the work, and to convincingly shape our class as a space that supported her growth and development. As she described:

> I thought this was interesting about Ellie's class. The very first day she said that she'd been talking with her mom the night before and her mom had asked if she was nervous about class starting the next day, and it was such an I'm a human being statement. She has a mom, she gets

*nervous before teaching—it was such a window into, okay, this is who our professor is, and it made a massive impact. I think I told my mom—because I said that admitting that I might have been nervous—that you don't have to come out and say, "I'm your professor so I'm clearly invincible" . . . just letting yourself be vulnerable in front of other people, it sort of relieves everybody of the stress, and it was a personal lesson for me that I don't have to go into new jobs and say I know everything I'm doing. I can go in and say I'm nervous, which is natural because I'm brand new here and I don't know what I'm doing. Or . . . just admit that to yourself and other people—I remember that very clearly.*

### One Principal's Work and the Importance of Relationships

This idea of being vulnerable—of being human—as a support to leadership and building relationships reminds me of the story of one principal and her assistant principal, both of whom I've had the honor of learning with and from in the Cahn Fellows Program at Teachers College. In the program, I work with the Cahn principals and the allies (i.e., assistant principals or teacher leaders from their schools) those principals are mentoring during the fellowships to enhance the allies' growth, capacity building, and ability to support in turn the development of the teachers back in their schools whom they are privileged to help grow.

In this example, Meg, a sixth-year principal of a middle school in the Bronx, was working in the program with her assistant principal and ally, Lisa. Meg was working to support teacher leadership in her school, and was stunned when one teacher leader asked, "Do you want us to facilitate the process for teachers in our grade-level teams, or do you want us to get someone to do the work that needs to be done?" Disappointed that her teachers seemingly wanted to be told exactly what to do, even though she was trying to support them in *making their own decisions* and *taking ownership of their work*, Meg shared with Lisa and me that she remembered being frustrated when she first took on greater leadership as a teacher, more than ten years before, because her principal told her *exactly how she wanted things done.* That was challenging for Meg, she shared, because she wanted to make her *own* decisions about how to lead her team of teachers and how to support their learning. After Meg recounted this experience, I asked, "Did you share that with your teacher leaders?" Meg admitted she had not, at which point Lisa chimed in: "Let them get to know you, Meg. They want to know who you are. They want to see you are human. Please share with them."

Indeed, as Lisa wisely understood, this type of connection could help support Meg and the teachers in this work. "Let [the teachers] get to know you," she encouraged Meg, and after a few minutes of reflection, Meg agreed. As we've been discussing, this emphasis on building relationships is exactly what I try to model and offer to leaders doing this very important work. Making herself vulnerable in this way—sharing herself and her prior experiences of growing as a teacher leader—made a tremendous difference to the teacher leaders in her school. Meg revealed that they subsequently shared more and more honestly, trusted her more, and made themselves more vulnerable in their efforts to grow.

*Thinking Out Loud*

As mentioned earlier in this chapter, another practice that you might find helpful in building relationships is *thinking out loud*. When you are holding a group or individual in the psychological sense to support growth, it's often helpful to pause and consider, *what do they seem like they need right now?* Sometimes asking them directly can be very productive and helpful. I also *think out loud* by sharing in the moment: "What was I thinking? Can you please stay with me; I need to ask for a minute to remember," or "I'm going to share what I'm thinking in my lefthand column—or what I'm noticing right now," or "Right now, I'm sensing that you might need a stretch break—how many of you are feeling that way?" Not only does this practice give you as the facilitator a chance to gather your thoughts and consider your next steps, but it also "pauses time" and gives the entire group a moment to reflect on what's been discussed. Importantly, thinking out loud helps to strengthen relationships by building and deepening the core values of trust and respect.

## MODELING

*Example is leadership.*

—Albert Schweitzer

In chapter 2, we considered the central importance of intentionality, or putting caring and purposeful thought into your words and actions, when working to shape professional learning environments that truly support growth. Being intentional, as you know, enables leaders to bring to the foreground all of the core elements in their work of supporting adult and leadership development. In the second growth ring, modeling works similarly, in that it brings together *and makes transparent* all of the components of this chapter: listening, seeing, using language, and building relationships. In other words, whereas intentionality refers to the deliberate developmental *thought* behind manifestations of care, trust, respect, and collaboration, modeling involves *embodying* these values through the actions described in this chapter and *explicitly sharing with others* the intentionality behind these approaches while leading and facilitating professional learning.

During and after my classes and workshops, leaders often comment on the power of modeling. Modeling real collaboration, vulnerability, developmental intentionality, and the value of listening with presence, seeing with sensitivity, and attending to language and interpersonal relationships helps them to *see and experience* the practices and processes that compose a learning-oriented approach to leadership development *while they are in the process of learning* about them. Also, they have shared that modeling enables them to more intimately understand the power of creating holding environments for others and the importance of growing oneself in order to be of best help to other adults.

When modeling learning-oriented leadership for groups and individuals, regardless of context, I do my best to embody the core elements in my actions and presence—because, as we discussed earlier, this kind of alignment is the glue that holds everything together in professional learning contexts. In addition, though, I am also explicit and clear about *why* I do what I do in order to pull back the curtain on my thinking, and to help the leaders I work with consider how developmental ideas and practices might translate to their own schools and leadership. Next, to help you understand *how* I model and the ways in which modeling has been meaningful for practicing and aspiring leaders with whom I've worked, I offer two examples.

## Modeling in Professional Learning Environments: Strategies for Your Practice

As I understand and practice it, modeling as a leader and facilitator involves being intentional and transparent about the way you:

- Use time.
- Use language.
- Make and use space.
- Listen.
- Offer feedback.
- See.

Actually doing all of the things we're learning about in this book and being transparent about the rationale behind your actions, words, and intentions *is* modeling, and, as such, is a powerful way to help adults learn about and *feel* the power of attending to adult development in your leadership.

To model and make things clear for leaders in my university classes, professional learning workshops, and academies, I employ all of the techniques discussed in this book, and I offer a kind of running commentary as I do so, inviting them to consider "renting" any of the practices and strategies they are experiencing. "Every move is intentional," I let them know, and suggest even that they might want to consider how this would work in their own settings. For example, I let them know that when one is facilitating workshops, seminars, or other initiatives, it's important to give adults choices as to ways they feel comfortable participating. Letting adults choose to reflect either by freewriting or freethinking, for example, honors their preferences and shows them respect. In addition, it is important to acknowledge to groups that you know that they participate in workshops or professional development meetings in very different ways. More specifically, I share with groups that I'm aware of the fact that some leaders *are* engaging in learning "even if they do not say anything to the group."

When we are fortunate enough to learn from effective teachers or leaders, we sometimes—consciously or unconsciously—adopt some of their mannerisms or techniques. Transparent modeling during professional learning, on the other hand, *explicitly encourages and supports* this kind of transfer, while allowing room for leaders to make the practices their own. After all, as you know, learning-oriented leadership is not a one-size-fits-all model, and no single way of leading can address every problem in every context. Rather, by surfacing the developmental intention behind a promising approach for participants to consciously think about and consider, modeling helps adults experience and see that approach's value and invites them to translate it into effective ideas and leadership strategies that will support them and others in their unique contexts. Indeed, as many leaders have shared with me, and as I describe further shortly, the straightforward but transformative power of simply saying "I'm doing this because . . ." has made a difference for many of the noble leaders I have had the honor and good fortune of knowing.

## Reflections on Modeling from Former Students

In my work leading professional learning and in my research, I have learned that leaders who participate in my classes and workshops really appreciate modeling. Moreover, as my colleagues and I have learned, this approach has even inspired educational leaders who took my university course on leadership for adult development five to seven years ago to be more transparent about the intentions behind their leadership decisions and actions with the adults they serve and support today.[7] Currently serving as principals, assistant principals, teacher leaders, professional developers, district-level leaders, and university professors, these former students have shared that modeling was a key feature of what made their course experience so meaningful, and that it was an important takeaway for their *own* leadership practice. As one course graduate, now a principal, explained about the modeling: "Just from that [the modeling] alone, the credibility of Ellie's teaching and leadership was incredibly powerful." Many of the leaders my colleagues and I learned from strove similarly to embody their values and visions after experiencing the modeling in the course.

Another former student, who now works as an educational consultant to help teams of teachers, schools, and districts use data to improve performance, likewise reflected that the modeling in the course gave her and her classmates the tools to pass forward these same lessons and experiences to the adults they now work with; in other words, the transparent modeling also helped them understand *how to model* for others. By "training the trainers," she explained, my modeling in the class helped equip her to lead her own work preparing others to meet the complex demands of teaching and learning today.[8]

In addition to this feedback from my former university students, I have learned again and again from the many amazing and dedicated educators I have worked with around the globe that modeling makes a big difference. In course evaluations, workshop feedback, and in-class surveys, aspiring and practicing leaders have shared with me that truly meaning what you say, and helping others understand what and why you do what you do, has the potential to bring people together and bring out what's best in ourselves and each other. In closing, I'd like to leave you with a few comments about just this idea, noted recently by several students in one of my courses:

> *Seeing the power of your work in uniting a group [of close to ninety people] around mutual respect and love for one another was moving. If I was a skeptic (and I was), you've got my attention and my trust now. Thank you.*

> *I think the biggest thing for me is just how reflective, and how genuinely sincere, I should be in my daily practice, and . . . if there is anything I could impart [to] my staff/students, it [would be] that they embodied the same.*

*We have the ability to inspire other teachers as you have inspired us. [You helped us] to be better, more committed, more strategic, and able to grow in this short time, no matter where we are.*

These words move me every time I read them, and I truly hope that my transparency in describing the creation of growth-enhancing professional learning environments in this book will be of similar help to you as you push forward courageously to support adult development in your own leadership work.

In the next chapter, I invite you to consider concrete strategies for conceptualizing and planning professional learning environments that support adult and leadership development. You will learn more about aspects of designing holding environments at both the individual and group levels that I have found essential to ensuring effective and meaningful workshops, classes, and learning initiatives of all kinds.

## TAKEAWAYS

+ *Listening* is perhaps the first and best way we let others know that they matter to us, that their views have merit and value, and that we are "with" them psychologically and developmentally. Listening in a developmental sense has to do with joining the person in his or her meaning making.

+ *Using language thoughtfully and with developmental intentions,* including paying careful attention to the words we use and how we frame our teaching and facilitation, is very important, in general, and especially so when considering how to shape holding environments for growth and leadership development.

+ Carefully watching and responding to the people in the room, or *seeing with sensitivity and intuition,* helps us address the needs of individuals and groups when effectively leading professional learning.

+ While, in many ways, listening involves attending to what people are saying, asking, and telling us about their experiences, seeing involves *attending carefully and caringly to nonverbal cues,* like reading their body language, homing in on potential problems or questions, and noticing the need for a break or a deeper dive into the material being discussed.

+ *Building relationships,* in its essence, really encompasses all you've read about thus far in this chapter and in chapter 2 (on the core elements), and all that follows. Building relationships is at the heart of creating holding environments at the individual and group levels—in any teaching, learning, and/or professional development environment.

✦ *Modeling* brings together and *makes transparent* all of the components of this chapter: listening, seeing, using language thoughtfully, and building relationships. In other words, whereas intentionality refers to the deliberate developmental *thought* behind manifestations of care, trust, respect, and collaboration, modeling involves *embodying* these values through the actions described in this chapter.

## REFLECTIVE QUESTIONS

1. How, if at all, might you employ any of this chapter's ideas about and practices for leading developmentally oriented professional learning to enhance your practice? In case helpful, I've listed them here: *listening with presence*, which has been proven to be a developmental support; *using language thoughtfully*; *seeing with sensitivity*, or attending to your own intuition about the emotional tone given off by people; *building relationships* by offering human connections through storytelling, listening, using language, and seeing through a developmental lens (also known as *the treasure of paid attention*, or the gift of attending to the individual); and *modeling*, which involves teaching with transparency and responsiveness.

2. Has there been something particularly important or useful to you in what you learned from reading this chapter, or is there something that you came to realize about your own work that you'd like to consider more deeply in your practice of facilitating adult growth and leadership development?

3. What additional features might you add to this second growth ring? How do those features assist you in your work as a leader?

# CHAPTER 4

# Shaping the Vision

*Using Space and Structure in Professional Learning*

In this chapter, I invite you to consider concrete strategies for conceptualizing, planning for, and building professional learning environments—*shaping the vision*—that will support adult growth and leadership development. These strategies are depicted in the second-outermost growth ring of the new leadership model outlined in this book (figure 4.1). As you see in figure 4.1, shaping the vision implies both creating and doing.

Put simply, this chapter presents three big ideas and practices (and strategies related to them) that will help you to implement your developmental vision with intention and mindfulness. In other words, this chapter is about 1) *designing* professional learning opportunities so that they support adult growth (internal capacity building) and leadership development, 2) *using space* with intentionality to nurture conditions that create opportunities for growth, and 3) applying the *pillar practices for growth*. Why, you may wonder, should you learn about and apply the pillar practices? These practices—teaming, providing adults with leadership roles, engaging in collegial inquiry, and serving as a mentor/developmental coach—as mentioned in previous chapters, compose a *learning-oriented model for school leadership* (described in detail in my earlier work), and they are a very important part of creating developmentally oriented learning environments.[1] While you may already be using these practices in some form in your leadership work, when implemented with developmental intention, they can serve as *holding environments for adult and leadership development* that support growth regardless of adults' ways of knowing.

Whether facilitating leadership in a district, a school, a university, a leadership team, a gathering of coaches, or any other environment in which the goal is to support adult learning and leadership development, you can employ the pillar practices as integral parts of the learning design. Toward the end of this chapter, you will get a taste of the pillars in action. You might

**FIGURE 4.1**

## The third growth ring: strategies for concepualizing, planning for, and building professional learning environments

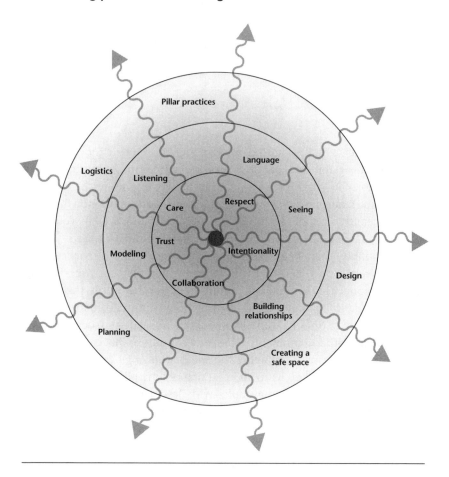

find it valuable, should you wish to learn more about these developmental pillar practices, to read my books *Helping Teachers Learn: Principals Practices for Supporting Adult Growth and Development, Leading Adult Learning: Supporting Adult Development in Our Schools*, and *Learning and Leading for Growth* (with Jessica Blum-DeStefano and Anila Asghar).[2] The first two are in-depth accounts of how leaders like you—principals, assistant principals, teachers, coaches, special educators, specialists, superintendents, and district leaders—actually employ these practices in their work and how you can use them to support adult growth, capacity building, and leadership development in your own context. The third describes how former students of mine, who enrolled in a university course about the ideas discussed in this book seven to nine years ago, are currently employing developmental ideas and practices in their various roles as educational leaders.

As you see in figure 4.1, the pillar practices are a vital part of this new learning-oriented model for leadership development. In this chapter, you will learn more about *how* the pillar practices actually work in professional learning contexts, and we will also explore ideas and concrete practices for intentionally designing and using *space* so that it can support adult growth.

To be a little more specific, we will discuss the components listed in the third growth ring of the model to help you understand how to design and use space when building professional learning opportunities with developmental intentions. There are five aspects of designing and using space that I have found to be essential to creating the conditions that support adult growth and leadership development. Accordingly, we will explore together: 1) ways in which we can work to create a safe space in teaching, learning, and professional development environments, 2) the importance of caring for logistical features when leading or facilitating other adults' learning, 3) the vital importance of planning before, during (in the moment), and after learning initiatives, 4) the intentionality behind the design of these holding environments, and 5) examples of the pillar practices in action to illustrate how you might invite adults to participate in them as supports for growth.

## CREATING A SAFE SPACE

In this section, I discuss the vital importance of designing and creating a safe space for leaders in professional learning initiatives. By *safe space*, I mean a space in which leaders feel free to take the risks needed to grow and learn. As you know, building these spaces for individual leaders and groups in any teaching, learning, and professional development environment is not something that any one of us can *make up* in the moment. Instead, it is something we need to be intentional about, something we need to consider carefully and caringly beforehand. Here, I'll share some ideas and one simple yet very effective practice for building safe spaces for growth in learning environments.

Most important, when building learning opportunities that support leadership development, we need to both create safe conditions and nurture them. Such carefully crafted spaces allow people to feel *accepted* for who they are and how they are making meaning of their experiences. Feeling accepted and being accepted are two very important ways we can hold adults well in the psychological sense, and meet them where they are in order to support their growth regardless of their way of knowing. These environments are also spacious enough to allow for movement, which helps us, as facilitators and teachers, to live and demonstrate the core elements (i.e., care, respect, trust, intentionality, and collaboration; discussed in detail in chapter 2) and likewise helps participants express them *for* and *with* each other. While especially important for socializing knowers, this kind of safe space is beneficial to all of us, regardless of how we make meaning. As I've learned from leaders, there's just something very precious about it.

## Being Proactive and Responsive

Before presenting an in-depth discussion of how you can help groups create a safe space once the workshop, program, or seminar begins, I'd like to share a few steps you can take *outside* the working space to build such an environment. First, it's important to send a welcoming email to those who will participate in the initiative. It's also helpful to build relationships by sending periodic emails with updates, expressions of gratitude, and gentle reminders about upcoming work when facilitating longer-term seminars to help leaders feel connected to the work, each other, and you. It also helps them to feel cared about and facilitates learning and growth. In addition, making yourself, as facilitator and teacher, available to address questions and concerns not only during the learning experience but also before and after can also help leaders to feel safe and cared for. Being responsive in this way, whether by email, in person, or by phone, helps to build and maintain a safe space and deepen relationships. We'll learn more about this in chapter 5, when we discuss the nuances of effective professional learning environments.

## Establishing Norms

While there are many ways we can work to create safe spaces, next we will consider one very effective practice for helping an entire large group, and smaller working groups within the large group (e.g., teams that work on design plans, small groups that discuss personal cases), work collectively to establish and nurture safe and productive spaces for growing. As you know, when we are designing professional development initiatives, it is very important—what my colleagues and I call an essential *precondition*—that leaders feel safe when sharing any kind of information or emotion.[3] In other words, leaders *must* have a sense of deep safety before we can even try to support their growth.

I want to offer a few thoughts about context and conditions since these might be issues you wonder about. When facilitating learning initiatives for groups that will be working together over an extended period of time (multiple sessions) or for groups composed of forty or fewer leaders, I normally ask the full group to engage in the process of establishing guidelines and norms that will help to make the space safe and productive. However, when there are more than forty leaders participating and when leaders will be working in smaller teams or groups and sharing their ideas, thoughts, and feelings in that forum, the smaller groups engage in the process on their own with my guidance.

In both cases, building a safe space involves developing shared understandings of group norms and confidentiality agreements. This is usually one of the first steps in forming a working, trustful group. However, should you elect to adopt this process, it's important to offer groups opportunities to periodically review the norms they've established. This allows individuals to add ideas (thoughts and feelings) and also enables the group as a whole to a) revisit norms, b) consider their work as a group in relation to upholding norms, and c) make decisions about whether or not they want to modify or adjust norms in light of their collaborative work so far.

Here, you are invited to consider this practice as an essential feature of designing and making use of space. Toward the end of this section, I share some principals' experiences of participating in this process and how it was meaningful to them.

When I invite individuals and groups to engage in the process of establishing norms, I introduce its importance by explaining the need for confidentiality. Because the environment becomes one in which personal and sometimes sensitive thoughts, feelings, experiences, and ideas are shared, participants need to agree on what will be shared outside the workshop and what will not. The workspace should be considered as almost sacred. Norms concerning the way discussions are conducted should also be established. For instance, just understanding that adults differ in how they make sense of being interrupted can be helpful during collaborative work. For one leader, being interrupted while sharing experiences could feel safe, supportive, and energizing (as if teammates were just so engaged and interested that they had to interject). For another colleague in the very same group, however, being interrupted might feel disrespectful (as if teammates weren't really listening or caring). Sometimes interruptions can even cause leaders to shut down and stop sharing. This is one example of how "letting others in" on your expectations and preferences can help groups to build safe spaces. Sometimes—actually, lots of times—as groups continue to collaborate in large or small groups, members begin to share their needs for safety in relation to their ways of knowing and the kinds of supports and challenges they need from group members to best grow and learn.

Of course, building safe spaces by developing norms also helps leaders to get to know each other before sharing the more personal and private aspects of their lives that often come up in developmentally oriented professional learning environments. It also deepens trust within groups, as discussed in chapter 2.

In exhibit 4.1, I offer a protocol I use with leaders to establish norms and build safe spaces for working productively together. It also highlights the importance of inviting groups to decide collectively on the way they choose to manage confidentiality. I hope you find it useful in your leadership work, and please feel free to adapt or modify it as you see fit.

### Observations from Participants on Establishing a Safe Space

To point to what leaders have shared about the value of building a safe space and what it has meant to them, I offer two brief examples.

While I was facilitating a developmental leadership academy, one of the senior teacher leaders, who was not accustomed to using protocols to share, worried that doing so would be "confining and limiting." After she shared this with me, I explicitly voiced appreciation for her courageous honesty and asked her to "rent" the idea. At the end of that session, she offered the following to me and all of her colleagues in the academy: "While I was initially resistant to using a protocol to guide our conversation—I resist these kinds of structures—my experience of having it guide our conversation was that it was liberating—to my surprise! It was freeing, not just for me, but for all four of us [in the group]." She continued, "Having guidelines and the protocol, allowed me, and I think us, to feel free. We knew we'd each have a chance to share and to be of help. It helped to begin to develop a feel for what real collaboration and sharing is like. Thank you! I'm going to use this with my team."

Next, it might also be useful to consider an example of how leaders' *experiences* with safe spaces and this particular protocol have helped them to create and design safe spaces for others. As mentioned in chapter 3, I have the honor of serving as a faculty coach to New York City principals who have participated in the Cahn Fellows Program (a fifteen-month program in which exemplary principals engage with an assistant principal or teacher leader—or ally—from their own school around a problem of practice).

As their faculty coach, I work to create holding environments within their sessions with and for them (including use of the safe space protocol),

## EXHIBIT 4.1

## Protocol for building a safe and productive learning space

When you are designing safe spaces and using this kind of protocol, it's wise to allocate specific amounts of time for each step in the process and to post timing in a location where leaders can easily see it. Of course, you'll want to check in with them as they move from step 1 to 2 and so forth to see if anyone needs a little more time. While the amount of time for each step is not listed here, I'll share the timing that usually works well for groups. For example, if leaders are working in smaller groups of four, you might want to allow ten minutes for initial introductions—if group members haven't worked together before and/or do not know each other. Ten to twenty minutes is usually enough time for discussion of a safe learning environment and confidentiality for groups of four. However, times will vary depending on the number of group members in each group. When working with larger groups as a whole, I normally allow thirty minutes for this kind of discussion and skip the introductions. The following is a general protocol for how you may want to invite groups to engage in this process.

1. Invite group members to freewrite or freethink privately for two minutes in response to the following questions: *What constitutes a safe, productive, and supportive team learning context or group for you? What makes a group learning space unsafe for you and your learning?* As you know, and as discussed in chapter 3, giving adults a choice about whether to write or to think privately (without writing) is important and empowering—and connected to helping leaders feel respected and safe. If leaders choose to write, I usually invite them specifically to *freewrite*. You'll recall that this means jotting down what comes to mind in response to a question without censoring one's thinking and/or feelings.

2. Before inviting group members to take a minute or so to share—whatever each individual feels comfortable sharing with the group—the group will want to ask one member to volunteer to take notes. With larger groups, a note taker sometimes records important points on easel paper for the whole group to reference, while in smaller groups it is generally helpful for the note taker to type the norms and share electronically with the team. You'll want to advise groups that the idea here is not to capture every word each member shares verbatim, but rather to capture the essence of what is said, with direct quotations—if needed—when possible.

3. Invite group members to share their thinking with each other one by one. Usually each person can do this in a minute or so. In larger groups of forty or fewer, I usually ask for volunteers to share, and after a few minutes, I ask, "Does anyone have anything they'd like to add that hasn't made it to our list?" Whether you're working in smaller groups or with a larger group, inviting leaders to develop a shared understanding of norms or ground rules for engaging in group discussion is a design feature that helps to create a safe and productive learning space. This is especially important because in these kinds of professional learning environments, members will be sharing their personal and often sensitive experiences.

4. At the next seminar—when leaders meet over time and for more than one workshop—making space to review norms and revise or add to them is essential, as previously noted. When facilitating for groups of forty or fewer leaders, I take notes on easel paper about what was offered, type the list of norms and confidentiality agreements, and distribute them to all in the workshop either during the next

*(continues)*

**EXHIBIT 4.1** (*continued*)

session or via email beforehand. When participants work in smaller groups to develop their own set of group norms, they distribute the notes from the previous meeting either via email or at the next gathering so that all group members can add to or revise them, as needed, and review them. As mentioned, creating space for group members to periodically revisit their norms and check in with each other around these important issues can strengthen collaboration, build safe holding environments, and support growth and leadership development.

5. After the group engages in the *safe and productive group learning space discussion*, the group will want to reach a shared understanding of what kind of confidentiality agreement they'd like. After the group has agreed about how to handle confidentiality, the note taker will want to restate the agreement to the group to see if all members agree with the wording and sentiment. Once agreement is reached, the note taker can add this agreement to the document, along with the group's thoughts and feelings about what constitutes a safe and productive team learning space. Group members may wish to discuss how they want to handle confidentiality around issues discussed in the larger group with others who are also participating in the seminar.

*Source:* Adapted from Drago-Severson, *Leading Adult Learning*, 93.

and this year, several principals and assistant principals found the protocol and process so meaningful that they decided to employ it with the teachers in their schools whom they appointed as grade-level team leaders. As one pair recently shared, "This process of developing ground rules and norms really helps us to help team leaders to help their teachers feel safe."

## LOGISTICS

In addition to creating a safe space, there are many—seemingly small, yet very important—*logistical* details that I attend to when designing professional learning opportunities. For example, the *setting* of any teaching, learning, and professional development environment plays a significant role in how people *feel* when they are with you, and it is important to do what you can to *maximize the space* and make people comfortable when asking them to engage in the hard and meaningful work of growing themselves and each other. This section is about the logistics of doing just that—anticipating and caring for the conditions that support adult and leadership development.

We all know what it feels like, for instance, to be too cold, too hot, too hungry, or too crowded to really learn or pay attention. There are, of course, things about space that we cannot control since we don't always have a say in the rooms we use, the furniture or technology available, or even the temperature. Yet recognizing, caring for, and addressing those things that we *can* influence does make a big difference for the adults we're working with, and also serves as a demonstration of care.

Accordingly, next we'll focus on some of the ways you can attend to the details of physical space to better shape it as a holding environment for adult and leadership development.

## Maximizing the Space

In addition to gathering all of the supplies I typically use in a class or workshop (including markers, poster paper, etc.) well ahead of time, when designing professional development environments I seek to care for and anticipate leaders' physical needs, the layout of the space, and the smaller but essential details that allow me to better connect with and get to know the adults I'm learning with and from. To help illustrate how you might do some of these things in your own noble work, next I offer a few mini-examples to describe some of the strategies I employ.

## Caring for Physical Needs

You might be surprised to learn how often the temperature of a room comes up in leaders' comments or feedback. While we don't always have control over the physical details of a space, it is very important to listen to what leaders are saying about their physical needs (comfort levels) and do what we can to make sure they are comfortable. I can remember, for instance, teaching a summer course in a room that was *extraordinarily* air-conditioned. Despite reaching eighty or ninety degrees outside, it often felt like a brisk winter morning in our classroom! When I realized that making adjustments to the thermostat in the room didn't effectively address the problem, I made sure to advise leaders—who typically came dressed for a warm summer day (shorts, tank tops, sleeveless shirts)—ahead of time to wear layers. In addition, sometimes members of my teaching team even brought extra sweatshirts or wraps for them.

I've also learned that providing food—even just some candy, dried fruit, or nuts—goes a long way with leaders, especially when you're gathered in the afternoon (i.e., after lunch) or for many hours at a time. Like caring for the temperature, appreciations about candy pop up in nearly every evaluation! Even years later, as my colleagues and I have learned through research, my students reflect on how much they appreciated candy. As one former student shared: "I loved that Ellie had candy! . . . Because you know what happened was, [our] class was at four o'clock, and between the hours [of] two and four, I'm usually headed downhill. (Laughs)

The attention span is not there. And the fact that she had candy kind of perked me up a little bit." Many others have shared that they now go out of their way to provide little refreshments at meetings and professional development initiatives, because you can't care too much about keeping people comfortable. It makes a *big* difference.

## Arranging the Physical Layout

I also pay careful attention to the physical layout of the room—how the tables are arranged, the number of chairs at a table, the way the chairs are facing in the room, the amount of space between tables, etc. Again, I realize that we don't always have control of the furniture or physical dimensions of a room. For instance, I've facilitated sessions in auditoriums with fixed rows when tables and chairs would have been far more conducive to meaningful group work, but the big idea here is to make the best use of what you can and do have.

As a more specific example, I recently facilitated a workshop with two colleagues on some of the ideas you're reading about in this book. The registration list suggested the workshop would be very well attended—a record high—and we were scheduled to facilitate in a beautiful, new, very large hotel ballroom. Still, when my colleagues and I got to the space, I noticed that it was crammed full of tables. There were at least twenty or thirty extra chairs and three or four too many tables for the number of registered participants. Realizing that the room would simultaneously feel overcrowded *and* empty as a result, we quickly went to work rearranging the space, and asked that the extra tables and chairs be removed. The additional space also allowed us to create walkways between the tables—which are always helpful when you're cruising the room during group work, as they allow you to mingle and connect with people from close up.

## Creating Opportunities for Connection

In addition to creating these kinds of connection-building walkways—to make sure I can reach people (in the physical sense) and that they can likewise reach out to me to talk or ask questions—I also ask participants to wear nametags and/or use name tents *large enough to read from a distance* in bigger workshops and courses. As you know, calling people by their names means a lot, and leaders notice when you do it. So, either providing or asking leaders to create these large nametags allows you to easily learn their names while you're facilitating, and also helps newer groups get to know each other a little better. Importantly, in the spirit of modeling and fairness, my coteachers and I always wear these nametags too. Every day!

Additionally, when facilitating particularly large groups in smaller rooms ($n$=100 in educational leadership prep classrooms only), I suggest a no-laptop/technology policy, for the logistical reason of avoiding the confusion and hazard of too many power cords. It's mostly dangerous when space is limited, and I don't want leaders to be hurt. In addition, in these fast-paced programs, it helps leaders to focus and to have a tiny break from being always connected through phones, laptops, and PDAs. While stepping away from technology is not always easy, it seems to mean a lot to the very busy leaders and educators I have the honor to work with. While I don't generally request this policy in more intimate settings because I know that leaders, like all adults, learn in different ways, I have learned that limiting technology, especially in this intensive learning context, can support more meaningful person-to-person connections when we are discussing deeply personal issues of growth, challenge, and problems of practice. Call me old-fashioned, but there's just something about being face-to-face, rather than screen-to-screen, when leading or being part of a group that makes me and the leaders themselves feel closer and more connected. Leaders share that this is often a meaningful change of pace for them as well when working in small groups or pairs. In our very digital world, finding time to slow down and step out of the information stream—to talk, reflect, and connect—can be precious in and of itself.

In each of these examples, I described specific strategies that I employ to make the most of the physical spaces I lead and teach in. I hope that they, as well as the concept of attending to logistics, are helpful to you in your own practice and leadership. Just like all of the other ideas in this book, they are yours to "rent," adapt, or try out if you find them meaningful—and I hope that you do.

## PLANNING

*Preparation, I have often said, is rightly two-thirds of any venture.*

—Amelia Earhart

As you will learn in this section, *planning* for teaching, learning, and professional development initiatives involves both the preparation that comes *before* the delivery of content, and the in-the-moment adjustments that get mapped out *during* the session itself.

Like Amelia Earhart, I have found that preparation is key to any successful endeavor, but you still might be surprised to learn just *how much* time I spend preparing before every course, workshop, individual class session, or professional learning opportunity. For example, the doctoral students I invite to teach with me often comment on how carefully we map out every minute of the time we share with students in the class. As one of my doctoral advisees once shared with me, "Everyone plans, but you *plan!*" Imagine stretching that word out as long as you can while you're saying it—that's what we're talking about here.

## Mapping Out the Minutes

When I am entrusted to facilitate the learning of a group of dedicated, gifted, and busy leaders and educators, every minute is precious (and I take that truth very seriously when planning for any teaching, learning, or professional development environment). To maximize my time with leaders, I literally *map out every minute of the day*, carving out space for introductions, questions, mini-lectures, small and large group discussions, private reflections, *more* questions, and appreciations (among other things). I do this when planning for every professional learning initiative, regardless of context, although the map looks different, of course, for different venues. In large part, this planning involves finding room for all of the strategies and ideas we've been exploring in this book, and lovingly making sure that leaders will have the most and best opportunities to learn and grow during our time together and beyond.

Mapping the time in this way is also about balance, about differentiating modes and activities to meet the developmental needs of learners with diverse ways of knowing—a topic you will learn more about in the upcoming section on the intentionality of design. For now, though, the big idea is that planning allows you to consider in advance the different activities you would like to incorporate (just as you would when crafting any lesson plan) and the amount of time you realistically expect it will take to complete them. While you inevitably get better at estimating times with experience, thinking carefully about how long learners will need to complete an activity (e.g., finding partners for a pair-share, reflecting privately in journals, or reporting work back to the group) is essential when designing the flow of a session.

It is also important to be generous and realistic about building breaks and transition times into your map. Scheduling and signaling upcoming opportunities for one- or sometimes two-function breaks (meaning breaks in which learners have time to do one or two things—like run to the bathroom, get water or coffee, check for missed calls, etc.) allows adults to hang in there with you and better focus on the serious work of learning and growing together.

**Flexibility and Replanning: "The Coach's Playbook"**

As carefully as we might plan ahead of time, it is also essential to "go with the flow" when leading adult and leadership development. Adjusting plans in the moment, especially plans as carefully and deliberately crafted as those just described, can be difficult for many leaders, but it is important to remember always that the purpose of learning-oriented professional development is meeting the needs of the learners (as opposed to successfully "finishing" any plan or schedule). Often, in the middle of a session, I'll realize that a group has more questions about a topic than I anticipated, or conversely, that they're ready to move on without additional discussion. Related to seeing, as we discussed in chapter 3, this type of sensitivity and responsiveness involves quickly adapting by adding more or less time to activities, adjusting the order or even content of mini-lectures, and/or reshuffling plans.

Yet, just as discussed earlier with preplanning, these adjustments are also carefully mapped out in detail. Before every class, workshop, or academy session, I always print out a copy of the presentation slides I use in handout form. I keep these with me as I facilitate, jotting down notes, observations, reminders, and other such things. Often, when I decide to adjust the map of the day, I rely on these handouts to cross out certain slides, indicate new timing allotments, or signal a new order. One of my coteachers calls my handout packet my "coach's playbook" because of all the circles, arrows, and *x*s I use when reshaping the day's plan in accordance with learners' needs. In some ways, that's not too big of a stretch, because a "win" for me is when leaders get the most out of our time together, and have a positive and meaningful experience. I truly feel that planning—before, during, and after professional learning sessions of all kinds—is essential to making that happen.

## INTENTIONALITY OF DESIGN

As facilitators of any teaching, learning, and professional development environment, we are all professional learning designers in one sense or another. And, as you know, when planning for and designing these environments, it is important to consider how participants' ways of knowing will affect their experiences. Constructive-developmental theory helps us understand that adults will experience the same activities differently, so being intentional about attending to developmental diversity is key when designing holding environments and professional learning opportunities. More than simply striving for balance in your facilitation, *intentionality of design* involves deliberately employing a variety of instructional approaches to meet people where they are developmentally, and voicing this aloud as a show of respect and transparency. As a wise mentor of mine once reminded a class I was in, "I'm going to use a variety of practices to support your learning. Please remember that what you love, the person sitting next to you might not find meaningful."

This section focuses on the importance of being intentional about how we as developmental learning designers create opportunities for learning, growing, and developing—not just by introducing content but also by considering *how* we will teach it and *how* will we invite leaders to engage in learning activities, applications, and processes. In some ways, this is an extension of planning, with an emphasis on intentionally designing and including practices in your session(s) that support the development of leaders with diverse ways of knowing. In chapter 2, you learned about intentionality as a core element that informs how we think about building and sustaining environments for growth. There, we focused on intentionality as it relates to being deliberate about creating holding environments that meet adults where they are developmentally, and I mentioned the importance of working to *purposefully* bring people together in ways that support their learning when shaping contexts in which they can grow. Developmental intentionality, as you know, in its largest sense connects intimately to employing theory to inform practices and to shaping holding environments for growth.

Here, we focus more specifically on the developmental intentions behind a few of the structures and practices I use in professional learning initiatives and why I employ them. A large part of being intentional in design is considering how to employ the pillar practices for growth (which you'll learn more about shortly). First, though, I offer a number of related strategies that can support adult and leadership development when employed intentionally.

### Inviting and Respecting Diverse Forms of Participation

As we've discussed, one big idea associated with being intentional in design is offering adults choices about *how* to participate in larger groups. Related to this idea is the importance of not forcing leaders into "public" speaking, and respecting different forms of contribution and learning. For example, during the second week of a learning initiative I was facilitating with a very large group, one leader approached me and asked to talk. While she had never volunteered or commented aloud during class, she wanted to assure me that she was "paying attention" and "with me and the class." She explained that the freewrites/freethinks (defined in chapter 3) and pair-shares, which we had engaged in multiple times during each session, were "really meaningful and important" for her, but she felt "less comfortable talking in front of the large group." As she shared, "I am learning so much and I am thinking about the ideas deeply. I'm just quiet. And I hope that's okay." Providing diverse opportunities for leaders to think about, engage with, and learn from the ideas and from each other is one important way to signal to learners that such diversity is indeed okay.

Accordingly, when I design professional learning opportunities, I intentionally incorporate multiple kinds of modalities, including:

- Private time to digest through journaling or reflection
- Opportunities to discuss ideas and questions with one other person or a very small group
- Application exercises that invite leaders to translate their ideas to practice in teams
- Quick, instructor-led check-ins
- Invitations to share out with larger or whole groups

For example, offering and thinking carefully about building in different kinds of venues for reflecting in writing and with colleagues can be supportive of growth and learning. Opportunities to engage in freewriting in response to prompts, questions, and/or insights can support individuals regardless of their way of knowing. Balancing different ways to invite adults to engage in dialogue is also important and intentional. First, I usually invite adults to engage with one other person (dyads) when sharing or discussing ideas. "Hopefully, you can find one person you do not know so well," I tell them. Then, I typically invite leaders to find two partners (triads) or engage in small groups of four (quads). Finally, I invite leaders to share anything they'd like with the larger group. I've found that moving from the comfort of sharing with one other person to more public reporting supports learning and eventually development in these kinds of contexts.

## Attending to Ways of Knowing

While leader preferences for one way of learning over another might be attributed to many things, one important aspect to keep in mind is that adults with different ways of knowing will experience different practices in qualitatively different ways. To support their growth, we must differentiate the practices we employ in professional learning and infuse the pillar practices with multiple kinds of developmental supports and challenges. In table 4.1, you can read about the supports and challenges that often help adults with different ways of knowing as they engage in the pillar practices. This table is similar to table 1.2; however, it's offered in this chapter in

**TABLE 4.1**

## Pillar practices as holding environments that support adult growth and leadership development

| Pillar practice | Instrumental knowers | Socializing knowers | Self-authoring knowers | Self-transforming knowers |
|---|---|---|---|---|
| Teaming | **Supports:** Provide clear and explicit guidelines and norms/rules for engaging in dialogue; develop concrete goals establish some step-by-step procedures, a timeline, and deliverable dates. | **Supports:** Establish ground rules/norms for engaging in difficult conversations; model engaging with conflict while sustaining positive relationships; explicitly acknowledge and confirm value of contributions. | **Supports:** Provide opportunities for creating and designing options and proposals; allow for demonstrations of expertise and competencies for promoting, analyzing, and critiquing goals and ideas. | **Supports:** Value sense of independence and provide opportunities for deep inquiry and self-expression; include a broad diversity of team members, perspectives, and forms of participation; provide team structures that are open to change and adaptation. |
|  | **Challenges:** Create opportunities for consideration of multiple perspectives; engage in tasks requiring abstract thinking; offer multiple options as solutions and ways of collaborating rather than one "right" way. | **Challenges:** Encourage voicing of ideas/perspectives *before* learning from authorities/supervisors; invite into lead role with support; invite perspective broadening and value generation in supportive context. | **Challenges:** Encourage critique of one's own value and belief system; pose questions about potential value of conflicting or opposing ideas and ideologies. | **Challenges:** Support in sorting through multiple points of view; challenge learner to cope with and manage hierarchy; encourage identification beyond team to authorities. |

| Pillar practice | Instrumental knowers | Socializing knowers | Self-authoring knowers | Self-transforming knowers |
|---|---|---|---|---|
| **Providing leadership roles** | **Supports:** Offer concrete goals and rewards; model leadership and explicitly make thinking transparent; share rationale behind actions; model sharing rules, purposes, and goals with community and point out value and intention behind doing so. | **Supports:** Explicitly acknowledge contributions; encourage looking inward toward self for decisions about how to lead; validate and recognize risk taking and achievements. | **Supports:** Provide opportunities to demonstrate competencies, design initiatives, and contribute to developing mission and/or vision. | **Supports:** Ensure team, group, or organization has culture of collegiality with shared power and room for creativity; provide room for using imagination and embracing original ideas. |
| | **Challenges:** Encourage consideration of different ways to achieve goals and alternative solutions; discuss multiple perspectives openly; encourage dialogue about value of analyzing alternative solutions. | **Challenges:** Encourage individual to turn toward self for generating own values, goals, and bench of judgment; introduce conflict and support as person works through it. | **Challenges:** Encourage through questioning the potential value and connection between perspectives, alternative proposals, and problem-solving strategies in direct opposition to one's own. | **Challenges:** Challenge knower to take authority when appropriate, even when knower might be unsure about doing so and even when it feels difficult to do so; acknowledge, assist, and offer support when challenging these adults to embrace situations when complex responsibilities require quick decisions; encourage and offer guidance on effective strategies for delegating work and responsibilities. |

*(continues)*

TABLE 4.1 (continued)

| Pillar practice | Instrumental knowers | Socializing knowers | Self-authoring knowers | Self-transforming knowers |
|---|---|---|---|---|
| **Engaging in collegial inquiry** | **Supports:** Share concrete examples of practice; provide detailed instructions, advice, skills, and information; establish steps to engaging in dialogue; establish some concrete goals. | **Supports:** Establish group norms; model engagement with conflict without destroying relationships; provide opportunities to voice and explore perspectives in pairs or small groups before sharing with larger groups or supervisors. | **Supports:** Establish opportunities for demonstrating expertise and competencies and for critiquing proposals, designs, and initiatives; create spaces for dialogue, engaging conflict, and sharing perspectives. | **Supports:** Offer opportunities to learn from diverse perspectives; ensuring shared values around discussion, process, and inquiry; provide freedom within the structure to experiment with different forms of inquiry; welcome conflict as means to greater harmony. |
| | **Challenges:** Encourage dialogue and exploration of multiple perspectives; create opportunities for generalization and transferability of broad, abstract ideas; encourage engaging in situations and problem solving requiring abstract thinking. | **Challenges:** Encourage the toleration of conflict and the development of individual beliefs and values; support voicing of one's own perspective as expert and leader. | **Challenges:** Emphasize the importance of tolerance and openness during debate; encourage sincere consideration of opposing viewpoints. | **Challenges:** Offer encouragement with developmental challenge to move from inquiry to action; acknowledge challenge of identifying or affiliating with authority or impersonal systems and create space for dialogue about it and encouragement to embrace it; acknowledge and discuss challenges and point to benefits and complexities of remaining committed when sense of purpose is unclear; encourage, coach, and challenge to remain sensitive to those without the same capacities for conflict. |

| Pillar practice | Instrumental knowers | Socializing knowers | Self-authoring knowers | Self-transforming knowers |
|---|---|---|---|---|
| Mentoring/developmental coaching | **Supports:** Name purposes and objectives for mentoring/coaching relationship; offer expertise and advise; share reasoning behind perspectives.<br><br>**Challenges:** Encourage movement beyond "correct solutions"; facilitate abstract discussion and consideration of others' needs/perspectives. | **Supports:** Explicitly acknowledge and confirm beliefs and perspectives; suggest "best" solutions to complex problems.<br><br>**Challenges:** Encourage mentee to recognize and establish own values and standards, and to tolerate conflict without feeling threatened. | **Supports:** Allow mentee to demonstrate own competencies, critique work, and move forward with self-determined goals.<br><br>**Challenges:** Engage in dialogue and offer additional goals, viewpoints, and problem-solving alternatives for contemplation. | **Supports:** Encourage peerlike and mutual exchanges; provide space for creativity and exploration; promote full relational and dialectic engagement.<br><br>**Challenges:** Embrace critical feedback rather than protecting self from it; appreciate the importance of learning from others, regardless of way of knowing. |

slightly different form to support you as we consider ways of knowing specifically in relation to using space and structure as you shape and design learning environments with developmental intentionality.

It might be helpful here to make a few connections between the practices we've been discussing and the pillar practices. For example, inviting adults to engage in freewriting and/or freethinking and then to talk with colleagues about their thinking, feelings, and assumptions is an example of employing collegial inquiry. Inviting adults to work in smaller groups over time, where they establish norms and various other kinds of agreements and work collaboratively, is an example of teaming as a pillar practice to support growth and leadership development.

As table 4.1 shows, intentionality of design is not just about implementing the aforementioned structures; it is also about employing them purposefully, with an eye toward differentiation and adjustment in order to meet the needs of a group at *any moment in time*. In addition, when adults *experience* these practices themselves, and when they see how they can build them into their own contexts, it helps them to understand the value of being intentional about making these spaces available for others. Differentiating the kinds of practices we employ to build robust holding environments and developmentally oriented learning opportunities—where time for reflecting, sharing, and engaging in dialogue is *prioritized in intentional ways*, and where feedback is an opportunity to both support and offer developmental challenges to help another person grow—is one promising way to build internal capacity and leadership.

As one leader recently shared with me during the last session of a developmental leadership academy, finding the right activity at the right time for leaders can make a big difference for their learning. "I was feeling very drained when I came here," she explained, "and one of my hopes was to be energized by *this* environment. And it worked!"

In the next section, we will further explore how you can employ the pillars as robust holding environments in professional learning contexts that support adult and leadership development.

## THE PILLAR PRACTICES: BACKGROUND AND DEFINITIONS

Next we will talk more about the four pillar practices for growth—teaming, providing adults with leadership roles, engaging in collegial inquiry, and mentoring/developmental coaching—and how they can serve as holding environments for individuals and in larger professional learning initiatives.

You may recall that these pillar practices (hereafter *pillars*), which I mentioned in the introduction and in the preceding section about planning, compose what I called in my earlier works a new *learning-oriented model for school leadership*.[4] While this model is an essential part of what you've been learning about in the preceding chapters, as you've seen in figure 4.1, this book expands on that prior work to offer you an even more robust model for creating contexts that support adult growth and leadership development, which includes these pillars and more.

In these next sections, I offer an overview of each pillar practice, followed by brief illustrations of the pillars in action in professional learning environments. In both cases, I'm offering "Tang" versions to be of help to you and your work designing structures and practices to support adult and leadership development. Do you remember Tang? It's the flavored powder we added to water to make an orange drink. Put simply, these sections, like Tang, are the *concentrated* versions of the pillars. The idea here is to offer a good taste of them and the more important aspects of their design and implementation. Should you choose to learn more about them, you might want to consider reading my prior work from 2004 and 2009, as I mentioned earlier.

### Why Use the Term "Pillar"?

I refer to these practices, employed with developmental intentionality, as *pillars* for growth for two reasons. First, they serve as a *foundation* or structure for supporting adults' growth and leadership development. Second, they *illuminate* important practices for designing and infusing professional learning environments with intentionality. In other words, these pillars can transform more traditional professional development initiatives into contexts that support adults with different ways of knowing. *How*, you might wonder? And *why*? Essentially, it's because each pillar involves creating opportunities for adults to collaborate and engage in dialogue and reflection as tools for professional and personal growth. While, as you will see shortly, the pillars can often work in conjunction, I have artificially teased them apart here to help us focus in on what is most important and distinct about each practice.

### What Makes the Pillar Practices Developmentally Robust?

While you may have implemented and/or experienced a variety of forms of teaming, providing leadership roles, collegial inquiry, or mentoring in your own leadership as coach, principal, assistant principal, superintendent, team leader, member of a professional learning community, or in professional development work in schools or other contexts, these practices can be re-envisioned with developmental intentionally to support adult growth and leadership development, as shown in table 4.1. Within this new model for learning-oriented leadership development, for instance, these pillars can assist you in:

- Focusing on leaders as meaning makers, within any context
- Enhancing safe spaces in which leaders can test and challenge assumptions
- Offering supports and challenges for growth and leadership development
- Using tools for reflections (i.e., protocols—both those offered earlier and those still to come) to help guide thinking and action
- Building structures and allocating needed time in professional learning opportunities for deep conversation, collaboration, and growing as well as learning together
- Meeting the diverse needs of individuals with different learning preferences and qualitatively different ways of knowing (i.e., capacities)

As you've learned from reviewing table 4.1, these pillars can be infused with developmental intentions. Hopefully, these ideas will be useful to you. Moreover, as you explore these practices, I invite you to consider how an understanding of adults' different ways of knowing and the four pillar practices might help with your noble work supporting other adults' growth and leadership development. And how might such understandings support your own growth and development?

Before we explore the pillars further, it is important to note that these practices have been developed, implemented, tested, and refined over many years with educators of all kinds—aspiring and practicing superintendents, principals, assistant principals, coaches, specialists, and teacher leaders in university classrooms; long-term teaching, learning, and professional development environments; and even longer-term developmental leadership academies as well as other venues. As emphasized earlier in the introduction, in these contexts practicing and aspiring leaders not only learn content, but they also experience the practices and see them modeled. Leaders have shared that seeing the pillars modeled and actually engaging in them while learning about them helps the leaders "know how to implement" them in their schools. Understanding how the pillars work, and the intentionality behind their design and how they are informed by constructive-developmental theory, is essential to shaping them as holding environments both in and out of more formal professional learning initiatives.

*Intentionally* designing environments that couple the practices and ideas you've been learning about with the pillars enhances opportunities to support adult growth and leadership development. Exploring and experiencing both (practices and ideas in this book) can help shape holding environments, effectively build developmentally oriented learning contexts, and in turn help leaders grow and pay forward these ways of helping others grow and learn. Leaders from all over the world have told me that the pillars you're learning about here have helped them to shape growth-enhancing school climates, build teacher leadership, grow effective professional learning communities where adults can increase their internal capacities, and grow themselves. In other words, being intentional in your design of learning contexts and employing the pillars to inform course design, teaching practices, feedback (written and verbal), and interactions with individual learners will assist you in supporting adult and leadership development across the system.

## The Pillar Practices Defined: Incorporating the Pillar Practices for Growth and Leadership Development into Your Design

In prior sections, we learned about different kinds of intentional strategies and structures to prioritize and utilize when building opportunities for growth and leadership development. What follows is an opportunity to learn more about how including the pillars in your learning designs can create conditions for growth. After a brief overview of each pillar, we will consider how the pillars in action can serve as vital holding environments within the larger context of professional learning sessions that offer developmentally appropriate forms of high support *and* high challenge.

### Pillar Practice 1: Teaming

When used intentionally to enhance adult learning and growth, the first pillar, teaming, is one powerful way to create opportunities to learn from different perspectives, and to question and understand one's own and others' assumptions and points of view when making decisions and pushing mutual work forward. Working in teams also enables adults to grow from collaborative decision making and reflecting on curricula, school missions, and teaching and learning philosophies.

Teaming offers a chance for individuals, organizations, and systems to grow together in general and from participating in teams in professional learning contexts specifically. As table 4.1 shows, putting certain structures in place can help team members with different ways of knowing create the conditions necessary to make teams developmentally robust holding environments. When implemented with intentionality, the team structure provides a safe context within which to experiment with one's thinking, grow internal capacity, and develop leadership.

For example, in my experiences and work with leaders who serve in different roles in learning environments, I have learned that for many of them one of the most challenging aspects of working on teams is engaging in conflict. Some leaders express that they wish they were "not so conflict averse," while others wish that the adults they work with would be better able to "engage in conflict rather than avoid it." Either way, conflict sometimes arises in teams, and it's often hard on people when feelings get hurt or perspectives are left unexplored.

A developmental perspective helps remind us that instrumental knowers will feel supported if teams have clear expectations and guidelines for how they will work together. Conflict for these adults is really a result of *not following the rules* ("if we all just follow the rules and do things the right way, we'll get it right!"). Teaming offers an opportunity for these adults to grow to consider more than their own concrete needs and desires, to develop the capacity to consider alternative points of view, and to understand multiple pathways to achieving team goals rather than one "right way."

Socializing knowers could find it uncomfortable initially to work with colleagues on teams, especially if they are required to share their perspectives on initiatives and practices and their views conflict with those of any "authorities" who are on the team. When invited to share out loud, these adults will often try to voice a perspective that does not contradict what valued others think and/or feel since conflict and disagreement are threatening to them. Providing opportunities for these individuals to share their thinking and feelings in smaller groups (dyads or triads) before sharing with the full team can support their growth. Modeling that conflict is a part of discussion and can lead to more effective outcomes will support these adults' leadership development and growth. Over time, working with colleagues in a team can enable socializing knowers to understand that conflict can be a means to developing better and more effective initiatives or solutions.

Self-authoring knowers will value teaming as an opportunity to learn from and critique colleagues' perspectives on teaching, instructional leadership, policies under consideration, and proposals for change. For them, conflict is a natural part of working together and can lead to more effective ways of collaboration and better decisions. To support these adults in their growth and leadership development, team members can encourage and gently challenge them to consider perspectives that diametrically oppose their own. In addition, supportively challenging these individuals to consider and critique their self-constructed goals and ways of approaching problems will support their growth and leadership development.

Self-transforming knowers will feel supported by colleagues on a team if they feel that there are opportunities for deep inquiry into proposals for change, student work, and leadership dilemmas. They will also work best in teams when team structures are open to change and adaptation. When conflict arises, these adults will seek to explore the paradoxes inherent in the conflict and work collegially to help the team sort through the conflict, build consensus, and return to a harmonious state. To support self-transforming knowers in their growth and leadership development, we can encourage them to manage the hierarchy that often exists within teams.

While I detail many additional strategies that support teaming in *Leading Adult Learning*, you've learned in this book that establishing norms and ground rules is one effective way to help create and sustain safe, productive teams.[5] This technique is a very important aspect of supporting growth, because it helps adults share individual feelings and expectations as well as build common expectations. As one wise leader shared with me, reflecting back on her experiences working with other adults: "No one ever taught us to work together." While the educators I have the honor of working with and learning from often feel very skilled in working with children and youth, many have shared with me that they never learned in their graduate work or professional training "how to work with adults." Yet we work with adults each and every day. Understanding how teams can be holding environments that support adults with different ways of knowing is one helpful tool, and my hope is that you find learning about the other pillar practices helpful as well.

### Pillar Practice 2: Providing Leadership Roles

The second pillar, providing leadership roles (PLR), is based on an important truth of contemporary leadership—namely, that we cannot lead alone and we need to help each other grow. Providing others with leadership roles allows for sharing power, decision making, authority, and responsibility. It helps leaders do their hard work better and can also support growth and internal capacity building.

Unlike the more familiar term *distributed leadership*, I use the phrase *providing leadership roles* because it conveys the idea of offering a leadership role with *developmental intentions* and of supporting the individual in that role so that he or she can succeed, develop as a leader, and grow from the experience. Rather than simply assigning tasks, PLR deliberately offers developmental supports and challenges to the person in the role. Having another person to "think out loud with" and to listen to the complexities and challenges of exercising leadership creates opportunities for growth.

Also, PLR considers the developmental match between the individual and the role in question. Considering the *developmental match* between one's expectations and adults' capacities to meet them will help to support adult growth. By standing alongside teachers, coaches, aspiring principals, colleagues, or other adults as they grow into and from a new role, you can help them build new expertise, skills, and capacities by offering appropriate supports and challenges. Not only does this support individual growth, but it also increases the collective capacity of a team, school, or system.

Another intention behind PLR is to offer differentiated and developmentally appropriate leadership roles to adults with different ways of knowing. As you know, leadership roles will be experienced differently, but they can support growth by providing supports and challenges like those shown in table 4.1. For example, those who are challenged by assuming authority (instrumental and socializing knowers) might initially require substantial support as they take on leadership. Self-authoring knowers might appreciate the opportunity to put *their* ideas into action, so one growth-enhancing leadership role for them might be to act as facilitator rather than leader. Self-transforming knowers will deeply appreciate assuming leadership roles that enable them to bring people together in the spirit of collegiality, collaboration, and community. Their growing edge in these roles is to delegate responsibility and to move to quick decisions when faced with complex situations. Leadership roles can be effective holding environments and can be carefully tailored opportunities for growth.

Leadership roles raise not only a person's consciousness but also a community's consciousness. Serving in lead roles, like a teacher leader or coach, enables adults to share their own expertise and knowledge and to grow from the experience of enacting leadership. By creating both formal and informal opportunities for adults in learning contexts, teams, schools, or organizations to build and share expertise, you can help others grow and develop as leaders.

### Pillar Practice 3: Engaging in Collegial Inquiry

Collegial inquiry (CI), the third pillar, is the practice of engaging with *at least one other person* in dialogue that involves purposefully reflecting on one's assumptions, beliefs, and values about teaching, learning, and leadership as part of the learning and growing process. In other words, CI is distinct from reflective practice because we can reflect on our practice independently, whereas CI can be done only with others. Educators of all kinds have told me that they employ CI and find it valuable and powerful, and that prioritizing spaces for meaningful, deep conversations in which they explore firmly held convictions, assumptions, and beliefs about teaching, leading, and life enhances growth for their contexts.

CI helps leaders push their own thinking and practice forward by exploring key questions and dilemmas with others. This kind of deep conversation helps us to uncover assumptions that guide our practice, to learn about our own perspectives and other people, and to grow from this kind of holding environment. This process also enhances the ability of a team, school, or organization to assess its *own* effectiveness.

CI provides opportunities for leaders to develop more complex perspectives by listening to themselves and others. As you might imagine, it is also an integral part of shaping developmentally oriented professional learning opportunities. In fact, CI can be employed to support growth in all kinds of teaching, learning, and professional development environments as adults engage in decision making and reflect on key issues (e.g., diversity, student work, assessment development, coaching protocols, proposals for change). Examples of CI include:

- Reflecting privately in writing in response to critical or essential questions, followed by discussion (a practice you've already read about)
- Engaging in the process of collaborative goal setting
- Reflecting collectively as a method of engaging in conflict resolution (e.g., identifying assumptions)
- Engaging in dialogue and sharing/learning from feedback about teaching, leadership, or important initiatives and/or ideas

As with teaming, using protocols and other tools can help create CI groups that are safe and productive holding environments that nurture the learning and growth of adults with diverse ways of knowing.

For example, leaders have shared with me that one of their biggest challenges with CI is offering and receiving truly honest feedback about practice. Many have told me that this is difficult for them as well as for teachers who are observing colleagues' practice. "It's easy," they explain, "to give positive feedback. But giving critical, constructive feedback can be extremely challenging." As we know, feedback is important—vital—to improving our instructional practice and leadership, and it can help us grow our internal capacities. Still, adults will experience and understand feedback in developmentally different ways. Therefore, it is crucial for us to consider how our colleagues each make sense of feedback in order to determine how to best support their (and our own) learning and growth.

Educators with an instrumental way of knowing, for instance, will tend to experience a valued colleague's or a supervisor's feedback on their teaching and/or leadership practices as an indication of whether they are doing things the *right* or *wrong* way. Instrumental knowers will feel supported if the person evaluating them offers examples of best practices, concrete advice and procedures for improvement, and specific skills they need to employ. Encouraging these adults to move beyond trying to instruct in the "one right way" and toward seeing multiple pathways for teaching a lesson or helping a struggling student effectively will support growth and leadership development.

Leaders with a socializing way of knowing will tend to understand valued colleagues and supervisors' feedback as expert advice. In other words, they see the supervisor as expert and will experience that feedback as advice they *should* follow in order to do good work and improve practice. Supervisors and valued colleagues' feedback will determine how these adults think about and evaluate their own practice. Helping these leaders feel accepted and cared for as individuals will enable them to take in feedback better and encourage them to take learning risks as they work to improve their practice. Supervisors would be wise to help these leaders understand that the feedback is offered to help with *improving practice* and is not about the leader as a human being.

Leaders who are self-authoring knowers have the internal capacity to generate their own evaluations of their instructional practice and their leadership. They have their own expectations for their leadership and teaching and their own standards for assessment. When receiving feedback from a supervisor, for instance, they will weigh it against what they think and feel. In other words, they will *listen* to feedback and then look internally to determine its value and to decide whether or not to implement the suggestions that have been offered.

Self-transforming knowers orient naturally to critiquing their self-system and practices. These leaders will want supervisors and evaluators to explore *with* them the inconsistencies in their leadership and instructional practices. They will feel challenged to grow and develop as leaders if supervisors and colleagues create opportunities to engage in dialogue and reflection *with them* to help them understand more deeply the assumptions, mental models, and intentions—including the strengths and limitations of each—that guide their leadership and instructional practice.

Table 4.1 offers additional developmentally appropriate supports and challenges that promote growth in adults with diverse ways of knowing as they engage in CI.

*Pillar Practice 4: Mentoring/Developmental Coaching*

Mentoring traditionally offers a more private, relational way of supporting adult development. This practice creates opportunities for broadening perspectives, examining assumptions, and sharing expertise. It takes many forms, including expert professionals paired with other adults, veterans with deep knowledge of a school's mission paired with new community members, and group or team mentoring structures. Most recently, given the changing and increasingly complex demands and expectations placed on principals, assistant principals, superintendents, and teacher leaders, mentoring (often referred to in the professional development literature as *coaching*) has become a prominent practice that is increasingly employed to support leaders and other educators. As you know, there are many different kinds of coaching. For instance, we have math and literacy coaches, improvement coaches, data coaches, content-focused coaches, as well as leadership coaches, peer coaches, and instructional coaches. While these differentiated forms of coaching are valuable and very essential, what I'm about to share is more about mentoring and what I call *developmental coaching*, or coaching that is developmental in nature and oriented toward building internal capacities in a longer-term relationship. As with the other pillars, this practice, too, has been found to support leaders' individual growth and to build capacity in schools and districts.

As you may already suspect, ways of knowing will influence what we expect of and need from mentors as well as what mentors and coaches are able to *give to mentees* (i.e., how our own internal capacities influence the resources we have to support others). Importantly, ways of knowing also influence the kinds of supports and challenges that help us grow. As mentioned previously, table 4.1 illuminates different kinds of developmental supports and challenges adults with different ways of knowing will need to grow and develop as leaders. For example, instrumental knowers will feel supported by mentors who help them meet concrete needs and goals. Over time, however, mentors can support growth by encouraging mentees to move beyond the perceived *right* way of doing things. Ultimately, more open-ended discussions about alternatives and abstract goals would help broaden instrumental knowers' perspectives and thinking.

Socializing knowers feel supported by mentors' explicit acknowledgment of their beliefs and ideas. Feeling accepted and cared for as a person enables these adults to take greater learning risks in sharing their dilemmas, concerns, and feelings. Mentors can gently support these mentees' growth by encouraging them to voice their *own* perspectives *before* learning about others'. In addition, modeling conflict as helpful and unthreatening supports growth.

Self-authoring knowers feel best supported by mentors who enable them to critique and analyze their own, others', *and their mentor's* perspectives, goals, and practices. To support growth, mentors can encourage these knowers to challenge their own philosophies without feeling internally conflicted.[6] Self-transforming knowers will appreciate a mentor who respects and acknowledges their capacity for independence and autonomy while simultaneously recognizing that they also have a need for relationship and interdependence. Supporting growth in these knowers can take the form of gently challenging them to embrace (listen carefully and deeply to) constructive and critical feedback as they sort through their sometimes-disorienting internal life (emotions and thoughts).

In summary, the ways in which we engage in the pillar practices, or any form of learning or collaborative work, vary according to *how* we make sense of our experiences. With appropriate supports and challenges, though, we can infuse these practices into professional learning contexts to support adult growth and leadership development. In the next section, you will see examples of a few of the pillars in action.

## THE PILLAR PRACTICES IN ACTION

Next, I share a few ways in which I have employed some of the pillar practices. Actually, many of the examples shared so far in this book involve the pillars (I just didn't frame them in that way), so you may find it helpful to review those now that you have a deeper understanding of the pillar practices and how they can serve as holding environments for adult and leadership development.

### The Use of Teaming, Collegial Inquiry, and Mentoring During a Mentoring Program

For the past eight years, I have had the honor of working with and learning from a group of experienced principals who serve as mentors to groups of five or six assistant principals aspiring to the principalship as part of the Advanced Leadership Program for Assistant Principals (ALPAP) offered through the New York City Educational Leadership Institute (ELI). I have the honor of facilitating the program gathering at the start (September) and closing (April or May) of the school year for these mentor principals and their teams of assistant principals (eighty to ninety-six leaders in total). In the example that follows, I will discuss the content and process of the opening gathering and how it shows *teaming*, engaging in *collegial inquiry*, and *mentoring/coaching* in action.

While this example focuses on New York City principal mentors and assistant principals, you might find it helpful to know that I also facilitate similar sessions with senior university professors who are coaches to professors who are new to the university, and education leaders (e.g., former and practicing superintendents, principals, and staff developers) who coach aspiring principals.

For more context, it might be helpful to know that in July of each year, I facilitate a daylong workshop for the seventy to eighty ALPAP assistant principals, during which they learn about constructive-developmental theory, ways of knowing, and the pillars so that they can apply these ideas and practices in their work to support adult growth and leadership development in their schools. This workshop also equips them to use a common language of development and capacity building with their mentors and provides a shared understanding of the pillar practices for growth, which they are simultaneously *engaging in and learning about* in this very program.

Also, for still more context, during the first three years of the ALPAP program I worked with the mentor principals in three-hour workshops four times a year. These sessions focused on learning about and employing developmental theory and the pillars, with special emphasis on mentoring, to inform their leadership and coaching practices. In these learning contexts, mentor principals engaged in teaming and in collegial inquiry about their coaching/mentoring practice, the challenges they encountered, and how to apply the pillar practices and theory to their mentoring relationships.

During the opening session in September (called "Building Meaningful Connections") and also during the closing session in April/May (called "Reflecting on Our Journey Together"), each principal mentor and his or her five or six assistant principal mentees sit at a table for the three-hour workshop. They work as *a team* throughout the session as they engage in collegial inquiry and the mentoring/coaching processes.

Each year, after sharing a meal and getting to know each other a little bit during the opening September gathering (this is the first time mentors are with their mentees), I invite the participants to engage in private

reflection through writing or thinking, and then to engage in collegial inquiry with their entire team about the following questions:

- What does mentoring mean to you?
- What constitutes a "good and productive mentoring relationship"?
- What are your hopes for this mentoring relationship? How do you
  hope to grow from your mentoring/coaching relationship?
- What kinds of developmental and logistical supports do you (assistant
  principals) think you will need from your coach this year?
- What concerns or challenges do you (assistant principals) have, if
  any, about the relationship at this point? (Often, leaders mention
  time—demands on their time as well as wanting to make time for the
  relationship.)

I pose these questions one by one, allocate a certain amount of time for
private reflection and team sharing, and then invite the teams to share out
what they'd like about each question to the entire group of ninety or so
leaders. In addition, I ask each group to have a volunteer record ideas so
that I can type up their reflections and give them back to everyone in
May—before they again engage in the process of teaming and collegial inquiry to reflect on their year together and their next leadership steps.

Both the questions and the process of engaging as a team in the practice of collegial inquiry are developmental in intention and action. The
questions and ensuing dialogue create a context for growth in three ways
(in addition to the event itself). First, they help the mentee to *clarify* his or
her thinking, and also to surface assumptions about and expectations of
the coach and the mentoring process. Second, this practice creates an opportunity for the mentor to learn more about each individual mentee and
the team in order to be of best support. And third, it creates a space in
which team members can learn from alterative perspectives. Importantly,
since everyone in the program has a common language for development,
individuals often disclose their way of knowing and ask for appropriate
supports and challenges so that they can build their own internal capacities
and develop as leaders.

Each year, just about all of the mentors let their teams know (and me
too, privately) that this experience of engaging in dialogue and in collegial
inquiry with their teams in response to these questions helps them to understand how their mentees make sense of the mentoring relationship and
the kinds of developmental and logistical supports they think they need

from their mentors. The mentees, each and every year, also let their coaches and me know how valuable this space is for them and how helpful it is to engage in this kind of dialogue with their mentor and their team. Most of them mention how this opportunity helps them to better understand their own thinking about the meaning of mentoring and the kinds of supports and challenges they need from their mentor and fellow team members to support their own growth.

As you can see, this example brings together teaming, mentoring/developmental coaching, and engaging in collegial inquiry. It also illuminates the interconnection and essential relationships between these pillars as they relate to the core elements in the first growth ring, and many components of the second. Employing the pillars with developmental intentions helps leaders build relationships by listening with presence, using language intentionally, and seeing. In addition, it creates a space for demonstrating care, establishing and deepening trust, and collaborating—and in turn, for supporting development.

Following are a few of the participating leaders' most frequently cited "strengths of the workshop" (these are direct quotes from evaluations):

- Time to reflect and share with peers and mentor—time to build community
- Strength as a presenter: motivating, helped bridge the relationship, provided a risk-free and safe environment
- Discovering what mentoring really means to others and me
- Having the opportunity to think, write, and discuss our hopes and concerns

Following are the "most significant discoveries" most frequently cited:

- [Learning about] my expectations and the expectations of my mentor
- How much you can learn from a group [team] experience
- How important our mentor will be in our development as leaders
- Putting a specific structure [in this space] to the process of mentoring
- The power of collective thinking [of the team]

Principal mentors and their mentees work as a team and one-on-one throughout the year to explore and learn from each other's perspectives, to grow from understanding their own assumptions, to develop their leadership, and to build internal capacity as they learn from each other. It is a privilege to be a part of this powerful and important work, and gratifying that many leaders have shared that the intentional holding environment of the workshop helped plant the seeds for their success.

## Mentoring in Action: Links in a Chain

Just as with ALPAP, one of the most rewarding aspects of my work involves mentoring or coaching leaders who in turn serve as mentors or coaches for others. By discussing, modeling, and developing the kinds of ideas described in this book with these leaders, I try very hard to nurture our relationships as holding environments—and as connective links in a chain of support—that can be passed forward, shared, and enhanced in leaders' unique contexts. Often, my work with mentors and coaches centers on the kinds of language and feedback that support adult and leadership development, as I describe in the following example.

Recently, I had the honor of working with a group of coaches who were very experienced retired and practicing principals, superintendents, and district leaders. They were working to support the growth and leadership development of teacher leaders, assistant principals, coaches, and professional learning specialists who were aspiring principals. Toward the end of our first two sessions together, after we had discussed ways of knowing and pillar practices for growth, we paused to share insights, questions, and personal reflections. One of the coaches (let's call her Jeana), a practicing principal who had been serving as principal for fifteen years and had been coaching aspiring principals for three, asked for help with a dilemma she was having with one of her interns (we'll call him Manny). Jeana shared that she was feeling "distressed" and "did not know what to do," because something did "not feel right" about her work with Manny. For more than three months, Manny had not followed any of the advice she generously offered from her fifteen years of experience. "I'm just not sure what to do," she confessed. "I want to be of help to him, but I'm just not sure it's a good fit."

"I'm so sorry," I told her, stepping into my mentoring role as coach to the coach. "That sounds very challenging, and I can see that you are upset. Thank you very much for sharing this with us." I then went on to ask, "Have you shared how you're thinking and feeling about this with Manny? What do you think might happen if you did share your feelings and thinking?" Just as we discussed earlier in the sections on trust and language in chapters 2 and 3, sharing one's true feelings and reactions can be a developmental support and a show of respect. In this case, engaging in this type of straightforward dialogue with Jeana served as a kind of model to help her lead a difficult conversation with her own coachee. "I didn't really consider it before now," Jeana acknowledged, and after I probed further about potential ways she could honestly discuss with Manny the feelings she'd shared with the group, Jeana had a kind of revelation.

"Wow," Jeana shared, "I never thought of actually telling him about how I was experiencing the relationship. I just didn't." She continued, "I'm reflecting on the question you just asked, 'What would happen if I told him how I am feeling about his not following my advice?' *What would happen?*" After a little more dialogue, Jeana decided that she would invite a conversation with Manny and that she would share what she was honestly thinking and feeling. She also wanted to learn about his experience. While she never thought of engaging in this kind of dialogue before, she said that she found our conversation very helpful, and that the questions posed—and the subsequent *thinking out loud and with the group*—helped her to realize how important it was to have this conversation with Manny. As other leaders have shared with me, having transparent, honest discussions about one's experience and expectations is crucial to shaping mentoring or coaching relationships as holding spaces for adults on both sides of the partnership.

As you know, even though they are sometimes difficult, these conversations can help to deepen trust. So, I aspire to make professional learning contexts of all kinds safe places for leaders to experience and experiment with honest conversations before translating them to their own mentoring relationships and leadership contexts. Like Jeana, leaders have shared that learning about how to frame mentoring conversations is very helpful in general and more specifically when helping other leaders grow and develop.

I hope the preceding examples help you with considering how mentoring and its various links in the chain can support adult growth and leadership development. By "links in a chain," I'm referring to the ways in which this example (and others in this book) involves helping leaders to connect what they are learning about and *experiencing* in the holding environment of our time together to their own practice and leadership in support of others. For example, as a mentor to mentors and a coach of coaches, I do my best to help leaders of all kinds experience the power of engaging in open, honest, and frank conversations about aspects of their work so that they, in turn, can engage in similar conversations with their own mentees. In Jeana's case, our conversation helped her to "think out loud" and come to a very significant realization about the importance of honest sharing. Adding a link to this chain of support, she was then planning to engage Manny in a similar kind of honest mentoring/coaching conversation with the hope that they could individually and collectively come to a new understanding of each other and the coaching relationship. Hopefully, Manny will in turn experience the power of such conversations as well and be better able to help those he serves and to offer developmental supports to help with capacity building.

From a developmental perspective, mentoring is a complex and personal endeavor that draws heavily on the ideas described in this book. And, as you know, what's at risk for others—and for us—in these kinds of relationships will vary depending on our ways of knowing. In actuality, all of the pillar practices have multiple links in the chain and can serve as holding environments that support adult and leadership development in diverse professional learning contexts.

## TAKEAWAYS

+ Put simply, considering these three big ideas and practices (and related strategies) will help you implement your developmental vision with intention and mindfulness: 1) *designing* professional learning environments so that they support adult growth—internal capacity building—and leadership development, 2) *using space intentionally* to nurture conditions that create opportunities for growth, and 3) considering the *pillar practices for growth* and employing them in leadership development initiatives.

+ Intentionality of design is not just about implementing the structures, but also employing them purposefully with an eye toward differentiation and adjustment in order to meet the needs of a group at *any moment in time*. Differentiating the kinds of practices we employ to build robust holding environments and learning contexts—where time for reflecting, sharing, and engaging in dialogue is *prioritized in intentional ways*, and where feedback is an opportunity to both support and offer developmental challenges to help another person grow—is a promising pathway to building internal capacity and developing leadership.

+ As illustrated in the third growth ring of this book's leadership model, there are five important strategies for designing and using space that you will want to consider when building learning environments that support adult growth and leadership development: 1) how we work to *create a safe space* in learning contexts, 2) the importance of caring for the *logistics* of the initiative, 3) the vital importance of *planning* (before, during—in the moment—and after learning endeavors), 4) the intentionality of the *design* of these holding environments, and 5) how employing the *pillar practices* in professional learning venues can support adult growth and leadership development.

✦ The pillar practices—teaming, inviting adults to assume leadership roles, engaging in collegial inquiry, and mentoring—are components of this model for learning-oriented leadership development. It's important to consider *how* the pillar practices, as part of this space, can enhance leaders' experiences in professional learning environments.

✦ *Intentionally* designing workshops, sessions, courses, and learning opportunities of all kinds that couple the practices and ideas you've been learning about with the pillars will enhance opportunities to support adult growth and leadership development. In other words, being intentional in your design of holding environments and employing the pillars to inform course design, teaching practices, feedback (written and verbal), and interactions with individual learners will assist you in supporting robust professional learning.

## REFLECTIVE QUESTIONS

1. What are some ways in which you currently design and use space in your teaching, learning, and/or professional development environment to support learning, growth, and leadership development that you think work especially well?

2. How, if at all, might you employ any of this chapter's ideas about and practices for using and designing space with developmental intentionality to enhance your work? In case helpful, I've summarized them here: 1) how we can work to *create a safe space* in teaching, learning, and professional development environments, 2) the importance of *caring for logistical features* when planning and leading professional learning, 3) the vital importance of *planning* (before, during, and after facilitating learning initiatives), 4) the intentionality of the *design* of these holding environments, and 5) the *pillar practices* and how they can support adult growth and leadership development.

3. What stands out as something important that you learned from reading this chapter or something that you came to realize about your own work in designing holding environments that support adult growth and leadership development?
4. What additional design features might you add to this growth ring? How do they assist you in leading, facilitating, and supporting adult growth and leadership development?

---

## APPLICATION EXERCISE: HOW WILL YOU IMPLEMENT THE STRATEGIES?

In this chapter, we considered various ideas and practices related to designing and making use of space in teaching, learning, and professional development environments in order to create opportunities for adult growth and leadership development. We discussed the ways these ideas and practices can assist in implementing your developmental vision with intention and mindfulness.

This application exercise is offered as an invitation to consider how you might apply some of the practices discussed here in your own work of designing and using space when building learning contexts with developmental intentions. By way of gentle reminder, I provide here the five important aspects of designing and using space that help to create conditions that support adult growth and leadership development: 1) how we can work to *create a safe space* in teaching, learning, and professional development environments; 2) the importance of *caring for the logistics* of learning opportunities; 3) the vital importance of *planning* (before, during, and after facilitating professional learning); 4) the intentionality of the *design* of these holding environments; and 5) the *pillar practices* and how they can support adult growth and leadership development. This exercise is a chance to use whatever ideas and practices you have found helpful from this chapter to develop and/or refine your own plan for supporting adult growth and leadership development in your practice. It's offered as an opportunity to reimagine and redesign one professional learning or professional development session or university class that you facilitate. How, if at all, might you change it now that you've read this chapter? The following questions might assist you as you consider ways to enhance your practice in light of what you've learned from this chapter:

+ How might you revise, adjust, and/or infuse the experience you offer to others with some of the intentional strategies and structures we discussed in this chapter to offer deeper opportunities for growth and leadership development?
+ What is one way that you will work to improve how you facilitate creating safe spaces for learning and growing?
+ How might you invite adults to engage in one or more of the pillar practices for growth in the teaching, learning, or professional development environment you facilitate?
+ How do you think colleagues in your workplace, students in your leadership preparation program, students in your classroom, teachers in your school, educators on your leadership team, adults in your district, or whomever you are working to support will experience the new aspects of your practice?
+ How can you best make sure that adults with different ways of knowing will be both supported and challenged to grow in the space you create?

# CHAPTER 5

---

# Nuances

*Little Things That Make a Big Difference*

---

> *It's the little details that are vital. Little things make big things happen.*
>
> —JOHN WOODEN

In this chapter, we will learn more about the nuances—the small things we do when we're actually in the room with leaders—that make up the careful detail work of facilitating professional learning to help support adult growth and leadership development. These nuances, which compose the outermost growth ring of this book's leadership model (shown in figure 5.1), add flavor and life to the elements we've discussed in the model's inner rings. This detail work matters tremendously when we're shaping developmentally oriented professional learning environments. Put another way, the little things we do as facilitators of growth and learning make a difference to adults in vital ways.

Nuances relate to the small actions and stances we take—in the space and in the moment—when leading professional learning and leadership development. So, once you've conceptualized and designed the teaching, learning, or professional development initiative, what do you do to continue shaping it when it's "live"?

There are many, many nuances that shape learning environments. Here, though, we will focus on five larger categories of nuance that are *very* important to leadership development: 1) being aware of the planes of listening, 2) welcoming questions and discussion, 3) extending personal connections, 4) being aware of pacing and transparency regarding time, and 5) acknowledging the need for refilling and reflecting.

FIGURE 5.1

**The outermost growth ring: nuances of facilitating professional learning to support adult growth and leadership development**

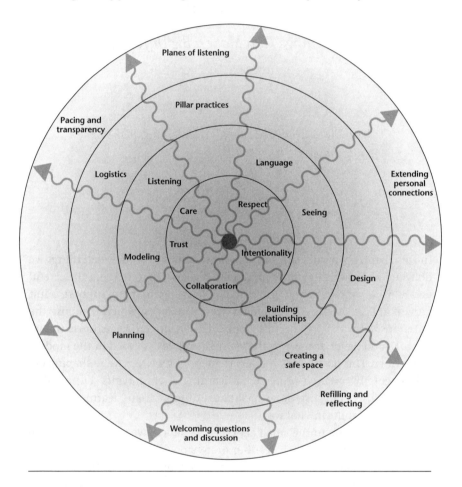

You might be thinking that some of these sound familiar and even seem closely linked to what we've discussed earlier in other growth rings, especially those covered in chapters 2 and 3 (e.g., listening with presence, building relationships). And, yes, you are right! In this chapter, we will expand on some of these earlier components as we consider how we can communicate the larger ideas of this model in the small things we do with and for others. And while there is some overlap between the concepts introduced earlier and the nuances presented here (for example, building relationships is related to the importance of extending personal connections), here we focus primarily on the *enactment* of the concepts in the other, inner circles. In other words, how does all of this *work* once you, as facilitator, are in the midst of a professional learning initiative? How do the components fit together? You might want to think about this chapter—as a dear colleague once put it—as "the narrative version of the squiggly lines" in figure 5.1 that reach from the central dot into each ring, connecting them all. The shading and squiggles are meant to indicate that all of the growth rings and their components are connected.

Even though the nuances are in the outermost ring, attending to them translates into being truly present in the space in ways large and small, which can help put the finishing touches on your careful designing, planning, thinking, and caring. Accordingly, we're about to learn more about the nuances that help to make the core elements and other components of the model visible.

One other way to think about nuances is to consider them as the adjustments we as facilitators make in the moment—when we *sense* something is needed or something is going on for learners, or that something needs to happen to enhance the space. This is really about *feeling the energy in the room and being sensitive to it, aware of it, and willing to care for it.* While we are in the room as facilitators, we need to be constantly moving from the "dance floor" (the doing) to the "balcony" (looking down on what's being done).

## PLANES OF LISTENING

In the previous chapters, we've talked a lot about the importance of listening as a developmental support, show of care, and signal of respect and interpersonal connection. In this section, I describe how your physical presence as a facilitator of professional learning can help leaders understand and *see* that you are listening deeply, and also help them to feel *heard*, which, as you know, is very important. Like all of the other nuances we will consider in this chapter, this idea of conscientiously and consciously considering your relationship to physical space when listening—or *planes of listening*—has deep roots. Connected to all of the core elements and the key concept of listening with presence, which we discussed in chapter 3, planes of listening also relate intimately to modeling, building relationships, and the other important techniques and values described in the second growth ring of the model. The big idea here, though, is that in addition to listening carefully and caringly, with developmental intention and with care from one's heart, mind, and soul, you can communicate a listening *stance* simply by the way you hold and carry yourself in a room, and in turn, join and hold others in the psychological sense. Next, I describe a few of the ways I do this when facilitating large group sessions.

I have learned, for instance, that it is very important to communicate a sense of being "with" an entire group, especially a large group, when facilitating the important and hard work of adult and leadership development. Listening is a key part of that, and listening with different stances and in different ways and locations in the space, can help. For example, I often find myself listening from a standing position, a sitting position, and sometimes even when kneeling as I take in what leaders are sharing. I do this to show respect when someone is offering a personal reflection or question, and also to signal to others in the group that this leader is now the central focus. Alternating my relationship to vertical space in this way was actually the inspiration for the use of the word *planes* in the model, and it is something I find myself doing quite often . . . and naturally. I also move around the room a great deal to different "anchor spots," as one of my teaching fellows calls them, so I can be *close to* leaders in different parts of the space. Like following the stage directions in a play, I make sure to hit "stage left," "stage right," and "stage front and back" to maximize my connection with each and every leader in the room. It's become a habit for me, and likely can become one for you, too.

Body language is also an important aspect of planes of listening. Just as we discussed in the section on listening in chapter 3, it is vital to communicate care, intention, and attention when you're listening with presence by leaning in and maintaining eye contact. Leaders often comment on how much this means to them saying, "I feel heard," "I feel cared about," and "I feel listened to, really listened to." This is also connected to modeling and transparency, because explicitly naming the importance of listening as a support and then demonstrating the power of genuine listening through your actions, presence, and posture can help others understand, value, and practice these kinds of listening techniques when they support the growth and development of others in their own work. Many have shared a sentiment expressed by one leader thusly: "This [practice] holds me and encourages me to share more—and more courageously."

Perhaps a quick example will help to ground these abstract ideas. As you've read in other chapters, my work with the Summer Principals Academy at Teachers College involves designing and leading an intensive summer course for a very large group of aspiring principals. With upward of eighty to one hundred leaders in the room, I do my very best to make sure that everyone feels important, cared for, listened to, and well held in the developmental sense. Often in this kind of course, small groups of leaders discuss application exercises related to content, future plans for implementing developmental leadership, and reflective questions. Representatives from each group then share important insights, strategies, or questions with the full cohort, and as they do so, I intentionally position myself in different parts of our large classroom to bridge some of the distance between us and to show that I am listening. In addition to being more proximal in my listening—and leaning in and watching carefully and caringly as others speak—I also sometimes sit at the periphery of the room. As you might suspect, this signals to others that the current speaker is at the center of our collective attention—and deserves the full focus of the spotlight and our listening ears.

## WELCOMING QUESTIONS AND DISCUSSION: VALUING LEARNERS AND THEIR IDEAS

The nuance of *welcoming questions* and *inviting and valuing discussion*, like planes of listening, is intimately connected to what we've learned about in chapter 3, especially how we listen with presence and how we use intentional language to facilitate adult learning and leadership development. Indeed, in this section, we will further consider how being physically and psychologically *present* in the room and unequivocally *open* to leaders as they offer questions, insights, and reflections enables us, as facilitators, to create safe contexts where leaders are and feel cared for, respected, listened to, and heard—all of which, as you know, matter a great deal in supporting growth and leadership development.

Although the concept of welcoming questions and discussion is closely linked to careful listening and thoughtful use of language, it might also be helpful to highlight its connection to modeling up front. We know that leaders in any teaching, learning, and professional development environment will also learn from *the way we model* our welcoming of questions and discussion as well as from *their experience* of having their thoughts, feelings, and presence valued, acknowledged, and appreciated. While I realize you know this already, I'm highlighting it here so that we are even more mindful of it as we learn more about how our physical presence (what we communicate consciously and sometimes unconsciously) and verbal response to questions and discussion can help to create a robust holding environment for leaders.

What we communicate as facilitators—in the words we say, through our body language and facial expressions, and in the way we respond to questions and discussion—can be a developmental support to growth and leadership development. Our way of welcoming leaders' thinking and feeling as they take in, contemplate, and make sense of content and processes will signal to them—auditorily, visually, cognitively, and emotionally—that we are *listening*, we are *hearing* their thoughts and feelings, we do *care*, we *value* what they are sharing, and we want to be of help. Like listening and the other nuances we will consider here, being mindful of what we communicate through our physical presence and words and attitude when leaders offer insights, questions, and reflections is a very important part of shaping growth-enhancing professional learning contexts. What we say, how we say it, how we respond to leaders, and the spaces we create for their sharing help them to see and feel that we as facilitators value them, their thinking, their feelings, and their presence, and that we want to support their growth and leadership development.

So how do we welcome questions and invite discussion? In addition to all the ways in which you already engage in these processes, I offer a few practices that leaders have found supportive of their growth. We can demonstrate that we value and welcome leaders' questions, thoughts, feelings, and comments by asking questions ourselves, making personal connections to the material, offering insights or reflections, and by many other means, such as:

- Responding to leaders' questions with positive affirmations, acknowledgments of their important questions, and gratitude (e.g., "I appreciate your asking that; thank you!" or "That's a really important question; I'm glad you asked").
- Listening carefully to what is shared and paraphrasing what the leader has asked in order to make sure we understand the question. This also helps ensure that other leaders in the space have heard and understood the question. It signals to all, as noted earlier, that the speaker has our collective attention.
- Inviting participants in the room to respond to what's been shared—whether it is a personal reflection or a question. If they do, as you'll see shortly, allowing leaders in the room to guide the discussion and share their expertise helps with learning and with building a collective holding environment.
- Giving generous amounts of wait time. I'll say a little more about this later.

- Expressing a feeling of having "goose bumps" when someone in the room offers a particularly poignant insight or a courageous sharing—especially about oneself and one's experience. This is something I have found that I now say automatically and sincerely when leaders share something with me or the group that I really connect to. (I literally get goose bumps all over, so that's why I say it.) You may want to consider how you could express a similar feeling when leading in your own context.

Next, I'll share a little more detail about some of these nuanced practices in case helpful to you when facilitating developmentally oriented professional learning experiences.

## The Importance of Truly Welcoming Questions and Discussion

As we discuss it here, welcoming questions and discussion is about more than creating spaces for questions (which we learned about in prior chapters); it's about truly valuing, appreciating, and inviting questions and contributions from those we work with. When facilitating learning sessions, I genuinely admire and welcome courageous contributions from leaders, and try to answer every question with some expression of gratitude, like those just listed. Leaders have shared how helpful it is and how much it means to them to have their questions not just addressed but *valued*. As one leader representatively expressed in a reflective post-session survey, "being able to ask questions and attempt to answer questions" was one of the most meaningful aspects of the experience—and it is vital to supporting learning, creating a holding environment, and to promoting leadership development.

As facilitators, we know that we're not only "on" during the formal learning time, but during breaks as well. In feedback and surveys, learners have voiced great appreciation for having the chance to ask questions privately during breaks and also before and after sessions. I've often been surprised by how much this kind of welcoming means to them. For example, when asked to describe the most meaningful part of the learning experience, one leader answered: "when I had an opportunity to ask Ellie [the facilitator] a question today during one of the function breaks." As you might imagine, it was a great honor to learn that, and to have been of help. Again and again, I have learned that even little welcoming encounters, such as these informal opportunities to connect and ask questions, really do make a big difference.

Another effective technique is inviting leaders to use Post-it notes to ask different kinds of questions on "parking lots" of poster paper placed strategically around the room. In any kind of professional learning session, there are times when it seems best to "hold" further questions in order to move a group forward and through more content; allowing leaders to ask lingering questions by sticking Post-its on the parking lots and then circling back to them is one powerful way to honor leaders' voices and perspectives without disrupting the session's momentum. Also, this technique allows leaders to ask questions in different ways (rather than voicing them as part of the mini-lecture). Typically, I ask leaders to post "burning" (urgent) questions on red or pink Post-its, "sizzling" (medium-importance) questions on bright orange Post-its, and "simmering" (more casual) questions on yellow. This color code also helps my teaching team and me better understand and address leaders' thinking and needs.

## Allowing Learners to Take a Lead Role

As mentioned, inviting leaders in the room to respond to others' questions and even to teach the class in response to a question can be a very powerful experience for individuals and the group. Not only does it allow leaders to share their expertise and knowledge, but it also enables them to build their own understanding of the material that's being presented, and enhances the holding environment in important ways. Next I offer some of the comments that leaders shared after engaging in this kind of process during a recent class session. As their reflections highlight, this kind of experience can be both meaningful and powerful for those who take the lead role and for the other leaders who witness it because it 1) supports learning, 2) models the facilitator's respect and care, and 3) illuminates for leaders the importance of creating a holding environment that is generative, that honors the collective wisdom of the group, and where all are teachers in different ways and with different gifts to offer. Of course, offering a mix of presentation strategies can help you meet everyone's learning and developmental needs.

> *I enjoyed listening to others [colleagues in the class] help to explain different concepts. Loved this! I also enjoyed discussing ideas with fellow cohort members and being able to ask and attempt to answer questions.*

> *I loved the way Ellie shared space with us [the full group of eighty leaders] to share our thinking . . . I was so intellectually stimulated, I felt like my mind was exploding with connections to other things I've been thinking about—mind-set, mindfulness, will, teaming . . . I feel like this was the missing piece! Thank you!!!!!*

*I like how Ellie welcomed us to "teach" the class. It shows she has hu-mility and still considers herself a learner, which I admire. The way this class is orchestrated has really made me rethink and reconsider how group learning experiences for adults can look different but still have the same positive effect. Thank you.*

### About Wait Time

Another very important way that you can signal to leaders in professional learning contexts that their thoughts, questions, and contributions are both welcomed and valued is by offering significant wait time after pos-ing a question or invitation to the group. Just as in the section on plan-ning, when we talked about stretching out the word *plan* to emphasize just how much planning goes into every course, workshop, and session, *wait time*—as we're talking about it here—is much longer than the few-second pauses most of us are used to. Sometimes, the amount of wait time I offer—as much as thirty seconds—can feel startling or unsettling to peo-ple at first, but I've learned that making this extra space allows for more ideas and voices to enter the conversation, and it is something that lead-ers have told me they really value and try to pass forward when working with other adults.

A twin to wait time is creating a space in learning contexts for silence—that is, allowing a quiet moment for processing, thinking, digesting, and considering. Silence also allows those of us who need a little more time be-fore asking a question—or those of us who might be more introverted—to gather our thoughts and/or the courage we need in order to share.

For example, Brooke McCaffrey, a kindergarten teacher who took part in one of my developmental leadership academies, particularly appreciated that the academy sessions "allowed for silence—a rare commodity in schools." Reflecting on her big takeaways from our four sessions over the course of the year, she explained, "I now realize the importance of silence for allowing busy brains to process new thoughts and information." More-over, as the leader of a team of eight teachers in her charter school, Brooke found the practice so valuable that she now uses it herself! I hope you, too, find this aspect of nuances helpful to your important work.

## EXTENDING PERSONAL CONNECTIONS

*Extending personal connections* is another very important nuance to consider as we transform teaching, learning, and professional development envi-ronments into contexts that support adult and leadership development.

Extending personal connections expands on what we called *building relationships* in chapter 3; it is about *connecting more deeply* to and with participating leaders while facilitating in the room. Naturally, this nuance is also enhanced by the ways in which we listen, use language, welcome questions, invite discussion, and more. In reality, like all of the components of the model, the nuances work synergistically to support growth and development. We are discussing them one-by-one here so that we can consider each as distinct as well as connected to each other and to components of the model as a whole.

So, how can we extend personal connections—an integral part of forming robust holding environments—in our learning contexts? While there are many ways we can do this, next I'll share some of the most important ways in which leaders have reported experiencing a feeling of "personal connection" in the moment and how that feeling supported their learning, created a space where they felt safe to take risks and grow, and modeled key features of relationships and connection that many of them then applied to their own practice. Feedback from surveys and conversations with leaders—even years after a learning initiative I've facilitated—have taught me that personal relationships really do need to be nurtured, enhanced, and cared for in professional learning contexts in order to support growth and leadership development. In other words, the ways that you recognize, honor, and build from your relationships with leaders *in the room as you are facilitating* helps deepen both connections and learning. As the head of a large charter school—who focuses on supporting adult and leadership development with his teachers and leadership team (principals and assistant principals)—eloquently put it, "I have learned over ten years that supporting adult and leadership development in my school, and I think any school, is really *all about relationships*. Without that and without caring for them and nurturing others, we cannot support adult development."

Extending personal connections while facilitating professional learning enables us to be *with* leaders as they learn and grow. This nuance helps with enriching safe spaces so that leaders are and *feel* respected, heard, seen, and cared for. Of course, as we have been emphasizing throughout this book, it is important to understand that adults with different ways of knowing will need different kinds of supports and challenges to grow from relationships.

### Exchanging Personal Stories: Extending Connections and Deepening Learning

One truly vital means of enhancing professional learning that supports leadership development is sharing personal stories—sharing your own stories and encouraging others to do the same. Doing so deepens relationships and extends personal connections in very powerful ways. As we discussed in chapter 3's example of how it was important for a principal, Meg, to allow her teacher leaders to "get to know" her, so too is it important to leaders in any teaching, learning, and professional development environment to learn from the facilitator's and one another's personal stories.

Sharing our own stories is important for several reasons. First, as touched on earlier, it makes us, the facilitators, more "human" and allows participants to get to know us a little better. This is especially important because in these learning situations, leaders often share personal and professional experiences that are private. Sharing our own stories opens the door for them to do the same, and also builds trust. Second, sharing personal stories helps learners to make connections to the content, practices, and ideas being discussed. For example, stories help break down complex concepts from theory and ground them in real-life experiences. Stories and personal examples also help to clarify concepts from the readings, allow leaders to feel personally connected to facilitators, and help leaders to think about how their own lives and experiences connect to the material and ideas. As you have probably noticed throughout this book, I often use stories about my life, my family, and my experiences with leaders and in schools to highlight key points or approach ideas from a more personal level. I also do this (and invite others to do so as well) while facilitating professional learning, and I have found that this is a very meaningful and helpful practice for all involved. I always learn so much from leaders' stories, and they often let me know that they appreciate what I share as well. As one leader reflected, personal stories are a vital part of extending personal relationships when shaping robust holding environments: "I appreciated the anecdotes Ellie [the facilitator] shared. They help bring to life some of the theory ideas I've [be]come familiar with through all of the readings. I also appreciate that they allow me to feel a more *personal connection* to my teachers and fellow learners." This comment is representative of what many leaders consistently report about how much they appreciate and learn from personal stories, as well as how this kind of sharing (and modeling) has encouraged them to use their own stories—both as participants in learning environments and as leaders in their own contexts—to build trust and support growth and leadership development. It's also important to recognize that inviting leaders to share *their* personal stories—as well as reflections and questions, as noted earlier—in small and larger groups contributes to extending personal connections throughout the space, illuminates the collective wisdom of the group, and supports leaders with diverse ways of knowing.

## Moving Beyond Nametags

Just as important to extending personal connections as sharing and exchanging personal stories, learning and using leaders' names—especially when they are no longer wearing nametags—helps strengthen connections and promote learning. Remembering someone's name makes that person feel cared about and for. While, in any large group, calling students by name is much easier when they are wearing tags with their names in large font, as discussed earlier, making an effort to move beyond *reading* leaders' names to *knowing* them helps demonstrate your care as facilitator for each leader as a unique and important human being. When teaching large classes, for instance, my teaching team and I work hard to learn every student's name quickly, sometimes even by studying photos of learners before and after each early class. We have learned that this kind of attention means a lot to practicing and aspiring leaders. In their evaluations and feedback, graduate students and leaders have repeatedly shared how much it means to them when members of the teaching team greet them by name even when they are not wearing their nametags.

## Additional Ways of Extending Personal Connections

There are so many small ways in which we, as facilitators, can extend personal connections while in the physical space of any teaching, learning, and professional development environment. For instance, making and keeping eye contact with *all* participants, even and especially those who are quiet or less extroverted or involved, helps to strengthen personal connections. Something special happens when you look into someone's eyes—for both parties.

There is something magical, too, about being physically near another person, and sometimes I even ask leaders for permission to touch them gently on the shoulder when demonstrating an example or raising up their contributions for the group. To be a little more specific, when working to demonstrate points connected to theory—such as what it means to "stand at the edges of someone's thinking and feeling and gently offer a little psychological push to help them grow"—I usually stand near someone and ask, "Can I touch you?" to illustrate that gentle push and to link theory to a gesture leaders will remember. Of course, it is important to be sensitive here to the way adults receive this kind of attention, so asking first is always the best policy.

In addition, introducing a sprinkling of humor builds and extends personal connections. Offering little jokes and being willing as facilitator to laugh at yourself, and to admit out loud, "I made a mistake," can lighten spirits and the mood of the room. In addition, this kind of humor strengthens bonds and personal connections.

## PACING AND TRANSPARENCY REGARDING TIME

Also connected to planning, or *p-l-a-n-n-i-n-g*, the nuances of *pacing* and *transparency regarding time* are crucial to keep in mind when you are leading any learning initiative. As we discussed earlier, even the most carefully considered session plan needs tweaking and adjustments in the moment, so *carefully responding to group needs* and *clearly signaling to learning leaders what to expect and what's coming next* are important ways you can make adults feel comfortable, cared for, and engaged. While listed here under the umbrella of a single category of nuance, there are actually many small things I do while facilitating that help keep learning sessions moving, and which offer leaders clear markers about timing and scheduling. I offer some of these strategies next in case you find them helpful for your own important leadership and work.

### Signposts, Signals, and Transitions

Whether you are beginning a session with an overview of the day or introducing an exercise for small groups, it is extremely important to clearly signal for leaders the steps of any process and the time allocated for each. Whenever I begin the day's learning, for instance, I offer (usually in the opening PowerPoint slides) an overview of what we will do first, next, and last. This helps provide an aerial view for leaders, just as it does for learners of all kinds. Signaling—as you're introducing them—the kinds of things leaders will be learning about and doing throughout the shared time helps keep everybody on the same page, and creates a common vision and expectation for the professional learning experience. Especially on longer days, and during afterwork sessions when leaders have already given so much to students and teachers all day, this transparency means a lot.

Being transparent about time is particularly important when beginning application, reflection, or small group work with leaders. I often structure activities with protocols, which I've honed over the past twenty years to help leaders work, learn, and grow together. One example is a protocol I use for assisting with the pillar of collegial inquiry, as shown in exhibit 5.1.

As you can see, offering clear directions for each step is an important part of helping leaders organize their time and efforts. When you're conducting this kind of activity with groups, it's also tremendously helpful to

**EXHIBIT 5.1**

## Sample protocol for engaging in collegial inquiry

*Checking in: applying ideas from your developmental leadership academy to advance your practice*

### Step 1: Reflect privately in writing.                    (5 minutes)

This is a quiet space to jot down thoughts about your application, joys, struggles, dilemmas, or challenges, and what you'd like help thinking through at this time.*

- What is working well?

- What challenges or dilemmas arose?

- What would you like some help with at this time?

> * Remember, this can either be in relation to applying ideas that center on pillar practices or ways of knowing, or shaping learning contexts to support adult growth.

### Step 2: Find a partner—someone you don't know so well, please.    (3 minutes)

Find a partner—preferably someone you don't know and would like to know better—and after brief introductions, the person with the SMALLEST HANDS shares first. ☺

### Step 3: First person shares (first speaker).                    (5 minutes)

Please explain the context and your application to your partner (from your journal writing).

- What is working well?

- What challenges or dilemmas arose?

- What would you like some help with at this time?

### Step 4: Listener offers help and dyad engages in dialogue.    (10 minutes)

Partner's role is to offer questions, informed by new or enhanced understanding of developmental theory in order to offer authentic supports, challenges, and help.

### Step 5: Step back and check in/check out.                    (5 minutes)

Please reflect on the process. How are you both thinking? Feeling? What went well? Next steps?

- Private writing/reflecting time                    (2 minutes)

### Please repeat the process—switch roles.

offer explicit directions about the timing for each step, and label this on presentation slides and easel paper around the room.

Verbal and auditory prompts are also effective signals for upcoming transitions. Marking time and pacing with verbal cues like, "We have about one minute left before the next person's sharing," or "In two minutes, we will move to share outs" helps ensure that all leaders have the time and space to benefit from the activity. This practice also serves as a small yet essential demonstration of care. Similarly, when I sense a group might not be ready to move on or transition, I ask them, "Does anyone need more time? Does two minutes sound like enough?" Asking these questions and then using the "close your eyes" technique—having all participants close their eyes and raise their hands to indicate their response in order to prevent potential embarrassment or discomfort—to get a sense of the room really helps with in-the-moment pacing. It also gently keeps leaders aware of the clock and timing as they engage in the deeply personal and meaningful work of growing themselves and each other.

Yet another effective strategy to help signal transitions involves a small set of chimes. Gently sounding the chimes is a warm, comforting, and caring way to signal that key transitions have arrived (when using protocols, for example), and can also be helpful when reconvening groups after breaks. As surprising as it might sound, I almost always receive positive feedback about the soothing tones of the chimes and their helpfulness. In fact, leaders sometimes even enjoy sounding them themselves or inquire about purchasing a set. It's amazing how quickly a room can quiet after hearing something so seemingly simple, but the chimes really do "soothe" a group into the next step of the day. As one leader explained, the sound of the chimes is so helpful in this regard because "it's not abrupt."

## Never Expressing Urgency Regarding Time

One of the other most important "little things" you can do when sharing schedule or agenda adjustments with leaders in professional learning contexts is framing changes in ways that don't express urgency around time. Saying to a group, "We only have five minutes for this," or "We may not get through all of this" makes people feel rushed and can diminish the potential for learning and growth. If, as described previously, it seems that leaders need more time to fully and deeply engage with an activity, giving it to them is more important than sticking to the agenda. There is *always* time to adjust, reprioritize, and reconfigure (as described in chapter 4's section on planning and as we will consider further in this chapter's upcoming section on refilling and reflecting). As with all of the nuances, and other aspects of the model, pacing and transparency regarding time involve first and foremost meeting leaders *where they are*, and making the learning experience as powerful as it can be for the unique and individual leaders in the room.

### An Example from Practice: Feedback from a Program Leader

After I facilitated a session for fourteen New York City principals and their mentees (e.g., assistant principals and teacher leaders) in the Cahn Fellows Program at Teachers College, the director of the program, who observed this session, kindly sent me an e-mail in which she offered some feedback about what she had observed and learned. In reading over her comments, I was inspired and humbled to see how helpful the idea of pacing and transitioning seemed to be for her and the leaders. To help you get a sense of what she shared, and also some additional techniques that she captured in her observations that I hope will be useful to you, I offer below an excerpt from her e-mail.

- The timekeeper role [I use this to help groups designate a leadership role and also to share responsibility for our work together] kept all on task and focused and seemed to free you up to really be with the pairs and group.
- "Whichever pair thinks it had the best day can go next" [when sharing] seemed to make the transitions go smoothly and also gave the group a fun way to gain a little insight into how others were feeling.
- Using the last minute or so for the pair [who was consulted by the group] to share any insights or next steps with the group seemed to keep them focused and keep their commitment to the project and each other strong.
- The thirty-second transition from pair to pair to jot down any insights/ notes helped group to focus and capture learning.

### REFILLING AND REFLECTING

*Refilling and reflecting* while in the moment of facilitating professional leadership development is another nuance that assists in shaping growth-enhancing learning environments. While this nuance is certainly an outgrowth of intentionality and planning—which we focused on in chapters 2 and 4, respectively—the big emphasis here is on *making space* while in the context of any teaching, learning, or professional development environment to pause, refill, and reflect before moving into new learning territory.

In other words, this nuance centers on creating the space, and thereby the opportunity, for everyone in the session—leaders participating in the space and the facilitator—to literally *take a breath* before moving into whatever is next on the agenda. You might be wondering why this is important. I've found that, in very intense learning contexts, these kinds of pauses allow everyone in the room to step back and reflect on what's been discussed, take an internal temperature of how they are thinking and feeling, and regroup from the very hard, deep work of learning, growing, and sharing.

You can think about the nuance of refilling and reflecting as a chance to move to places of deep thought where we can pause to step back and synthesize ideas previously discussed, consider upcoming segments, and care for ourselves and our energy levels. Creating these moments and naming them explicitly for groups by saying something like, "Let's pause for a few moments and reflect on where we've been before stepping forward," models the importance of stopping to consider learnings, questions, and insights, and of offering refilling breaks or "rest stops" for learners. These refilling and reflecting pauses can be silent moments in which everyone in the room is thinking quietly, or they can be opportunities for freewriting. I've found that leaders truly appreciate such spaces. As one leader recently commented (and her reflection echoes what many have voiced on this topic), "I appreciate writing reflections. It forces me to think deeply about my own feelings and views." Regardless of how each individual in the room uses this pause, it's very important for us as facilitators to be transparent about why we are creating it and to remind everyone that we are respectfully asking to "quiet the room" since "some people really need the quiet to think and reflect."

As facilitator, you can also use these kinds of pause moments to adapt instruction to audience needs as you check in with yourself to consider what might be best for the group before moving forward with the learning agenda. I have also found that sharing what I'm doing during these pauses helps make leaders more comfortable with the quiet space. Sometimes I say things like, "I'm pausing now because . . ." or "I want to share what's going on for me right now. I'm noticing *X* and thinking about what's a good next step for us in terms of learning . . ." or "To make my thinking transparent, right now I am wondering . . ." You might even consider voicing (as I do), "We have the plan, but right now I'm considering moving things around based on where we've been, what I'm sensing as your learning needs, and the energy level at this time."

As you might suspect, these moments are connected to what we have previously referred to as the "coach's playbook." This is the process I use in the moment to carefully adjust session plans to meet leaders' needs. As noted earlier, members of my teaching team use the nickname "coach's playbook" because the revisions on my PowerPoint handouts look like *x*s, circles, and arrows. For me, these marks represent the adaptations and refinements I consider in the moment regarding the next steps and activities that will best meet participants' learning needs. I use the playbook and the pauses to review where we've been, consider where we're going, and check in with members of my teaching team about their perspectives, observations, and suggestions. The pauses are also opportunities for me to gather the mental and physical energy I need to be at my very best moving forward.

In chapter 6, we will learn more about the importance of refilling oneself as a leader and facilitator of other people's growth and development. More specifically, we will think together about the importance of creating and securing holding environments for self-development and renewal. While we have been learning about creating holding environments for others, we have been moving from the central, personal dot in the model outward to focus in on the components of each growth ring. The arrows in the model have mirrored this approach. In the next and final chapter of this book, though, you will see that the arrows will circle back to the center. There, we will invest time in considering the importance of refilling the dot—the self—and caring for our own development, growth, and renewal, which in turn enables us to better support those processes in others.

## TAKEAWAYS

Nuances are the adjustments we as facilitators make in the moment, when we *sense* something is needed, something is going on for learners, or something needs to happen to enhance the space. Most simply, this chapter is about *feeling and being aware of the energy in the room,* and *being willing to care for it* in the little things you do and say. As facilitators, we need to simultaneously move from the dance floor (the doing) to the balcony (looking down on what's being done in order to gain perspective and insight). As you know, nuances are in some ways little things and in other ways very big things—because they make a tremendous difference. Nuances enable us to demonstrate and communicate our developmental intentions as we work to support growth and leadership development in adults with different ways of knowing. We've discussed these five nuances:

+ *Being aware of planes of listening:* In addition to listening carefully, caringly, and with developmental intention, you can communicate a listening *stance* simply by the way you hold and carry yourself in a room, and in turn, carry and hold others.
+ *Welcoming questions and inviting discussion:* Leaders in any teaching, learning, and professional development environment will learn from *the way we model* our welcoming of questions and discussion as well as from *their experience* of having their thinking, feelings, and presence valued, acknowledged, and appreciated.
+ *Extending personal connection:* This nuance extends the practice of building relationships, as it is about *connecting more deeply to and with* participating leaders while facilitating in the room.
+ *Being aware of pacing and transparency regarding time:* As an extension of careful planning, it is very important to clearly signal objectives, agendas, and timing for leaders in professional learning contexts, and to carefully respond to a group's learning pace and needs in order to help adults feel more comfortable, cared for, and engaged.
+ Acknowledging the need for *refilling and reflecting:* Within any teaching, learning, or professional development environment, making a quiet space to pause, refill, and reflect before moving into new learning territory supports private reflection and growth—and allows you time as facilitator to make any necessary adjustments, and to breathe and refill.

## REFLECTIVE QUESTIONS

1. What nuances do you employ in your noble work of shaping holding environments and leadership development?
2. How, if at all, might you employ any of the nuances we learned about here—namely, 1) planes of listening, 2) welcoming questioning and discussion, 3) extending personal connections, 4) pacing and transparency, and 5) refilling and reflecting—to inform and

enhance your important practice of supporting adult growth and leadership development?

3. What stands out for you as something important that you learned from reading this chapter or something that you came to realize about your own work and how *you* use different nuances when facilitating adult growth and leadership development?

4. What other nuances might you add to the list presented in the model's outermost growth ring? How do they assist you in creating holding environments and learning-oriented professional development?

---

### APPLICATION EXERCISE: ACTION PLANNING

This is an opportunity for you to apply your learnings from this chapter to your own leadership practice of supporting adult growth and leadership development. I hope you find this useful.

You might find it helpful to create an outline or narrative of your thinking and feelings in response to the following application invitation. This can serve as a starting point for exploring your ideas in greater depth as you step forward with implementing some new nuances and/or refining those you are already using in your practice.

Most important with this exercise is that you consider adding or refining your practice in ways that are *personally meaningful to you and your work* and *that will meet the needs of individuals in your school and/or work context.* The main purpose of this action planning is to give you an opportunity to develop your own ideas and to consider how using nuances in your leadership *with developmental intention* can support adult and leadership development.

In developing your design/action plan for employing nuances, you may want to consider the following suggestions and questions:

◆ Create a growth ring map. Please jot down the nuances you are currently employing in your practice. How do you think they are working to enhance teaching, learning, and professional development in your context? Why?

+ What other nuances would you like to include, after reading more about nuances in this chapter? How might you build them into your practice? What would feel like a good first step to you? A second?
+ How might these nuances enhance your professional learning initiatives? How might they support learners with different ways of knowing?
+ What questions/challenges/dilemmas seem especially important for you to consider in terms of implementing these nuances?
+ What is your biggest takeaway from engaging in this application exercise?

# CHAPTER 6

# Coming Full Circle

*Refilling the Self to Sustain and Support Others*

*The ultimate lesson all of us have to learn is uncondi-
tional love, which includes not only others but ourselves
as well.*

—ELISABETH KÜBLER-ROSS

*Who shall kindle others must himself glow.*

—ITALIAN PROVERB

Throughout this book, we've been exploring practical ideas and strategies
for how to transform teaching, learning, and professional development
environments into contexts for growth and leadership development. Developmentally oriented professional learning, as we've been discussing it,
involves creating environments in which practicing and aspiring leaders
can grow in order to increase their own internal capacities and develop
as leaders. The central idea is that by actually experiencing the conditions and practices that support adult growth in real time, practicing and
aspiring leaders will be better equipped to support others' growth in their
own contexts.

From the very beginning of this book, we have emphasized the importance of understanding and attending to adults' different ways of knowing
when shaping any teaching, learning, or professional development environment. We discussed how doing so helps us to create contexts that serve
as rich and dynamic holding environments that support growth, leadership development, and capacity building in adults who make meaning in
qualitatively different ways. Supporting this kind of growth is essential to

helping practicing and aspiring leaders develop the internal capacities needed to meet the complex challenges of being an educator today. Recall that by *internal capacities*, I mean the cognitive, affective (emotional), interpersonal, and intrapersonal capacities that enable us to better manage the complexities of leading, learning, teaching, and living.

As you'll also recall, creating these holding environments and leadership development contexts is especially important given the kinds of *adaptive challenges* that aspiring and practicing leaders encounter every day in their work. These adaptive challenges require the internal capacity to manage enormous amounts of ambiguity and complexity. They also require that leaders be able to engage in difficult conversations, manage conflict, and offer and receive constructive and critical feedback. Shaping professional learning environments that support adult growth can enable practicing and aspiring leaders to better meet these implicit and explicit demands of leadership, teaching, learning, and life. These spaces also support leadership development—as mentioned very early on, supporting adult development *is* supporting leadership development.

We also know that deliberately and purposefully building growth-enhancing contexts requires a significant investment of our time, energy, love, care, effort, and self. It is a vital and worthwhile investment, however, made with the hope of improving the world for children today, for their children, and for all of us.

But how can we sustain these holding environments over time? What can schools and districts, university education leadership programs, and *you* do to support and strengthen this work? In this chapter, we address these questions by recognizing that *refilling oneself* through self-development and renewal is *critical* to building and sustaining effective learning environments over time.

So far, as just noted, we have focused on the work of conceptualizing, designing, and creating holding environments *with and for* others. In the spirit of coming full circle, however, you will recall that one's "central dot"—the self—sits at the very heart of the new model for learning-oriented leadership development. Indeed, it is from the self that the rest of the model stems—from the core elements in the innermost growth ring (care, respect, trust, intentionality, and collaboration) to the outer growth rings. It follows, then, that replenishing oneself—*refilling the self*—is of vital importance in sustaining holding environments for *others* in the long haul. Consider an image similar to the model's growth rings: you know that dropping a small pebble in a pond can send ripples to the farthest shores, but once that pebble sinks to the bottom—once it stops moving, generating, and *putting forth*—the ripples will eventually fade and the concentric circles will dissipate. As you might imagine, the big idea here, then, is to keep oneself buoyed—*full and supported enough to keep growing and giving*. This may be the most important way that we can sustain this work for others and ourselves.

Along these lines, figure 6.1 depicts the arrows that we have followed outward from the center of the model now returning to the central dot. This illustrates the need to replenish oneself and to secure supports for one's own development in order to create supportive holding environments for others.

While I inarguably get so much energy and joy from the light and gift of leaders' learnings, and from being a part of and witness to their remarkable journeys and growth in the professional learning sessions I facilitate, I have learned that I also need to find other, more personal opportunities to renew, replenish, and grow myself in order to offer my best to others. I purposefully seek out these opportunities. And I have heard this very same sentiment echoed by nearly all of the courageous leaders I have had the honor and privilege of working with and learning from over the past years. They too need to make space to renew and restore themselves; they too cherish opportunities to grow themselves. And they often remark that while they know how important it is to care for themselves and to make

**FIGURE 6.1**

**Returning to the central dot: refilling the self**

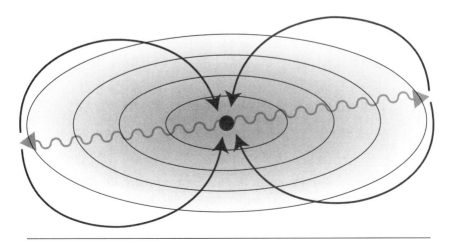

time for self-renewal, they are running so fast and hard that it can be really challenging to pause to do so. I know how this feels.

And so, in this chapter I highlight the vital importance of refilling ourselves, of creating holding environments for self-development and renewal. We will focus on both *why* it's important to create a holding environment for oneself, and *how* to do it (what strategies can be employed). I also offer suggestions for ways that schools, districts, and school systems can help support and sustain the important and essential work of building human capacity. The examples presented in this chapter all involve refilling—that is, securing holding environments for personal support, development, and renewal. By way of preview, I'll emphasize here that one very important aspect of working to support our own growth and development is that *we cannot do this alone.* In other words, one big takeaway of this chapter is the power and promise of growing oneself *through and in the company of others.* As you will see, many of the strategies offered for growing ourselves highlight the importance of having a reflective partner, critical friend, or group of colleagues to help us. This is essential, I think, because collaboration and dialogue—engaging in meaningful, deep conversations with other people—is one of the most important holding environments you can carve out for yourself. I also talk about how I do this for myself.

Next, I'll share a little more about why having a holding environment for renewing and developing the self, represented by the dot at the center of the model, is valuable and important. I'll also discuss three aspects of refilling: 1) securing supports for oneself, 2) prioritizing self-development, and 3) making time for self-renewal. While all three components are in some sense interrelated, I'll tease them apart here to shine a light on them as different but equally important aspects of refilling oneself. After this I'll offer some strategies for self-development and self-renewal, since these strategies are intertwined. They are the *how* of what we do to care for and grow ourselves.

## CARING FOR ONESELF WHILE CARING FOR OTHERS

*Knowing others is wisdom, knowing yourself is enlightenment.*

—Lao Tzu

As you know, self-development and caring for others' development are both important. To be of best help to others and their growth, we need to care for ourselves and our own growth—to refill the dot at the center of the innermost ring of the model. All of the other growth rings *begin with and rest on* self. We need to create and prioritize holding environments for our-selves, or we will not be able to give our best to others. We need to nourish the self, or we will starve and be unable to do the work that brings joy, hope, love, and life.

In schools, whether they are university education leadership prepara-tion programs or K–12 schools or systems, we as leaders of all kinds are constantly giving of our whole selves—giving the very best of what we have emotionally, intellectually, and spiritually—and drawing from deep within ourselves to do so. To keep doing this, we need to reignite our own pilot lights. To create holding environments for others, we need to refill the well, to grow ourselves, and to feel *well held* ourselves. Otherwise, we de-plete ourselves and end up trying to draw from an empty reserve.

As a director at a Science Education Fellows Program in Boston at the University of Massachusetts shared with me after I facilitated a workshop for teacher leaders, we can only give as much as we have. To give more, we need to *be* more. As she explained: "I realized, I think for the first time to-day, that I give so much of myself to my work and to others' growth and development. And I focus a lot of my time and attention on helping to de-velop my leadership team, and the teacher leaders grow and develop, and I love that . . . And I just realized that it's really important for me, and also for all of us on this leadership team, to create plans and make spaces for our own growth and development and learning." In my work and research with leaders of all kinds, I have learned that the need for this kind of refill-ing is a common one that can be met in a variety of ways: seeking and ac-cepting support from others, finding times to relax and renew, and carving out holding environments for self-development. Next, I offer a few exam-ples of why this kind of refilling is so important, and a bit later in the chap-ter we will explore more deeply *how* you can do this for yourself.

## Securing Support for Oneself

When working to create professional learning opportunities that support others' growth and development, it is critically important that you have supports in place for *yourself*, including people you can trust and lean on, because doing this work alone is hard on the body and soul. We all know what it feels like when we've been giving so much to others that we feel like our own energy sources are getting low, and we need a boost or to "recharge our batteries." We also know that, in order to help others grow, we need to have supports for our own growth. Before describing more practices or strat-egies we can employ to help us do this, I thought sharing two powerful ex-amples might be useful as a first step toward this important work.

I fly a lot in my work, and the idea of self-support reminds me of one of the first statements the flight attendants make when they are preparing passengers for a flight. They almost offer this as a warning, I think, because our nature as humans is often to reach out and care for someone else, especially a child, before caring for and supporting ourselves. The announcement, as you likely know, goes something like this: "Should something happen while we're in flight and the oxygen masks drop down, if you are traveling with a child or someone who requires assistance, secure your own mask first and then assist the other person." What the attendants are communicating in their own way is that it's important to care for yourself before caring for another, because if you don't, you will not be able to help that person. This connects to the ideas we're exploring here.

One other powerful example comes to mind. Last summer, when my teaching team and I were preparing for the intensive course we would teach together to a cohort of more than eighty graduate students in the Summer Principals Academy at Teachers College, we discussed the time, energy, and care that goes into teaching a large cohort in a very intensive two-and-a-half-week stretch. As a team, we shared the ways in which we manage our time during this period and how each of us was preparing for this "marathon," as I often refer to it. We had several new team members who had not taught the course before, so some of the veterans thought that sharing our own strategies for working so hard and carving out time to support ourselves would be especially helpful to the new team members.

Since my co-instructor, Jessica Blum-DeStefano, had taught this course with me twice before, she volunteered to be the first to share. She'd taught this course initially as a teaching fellow, just as the others on our team were doing now, so she could share based on her experiences. She knew the time commitment, the energy needed, the care given to students (not just during class time), the rhythm and intensity of the course, and the amount of investment required from everyone on the team to make the course a holding environment for these aspiring principals. This particular summer, however, was different for Jessica because a few months earlier, she had given birth to her sweet little son. Since she knew this year would be different for her, she had developed a "support plan" to secure support from trusted others so that she could still thrive—and give fully of herself—under these conditions. For example, as is the case with many working parents, Jessica arranged for child care during the days when she would be teaching and also before the course began while she would be coaching new team members. She asked her parents, husband, and friends if they could offer a little more support to her young son before and during the time she would be teaching the class, adding that she might need extra help during the weekend when she would be commenting on student papers. Jessica's sharing was very helpful to all of us on the team, and I hope it's helpful to you. It highlights the importance of making support plans for ourselves so that we can refill, renew, and care for our own development—and that of others.

### Prioritizing Self-Development

We all need to continue to grow, learn, and refill in order to bring our best and truest selves—our hearts, minds, and souls—to the important work of supporting others. Still, the ability to take such a learning stance—to show and embrace our vulnerability, authenticity, and journey as a leader—is itself a developmental capacity, and we cannot grow into our full potential as human beings unless we take the time to care for our own hopes and needs, including our needs for growth. I've found that educators and leaders (and I'm often guilty of this myself) too often prioritize serving others over nurturing themselves, so my hope is that this chapter and this book will help you to carve out and prioritize time to honor, cherish, and care for yourself as well as others.

In this section, I'll share a few ideas related to the importance of caring for our own growth—that is, our *self-development*—and then in a bit, we'll learn about *how* to do this. It might be helpful to first clarify the difference between self-renewal and self-development. Both are forms of refilling ourselves. Renewal is more about replenishing, or recharging, oneself and one's energies. Self-development relates primarily to growing our own internal capacities.

In preparing to write about the importance of and strategies for self-development, I not only reviewed what I've learned from leaders and from my own experience, but I also asked one of my doctoral advisees to help by conducting a literature review. I had hoped to learn a little about what the academic literature on leadership and/or leadership education says about how people support their own development. My doctoral advisee and I searched for *many* months to learn more about this topic. We looked at many sources in different bodies of the academic literature on leadership and leadership education and searched for many keywords including "transformational self growth," "self-development/self-growth," and "personal growth." Ironically, we found very little. It seems especially critical to discuss the importance of caring for one's own growth as the world becomes increasingly complex and the adaptive challenges we must manage require greater internal capacities. While some of us have the gift of working in contexts that purposefully support our own development, others do not. And even when we are in environments in which others are supportive of our own development, it is still important to consider how we can help ourselves grow as well.

I hope that these ideas and the upcoming strategies I share will help you consider how you can encourage those you serve, aspiring and practicing leaders, to think about how *they* can support *their* own development. And I also hope what follows gives you ideas for how we might join together in our workplaces to discuss ways to make our teaching, learning, and professional development initiatives spaces that invite questions about and secure structures for supporting self-development.

This will benefit all of us; it will help to grow our practices, schools, organizations, and systems. In turn, this will foster the conditions and holding environments that help adults to feel that they do not have to leave their schools or districts *in order to grow and develop*. Over the years, many graduate students have shared with me that one of the reasons they left their previous positions and went to graduate school was because they could not carve out environments *within these work contexts* to care for, nurture, renew, and grow their inner selves. Helping practicing and aspiring leaders to create conditions where they can do this will, in turn, equip them to create conditions for the adults in their care to likewise have space for—and to become aware of the importance of—caring for their own development.

### Making Time for Self-Renewal

Making time and prioritizing self-renewal is another very important way in which we can refill ourselves, or the "central dot." This practice can include other people, but sometimes it's as simple as doing little things independently that help us relax and unwind. Either way, renewal practices are things we do for ourselves, or *gifts of self-care.*

During professional learning initiatives, I save time toward the end of the experience to talk with leaders a little bit about the importance of renewal. Last summer, as I was introducing this topic, one leader asked, "What is renewal? What does that mean?" Sadly, I have been asked similar questions over and over again by aspiring and practicing leaders. While *defining* it is simple, *doing* it is not always easy and may not come naturally. Essentially, renewal means finding time to recharge by engaging in the kinds of things that bring light and spark to your day and step, and it often means doing things with others. For many years now, leaders who serve in all different capacities in schools and school systems have shared with me that renewing themselves is hard and something they need to "get better at." Whether I am facilitating professional learning for teachers, assistant principals, principals, coaches, superintendents, district leaders, or faculty in universities, one comment that these leaders consistently voice is that they "wish" they could make more time for renewal, but it's challenging given the increasing complexity and demands of their work.

In the spirit of helping, then, I will detail in the next section *how* leaders can do this—and how you can, too.

### STRATEGIES FOR CREATING HOLDING ENVIRONMENTS FOR SELF-DEVELOPMENT AND SELF-RENEWAL

*Few needs are as pressing and as often go unmet in our world as the need for a place to converse. We all require somewhere, some circle of companions, where and with whom we can enter into the demanding task of trying to say what we experience and to understand what others say in response.*

—Michael Himes

We know that it is vital for practicing and aspiring school leaders to create holding environments to nurture their own growth and renewal in order to best support the adults in their care.[1] And so you may be wondering, like many of my Summer Principals Academy students have voiced as their class comes to an end, "How we will all be able to sustain this momentum as we move forward?" Next, we will explore some real-life, practical examples of how leaders of all different kinds sustain themselves and thereby secure their abilities to attend to the care and growth of others.

Recently, a very experienced New York City principal, whom I am coaching as she participates in the Cahn Fellows Program at Teachers College, asked me a very important question: "What strategies do principals use to renew and grow themselves?" In different kinds of professional learning initiatives I've facilitated, with any group of leaders, some version of this question always seems to pop up, especially toward the end of these experiences. By way of another example, teacher leaders often have asked, "How can we create a holding environment for ourselves? Is it possible to develop without someone giving you the holding environment?"

To help answer this very significant and representative question, this section highlights leaders' experiences from the field about seeking out and creating holding environments for themselves, which involve different combinations of support, renewal, and self-development. My hope is that illuminating strategies and approaches leaders have shared with me in workshops, university courses, leadership academies, and my research over the past twenty years or so, as well as some of the issues that they faced when shaping contexts for their personal growth and renewal, will help you in the important work of supporting your own and others' growth and leadership development. Like these leaders, by increasing your own internal resources and capacities (i.e., self-development) and seeking out and prioritizing the supports needed for your renewal and rejuvenation, you can lead and support others even more effectively. I also offer my own thoughts about and experiences with self-development and self-renewal.

## Strategies for Self-Development

In this section, we will learn about different ways in which leaders secure holding environments for their own development. As mentioned earlier, one very important truth about working to support our own growth and development is that *we cannot do it alone.* Importantly, while a few of the practices and strategies that follow are ones that we can use by ourselves (i.e., without the company of colleagues), they are best employed *in combination with the other self-development practices that can be done only in the company of others.* I have learned from leaders and through my own self-development efforts that there is great power and promise of growing oneself *through and in the company of others.* Put another way, support and challenges from others do make a difference in our own growth.

I've grouped the ways in which leaders support their own growth into three categories: 1) supports for self-development at the individual level, 2) supports for self-development involving one other person (one-on-one, also known as a *dyad*), and 3) supports for self-development that center on engaging with colleagues in groups that meet regularly and over time. As you will see, the majority of these strategies for growing oneself emphasize the importance of having a reflective partner or partners, a critical friend or group of colleagues to assist in your work of self-development. Engaging in meaningful, deep conversation and inquiry with others over time is one of the most important and robust kinds of holding environments you can carve out for yourself.

### Personal and Individual Supports

Here are several ways in which we can support our own development independently (but, as just noted, you might want to combine these strategies with some of the others that follow in the next two sections):

- *Journaling regularly.* This form of reflection and questioning can be helpful in terms of moving your thoughts from inside to outside (i.e., moving them from being unseen—or the way things are; things we do not question—to being able to see them, reflect on them, and question them).
- *Reading.* This form of self-growth can support your development. This category includes reading about development as well as learning from other people's accounts of leadership, growth, and life journeys (this could include genres like self-help, nonfiction, fiction).
- *Meditating.* This category includes any type of personal practice (and there are many forms of this) that leaders engage in on their own, and in which you can train your mind to reflect in order to realize some benefit, including self-growth.
- *Practicing yoga.* Recently, there's been an increase in popularity for this method of self-growth and self-improvement in the Western world. Yoga, in a variety of forms, focuses on developing and growing oneself as a person. The umbrella term *yoga* refers to multiple practices for self-growth, self-development, self-realization, and fulfilling our human potential. This is a practice that leaders have cited as being helpful to achieving greater self-understanding.
- *Attending conferences, taking courses, and serving on various committees and boards.* These are other ways in which leaders feel they support their own growth.

While all of these strategies are popular with leaders for supporting self-growth, there is one caveat to mention here. Many leaders, serving in very different kinds of leadership positions, have shared that while they find the practice of reading helpful, they would much rather "talk to someone to support" their growth rather than read about it. These leaders highlight, and I agree, that while these practices are valuable, there's no substitute for engaging in purposeful and deep conversation with at least one other trusted person.

### Dyads

Many leaders emphasize the value of "connecting" with one other person—a relationship known as a dyad—to grow themselves and to support another person's growth. Those who don't have this connection say they "wish" that they did. Having a thought partner—someone to talk through dilemmas, sticky points, the challenges of leading and helping others grow, and the challenges of learning to grow oneself—is vital to supporting self-development. I've learned this from others and have experienced it myself. As one leader put it, expressing a sentiment shared by others, "Having the opportunity to talk with a few very close friends and colleagues about the kinds of things that keep me up at night has been a gift to my own growth."

Mentoring is another form of collaborating in a dyad to support self-growth. Aspiring school leaders, who are teachers wanting to be better leaders in teams and in professional learning communities (PLCs), and assistant principals who deeply want to become principals, have shared that they love—really—the chance to grow themselves by working with mentors.

However, I've also learned that some leaders, whether they are principals, assistant principals, or teachers, hesitate to ask for mentors to support their growth. Why, you might wonder? Well, some initially think that if they express the need for a mentor, others will see them as "having a deficit." Needing help to grow is not always easy to ask for. Yet framing mentoring as a holding environment for both mentor and mentee can help. Leaders, both mentors and mentees, have appreciated the idea of *co-mentoring* (i.e., acknowledging that both parties have gifts to share and can support each other's growth) as a new approach to mentoring and a holding environment for self-development in which both partners can grow and share their unique gifts and domains of expertise. Co-mentoring can help promote the understanding that, as one leader shared, "having and wanting and needing a mentor is not a competency deficiency." Other leaders have explained, "We need to change the institutional perspective on mentoring. It is not a weakness, not a deficit," suggesting that the "institution" needs to shift accordingly to a co-mentoring model and perspective. As Barbara Chase, head of Andover Academy, shared, engaging in mentoring relationships is "like teaching . . . it's learning more about yourself by working with other people."

Another strategy that leaders use in dyads is to write in journals and to share one-to-one with a colleague. Engaging in this form of collegial inquiry, leaders say, helps to support their own growth.

### Growing With and Through Groups

Leaders across the system, regardless of role, have shared how what I call *collegial inquiry groups*—in which they engage in meaningful, deep conversations about practice—support their development and serve as a valuable source of renewal. In general, these groups meet regularly for several hours each month (or week or every two weeks) throughout the year. In addition, teachers, principals, assistant principals, coaches, mentors, and mentees have noted that they support their own growth by engaging in these groups as critical friends. As we've discussed earlier, many explained that using a protocol and responding to questions creates a context for growth.

As with the dyad relationships just described, leaders who don't have this opportunity for collegial inquiry have expressed a "wish" to be members of such groups, which they believe would help them in their work and assist them in self-growth and renewal.

For example, teacher leaders in several professional development contexts have expressed that it is hard to "collaborate" with "one and only one other person." They have voiced a desire to have ongoing time with "groups of teachers" and said that they really appreciated the "chance to be with teachers from different divisions" during workshops or seminars. This sentiment resonates with the majority of professional learning participants, who similarly express a strong desire to strengthen collaboration between administrators and teachers to support growth.

In earlier chapters, we've learned about how much these opportunities for self-development matter. For instance, we learned about how principals who participate in the Cahn Fellows Program at Teachers College with their assistant principals (and/or teacher leader "allies") value engaging with colleagues in a group over a fifteen-month period. These groups remain consistent over time and are facilitated by a faculty coach—in this case, me. From surveys taken after each group meeting, we've learned that what the leaders value most about the group is that they grow themselves from having "a safe space to talk and think out loud," and "the opportunity to share problems and leadership dilemmas" and "learn from colleagues' perspectives, insights, and questions." They have also shared that being a member of these groups helps them to feel "renewed" and better "able to tackle challenges." Last, and very important, they share that being part of this kind of professional learning environment, where they are *experiencing* the practices that support their own growth, helps them to use these very practices with their teachers to help the teachers grow. What these principals and their allies voice about the ways in which groups support self-development is similar to what other leaders have expressed on the same subject. We've seen examples of this throughout this book.

In chapters 1 and 4, for example, we emphasized that the opportunity to share perspectives and experiences enables us to learn and grow. Considering alternative perspectives, understanding our own assumptions and how they guide our behaviors, and contemplating questions offered by colleagues can help us grow. Having the chance to think out loud and to be listened to by colleagues—"a rare and treasured opportunity," as one leader put it—supports our self-development.

We've also learned that engaging in dialogue with others in groups and/or in dyads provides a holding environment. Leaders have voiced that they grow from the questions their colleagues ask, and that they find them useful in facilitating reflection on their own assumptions about leadership practices. Reflecting and engaging in dialogue in the company of colleagues enables leaders to grow from probing their own thinking and assumptions as well as from testing new ideas and ways of acting. In other words, having a heightened awareness of our own assumptions allows us to examine the influence they have on our performance, thinking, and feelings—and to eventually test these assumptions. This is part of helping oneself to grow.

In addition, leaders have voiced that being part of a stable group over time reduces their feelings of isolation and enables them to better support adult growth in their own workplaces. They've also shared that this kind of opportunity for self-development helps them to better manage adaptive challenges and to improve their instructional leadership. Leaders of all kinds who engage in these types of groups consistently emphasize the group as a support to their growth and leadership development and report that having experienced this kind of space helps them to create similar kinds of holding environments for other adults in their care.

### Strategies for Self-Renewal

The majority of school leaders wish for "more time" for renewal, and many ask for advice about "how others do it." In this section, I offer some of the more common ways in which leaders renew and restore themselves. Many leaders point to the importance of making time to:

- Be with family and friends, making this a priority
- Reflect privately (reflecting in mind and/or in writing)
- Occasionally take time away from work for at least part of a day during the week, or set aside some time during a weekend (some refer to this as a "Sabbath")
- Exercise
- Read the newspaper or a book or participate in a book club
- Watch their favorite TV shows or movies to clear their minds
- Attend retreats, especially during holidays, vacations, and summer break

- Take some time off from work during vacations, meaning that they make sure that vacations really involve a *break from work*
- Travel

Of course, there are more strategies and practices that school leaders employ to renew themselves. As noted, the preceding list highlights the most common ways in which they rest, restore, and rejuvenate themselves based on what I've learned from working with them. Next, I'll highlight a few big ideas related to renewal as a form of refilling.

Having a balance—or for some, developing a better balance—between work and family is central to renewal. Many leaders have shared with me that one of the main ways they renew and "nourish" themselves is through their "intimate relationships with family and friends," a practice that is captured eloquently by one school leader in particular, Mary Newman: "I also nourish myself through . . . intimate relationships with family and with friends . . . and travel [with them] . . . I try very hard, and always have, to keep up a very rich personal life. And if I don't, I don't have as much to bring to my work. Both the work and the home are really of primary importance to me."

Another renewal strategy I'd like to highlight has to do with taking time away from work in order to recharge. This might mean time away for leaders to focus on other aspects of their life and relationships, or time away to reflect on their work. Regardless of their leadership positions and contexts (K–12 schools, districts, or universities), school leaders have emphasized the importance of taking time off as a "highly effective and necessary" renewal strategy. Many have also shared that taking some time away from e-mail ("staying off the grid by unplugging") to recharge is essential to self-renewal. The majority of leaders have stressed that securing some time away from work to get their "batteries back up" is of vital importance to help them feel rejuvenated. The amount of time varies; it might be a couple of hours, a few days, or a week or two.

Writing is another strategy that teachers, assistant principals, principals, coaches, district leaders, and university teachers use frequently to renew themselves. For many, regular journal writing is one way they support self-renewal. In addition, leaders have told me that they find that writing proposals, articles, and books helps them to feel refreshed and restored. Some have mentioned that writing helps them to feel inspired.

As you know, setting aside time and space to renew helps us to feel replenished. It also gives a little more distance from the adaptive challenges we face every day. In effect, self-renewal helps us to step back and refill ourselves so that we can continue giving and supporting others' growth and learning.

## Speaking for Myself

In this section, I'll add to the strategies that have been offered by sharing a few of my own and some thoughts about them, in case useful to you in your work of self-development. I, too, engage in a variety of practices to support my growth. While some of these are at the individual level—reading and journal writing, for example—I will focus here on those strategies I use that involve other people. As I discussed this section with a dear friend, India Koopman, she reminded me of something that's very important when thinking about supporting our own growth: "We all need help analyzing ourselves and growing from that." Her wisdom reminds me of how vital it is to grow in the company of others.

As part of my self-development strategy, I purposefully and intentionally put myself in personal and professional learning situations and relationships that support my growth.

I'll begin with the interpersonal relationships in which I feel both well held and appropriately challenged to grow. For example, I am blessed with a husband, a few brothers, a cherished mentor, and several very close friends, all of whom have known me for a long time and have watched me grow from the holding environments they have so generously given me. In these one-to-one relationships I intentionally ask for feedback, for help, and for these individuals to stand at the edges of my thinking and feelings for the purpose of helping me grow. And I *actually ask them* to help me grow. In these relationships and holding environments, I share what's in my soul, my thoughts and feelings, and I feel comfortable being vulnerable and open to their perspectives, insights, and developmental challenges for growth. I also feel that they listen oh-so-closely to my thoughts and feelings without judgment. I *trust* that what they offer in terms of perspective, thinking, feelings, questions, and insights comes from a place of wanting to help me grow. Importantly, I also feel that they accept me for who I am and how I am making meaning in the moment. In these relationships, we engage in deep and meaningful conversations fairly regularly, and especially when either one of us needs to talk. These relationships serve as holding environments for both of us.

Speaking from my side of the relationship, I can say that I feel safe and supported in my own development. I share the kinds of things that keep me up at night. I ask for feedback. I work to be open and to open myself up. With these individuals, I share personal and professional puzzles and dilemmas. Sometimes I ask for help in the following ways: "Can I just think out loud with you?" "Can I share something with you?" "I'm stuck . . . Can you please listen and help?" "I know I need some perspective on this. Can you please help?" "Can I just vent?" "Can we think together about this?" They do the same with me. It's *reciprocal*.

Many years ago, it was very difficult for me to ask for help. I have learned the importance of doing so and find it a great support to my own growth. With these few people, I can share what a friend of mine calls "close to the bone" and "raw" feelings and thinking. Doing so helps me to clarify my thoughts and feelings and thus to understand better what I am *actually* thinking and feeling. I learn from another person's perspective and carefully consider it as well as that individual's questions. I grow from carefully considering the different perspective offered to me out of and with care.

I also grow from being part of stable groups in which we purposefully explore our beliefs and values and assumptions as part of "the work." For example, I'm part of long-term research and writing partnerships. In these groups we do a lot of work, and we also support each other's growth and development. These groups for me—and I think for my colleagues—serve as holding environments in many of the same ways as the relationships I've just described.

There's one other way in which I seek to grow myself that seems important to mention here: I purposefully put myself in learning situations that are aimed at supporting the kind of growth and development we've been learning about in this book. One example is that I am currently participating in the Immunity to Change Coaching Program, which is designed and facilitated by Robert Kegan and Lisa Lahey. In this advanced program, I am working to learn how to be a more effective developmental coach, and as I am learning, I am also being coached. This kind of coaching—I refer to it as "soul work"—is developmental coaching aimed at helping adults to grow their internal capacities. In this program I can feel myself growing from being coached, from learning from the leaders/facilitators, and from being part of a cohort—a group that's stable and working together for an eleven-month period. It is an extremely powerful and meaningful support for my growth. I highly recommend it!

I hope you find these additional strategies helpful. I think what I find most meaningful about the aforementioned holding environments is the quality of care, love, respect, honoring (acceptance), and listening that infuses them all. As we've discussed earlier, in these spaces I feel that people, others and myself, are *listening with presence*; we listen not just to what is said but to and for the *meaning* it holds for the speaker. In these relationships, sometimes we "talk about nothing and everything," as my husband, David, says. The relationships do support my own growth, and I hope that my partners in them feel supported as well.

I want to end this section with one last thought. I've been asking a lot of people lately about how they support their self-growth. "What is one way?" I've been asking. Many have said that they "need time to think about it." Many have paused and said, "That's a great question. I'm not sure." The leaders in professional learning sessions of all kinds have shared the strategies we've just discussed.

When I asked my husband, however, he did not hesitate at all. He immediately replied, "Being married." I'm sharing this with you because I truly believe that we grow most from *being in relationship and in relationships*. By this I mean that we grow from being surrounded by and connected to and *with* others in both general and deeply personal ways. By honestly sharing our selves, our lives, and who we are continually becoming with those around us, we are able to support and be supported in vital and meaningful ways. This, in essence, is what we've been learning about in this book.

## CREATING OPPORTUNITIES FOR GROWTH IN SCHOOLS, DISTRICTS, AND SCHOOL SYSTEMS

*If you can dream it, you can do it.*

—Walt Disney

We need to create ongoing holding environments where education leaders in all contexts—universities, schools, teams, districts—have the opportunity to continuously reflect on and engage in purposeful dialogue about their leadership in the company of colleagues and in light of the complex challenges they face. As we've discussed, this type of self-reflection and dialogue creates a context for growth. In this section, I'll share some recommendations and reference larger systemic supports needed to help make them a reality. These recommendations are for those who lead and facilitate professional learning initiatives for teachers, principals, superintendents, assistant principals, coaches, and curriculum and improvement specialists in schools and districts; those who are involved in leading professional learning communities for teachers; those who lead and want to create teams; those who prepare aspiring and practicing leaders; and those who teach practicing and aspiring school leaders, district leaders, and policy makers.

## Implementing and Supporting Collegial Inquiry Groups

First, districts, K–12 schools, and university education leadership programs can support the creation of *collegial inquiry groups* in which practicing and aspiring leaders (i.e., principals, assistant principals, superintendents, teachers, mentors, coaches, and professional developers) purposefully reflect on their leadership challenges and how to support adult growth to build capacity as they meet together on a regular basis. These groups can be composed of leaders who serve in the same roles, and they can also be mixed groups. Over time, this context can help leaders (and all adults, for that matter) to grow and to renew themselves as they develop a new relationship to their own thinking and assumptions and learn from each other and from thinking out loud. This context is one in which leaders and colleagues can support and challenge each other in a psychological sense (i.e., by listening and by asking questions that help with considering alternative perspectives) as they strive to grow and sustain themselves in order to meet the demands of twenty-first-century leadership. Creating these ongoing and stable holding environments will enhance possibilities for them, their communities, teams, schools, school systems, and other organizations. These holding environments can, over time, help leaders to increase their own internal capacities. By creating spaces in which leaders can reflect purposefully on beliefs, values, and assumptions about practice in the company of colleagues who can offer appropriate supports and challenges, these robust environments can support the growth of adults with different ways of knowing. Leaders who participate in these collegial inquiry groups will be better able to manage the adaptive challenges they encounter every day in their practice.

In addition, these collegial inquiry groups could be effectively incorporated into university education leadership preparation programs. Universities could also offer these kinds of collegial inquiry groups to districts, schools, and other educational organizations. This would be an important opportunity for schools and universities to partner in an effort to more effectively support *all* educators as they strive to build their own and each other's internal capacities and tackle the adaptive challenges in their complex work. Policies would need to be developed and resources allocated to support these groups at the school, district, and university levels.

## On Teaching This Model, Ways of Knowing, and Pillar Practices

As noted in chapter 2, when I've presented the ideas and practices we've been learning about in this book at annual conferences such as Learning Forward (formerly known as the National Staff Development Council) and to other leaders both domestically and in other countries, these leaders, regardless of their particular roles, have found them important and helpful.

Thus, teaching adults about this developmental leadership model that focuses on how to create holding environments in schools, districts, systems, and education leadership preparation programs will help to transform any teaching, learning, or professional development initiative into a context for growth and leadership development. As we've been learning throughout this book, one important way to support the growth of leaders in their work contexts is to create opportunities where they can not only *learn* about the practices and processes that support growth but also *experience* them. This kind of experience, as we have seen, can help them to shape holding environments for growth and leadership development for the adults in their care. While this is hard work and requires authentic engagement, it is well worth the investment. I hope you find it worthwhile and meaningful. I have faith in you! I know that you can continue to make a real and permanent difference. As one aspiring principal shared, and this has been echoed by many leaders, "Thank you for sparking the fire to go out in the world and set the world on fire."

## NEW BEGINNINGS:
## RESPECTING THE PROCESS OF GROWTH

*We don't receive wisdom; we must discover it for ourselves after a journey that no one can take for us or spare us.*

—Marcel Proust

In this chapter, we've been focusing deeply on the importance of making time to *refill ourselves* with energies and passions for development by caring for our own renewal and by securing, prioritizing, and safeguarding ways to help ourselves to grow. To ensure the growth and development of others, we must also attend well to restoring ourselves and to caring for and supporting our own development. Put simply, in order to best support the growth and deep personal learning of others, we need to support these very same things in ourselves. As we've been learning throughout this book, our own internal developmental capacities influence *how* and *the extent to which* we can make ourselves and our gifts available in support of others' growth.

In the concluding pages of this book, I want to share with you one additional story to highlight an idea that is vital to crafting environments for others to grow while in our care. Marcel Proust's wisdom in the opening passage reminds us that there are certain lessons and ways of growing from which no one can *spare us*. This wisdom is highlighted in the story I'm about to share with you and in the lessons offered within it.

Some of you may already know the story of the novice entomologist whose interest in insects, and especially butterflies, was equal to her admiration and appreciation for the transformations that move the small creatures through their different life stages. *Butterflies*, as well as moths, develop through four distinct *stages* of life: egg, larva (the caterpillar *stage*), pupa (the *chrysalis* phase), and adulthood (the butterfly stage). Female Monarch butterflies lay their eggs on milkweed, as milkweed is the only plant that Monarch caterpillars can eat. Four to six days after the eggs are deposited, they will hatch. The hatched Monarch caterpillar will shed its skin five times during the larval stage as it passes to the pupa stage of metamorphosis. Under the caterpillar's skin at this stage is a jade-green casing called a chrysalis. It is within this chrysalis, only about one inch long, that the caterpillar will undergo a miraculous transformation to finally emerge as one of the most beautiful butterflies.

Her great admiration and strong appreciation for the life transformations of the Monarch butterfly led the budding scientist to cut open a Monarch chrysalis near the end of its pupa phase. She wanted to release to flight the beautiful butterfly that was beginning to stir within the chrysalis. Could she somehow make the breaking-out-of-chrysalis experience a little easier, less complicated, or less difficult for the new butterfly? This story of scientific curiosity and experimentation is also a tale of development interrupted. Development occurs during moments of struggle over time as much as it also takes place during periods of apparent rest. Just as growth and development can best take place within safe and secure spaces—such as a chrysalis or holding environment—where both supports and challenges are present, so too must growth and development take place at their own pace and in their own time. Our development depends on our readiness for growth, just as attention to facilitating our development depends on the timing of interventions—supports and challenges to grow—that might guide the best of intentions and intentionality.

Rather than allowing the new butterfly to struggle toward finding its own strength—to develop its still-frail wings so that flight would be possible—our entomologist carefully cut the chrysalis open with the intention of making it easier for the butterfly to emerge to freedom. However, instead of fluttering its way to bursting life in the skies above and fields beyond, the freed butterfly fell to the ground and to its end. The strength that the Monarch butterfly needed in order to live and grow was not allowed to fully develop. By interfering with the process of development and growth achieved through struggle, the student of butterflies interrupted the natural life cycle of the butterfly she loved.

So, you may be wondering, "Why this story? Why now?" Well, there are several reasons. First, I have discovered that it's not always easy for us as leaders to hold ourselves back and refrain from easing another person's struggle—struggle that is crucial to developing strength over time. On occasion, even today, I find myself offering solutions to necessary problems and challenges being faced by people who *need to grow their own strength* for problem solving. How can we build confidence in ourselves to overcome issues and obstacles when the necessary challenges are removed from our path by someone who cares so deeply that they do not want us to struggle or face adversity? As leaders, we all might be striving to be of help and support to others in need of development. Yet, as is too often the case when we care deeply for another person's welfare, we can sometimes find ourselves hindering that individual's growth and development as a leader. Struggle is necessary to the development of the capacities and capabilities that will help us to overcome adversities. Holding back requires patience, presence, and intentionality. While it is not easy to stand by and with someone as he or she struggles through to growth, it is essential that we do. What we are considering is a question of someone's *readiness* for growth and development; this readiness informs our decision that the timing is right for us to offer support *that will feel like support to the developing leader* during the growth process in which he or she is engaging.

Second, the timing of our intervention within the safe and secure space that we are creating must be right *for the leader who is doing the growing*. Growth cannot be forced, nor can the growth process be quickened. Yet it can be made easier and much more effective within the holding environments that we create for the miracles of emotional, psychological, and cognitive metamorphosis to take place. We can create the conditions for growth, and then we can invite leaders to engage in their own development within the safety and security made available within those holding environments. We offer developmental supports and challenges for growth.

We differentiate the kinds of supports and challenges that we offer to others who make meaning of their work and lives in ways that are qualitatively different from our own ways of knowing. Yet we stand *with them and for them as they struggle* toward developing in themselves greater internal capacities for growing and leadership.

It is important to keep in mind that sometimes, no matter how much we may want to support the growth of another person, the readiness or timing may not be right for that individual. If we rush the process, the leader in development may withdraw. This leader must be *ready to grow*. The *timing must be right* for the leader. We must be patient with the process of growth. I offer the story about the butterfly released too soon from its chrysalis as an illustration of these lessons. It is also an assurance that, given time, ultimately the butterfly will emerge—reminding us of the possibilities for transformation in others and in ourselves.

## AN INVITATION

In closing this chapter and this book I invite you, as I do in all professional learning sessions, to "make a promise to yourself" about one way you will renew yourself and one way you will help yourself to grow in order to refill. Thank you for giving to the world and the future.

## TAKEAWAYS

- Replenishing oneself, or *refilling the self*, is of vital importance to sustaining holding environments for *others* in the long haul.
- A very important aspect of supporting our own growth and development is that *we cannot do it alone*. In other words, one big takeaway is about the power and promise of growing oneself *through and in the company of others*.
- We need to create and prioritize holding environments for ourselves or we will not be able to give our best to others.
- When working hard to create holding environments and professional learning initiatives that support others' growth and development, it is critically important that you have supports in place for *yourself*—including people you can trust and lean on—because doing this work alone is hard on the body and soul.

- We need to continue growing, learning, and refilling in order to bring our best to the important work of supporting others.
- Leaders support their own growth in three ways: 1) engaging at the individual level (e.g., reading, journaling), 2) engaging with one other person (a dyad), and 3) engaging with colleagues in groups that meet regularly and over time.
- Making time and prioritizing self-renewal is another very important way in which we can refill ourselves, or the central dot. This kind of refilling and renewing can include other people, but sometimes it's as simple as doing little things independently that help us relax and unwind.
- To sustain this work, school districts, K–12 schools, and university education leadership programs can support the creation of *collegial inquiry groups* in which practicing and aspiring leaders (i.e., principals, assistant principals, superintendents, teachers, mentors, coaches, and professional developers) reflect purposefully on their leadership challenges and how to support adult growth to build capacity as they meet together on a regular basis.
- To sustain this work, I recommend teaching adults about this model for learning-oriented leadership development to transform any teaching, learning, or professional development environment into one that effectively supports adult growth.

## REFLECTIVE QUESTIONS

1. What practices do you employ to renew yourself? How are they working? After reading this chapter, are there any new strategies you'd like to adopt in order to refill your central dot?

2. What are two ways in which you support your own development? How are these working? How do these serve as holding environments for your self-renewal, growth, and/or learning?

3. In what ways, if any, does this chapter help you in thinking about the process of self-renewal and self-development and their relationship to supporting those in your care? What ideas and practices would you like to incorporate into your practice to help others support their self-renewal and self-development? What ideas and practices would you like to add to your own to better support your refilling processes?

4.  What structures could you implement in your organization to better support self-renewal and self-development? How, ideally, would you reshape conditions to better support implementation of your ideas? What small steps could you take toward securing the needed resources to create these kinds of holding environments?

## APPLICATION EXERCISE: ATTENDING TO WAYS OF KNOWING TO ADVANCE SELF-GROWTH

In case helpful, I offer the following protocol as a closing application exercise. It is what I call a "pair-share" protocol, an example of how to structure a holding environment for yourself with a colleague. I truly hope you find this helpful. Please feel free to contact me about any of the ideas and practices we've explored in this book. I would love to learn from you.

### Preparation

+ Think about an aspect of yourself that you would like to grow. In other words, think about something or some side of yourself that tugs at the limits of your own capacities. What is that? In what ways would you like to develop yourself? What kinds of supports and challenges do you think you need to facilitate your own growth?

+ What do you see as your own growing edge? What presents a developmental challenge for you in your practice? Are there ways in which you'd like to grow yourself to better meet this challenge? How might a reflective partner, the person joining you in this exercise, help you?

### Process

Complete the process twice, so that each person has the opportunity to play both the coach and the coachee.

1. Reflecting privately in writing
   a. This is a space to jot down thoughts about your experience, questions, and struggles—from a developmental perspective.                                    (5 minutes)

2. Partner check-in
   a. After sharing how you are feeling about this exercise in general, please decide who will share first. ☺                 (5 minutes)

3. Partner share
   a. Please explain the context, how you'd like to grow yourself,
      and your challenge to your partner. Please explain the kinds of
      supports and challenges you think you would benefit from.
      What do you need help with right now?
      (Partner will serve as developmental coach.)         **(15 minutes)**

   b. The coach's role is to offer questions, informed by a new
      or enhanced understanding of developmental theory
      and holding environments as well as ideas and practices
      discussed in this book, in order to offer authentic
      supports and challenges to the coachee.              **(15 minutes)**

4. Step back and check in/check out
   a. Please reflect on the process. What is the coachee feeling?
      Thinking? What is the coach thinking? Feeling? What
      went well? Next steps?                                **(10 minutes)**

   b. Private writing/reflecting time.                      **(5 minutes)**

# Notes

## Introduction

1. Robert Kegan, *The Evolving Self: Problem and Process in Human Development* (Cambridge, MA: Harvard University Press, 1982), 115; Robert Kegan, *In Over Our Heads: The Mental Demands of Modern Life* (Cambridge, MA: Harvard University Press, 1994), 331–337; Robert Kegan, "What 'Form' Transforms?: A Constructive-Developmental Approach to Transformative Learning," in *Learning as Transformation: Critical Perspectives on a Theory in Progress*, eds. Jack Merizow and Associates (San Francisco: Jossey-Bass, 2000), 35–70; Eleanor Drago-Severson, *Helping Teachers Learn: Principal Leadership for Adult Growth and Development* (Thousand Oaks, CA: Corwin Press, 2004), 1–175; Eleanor Drago-Severson, *Leading Adult Learning: Supporting Adult Development in Our Schools* (Thousand Oaks, CA: Corwin Press, 2009), 5–12.

2. D. W. Winnicott, *The Maturational Processes and the Facilitating Environment* (New York: International Universities Press, 1965), 5–22.

3. Kegan, *The Evolving Self*, 115.

4. *The King's Speech*, directed by Tom Hooper (London: See-Saw Films, 2010).

5. Gordon A. Donaldson Jr., *How Leaders Learn: Cultivating Capacities for School Improvement* (New York: Teachers College Press, 2008), 8–15; Thomas R. Guskey, "How Classroom Assessments Improve Learning," *Education Leadership* 60, no. 5 (2003), 6–11; Robert Kegan and Lisa Laskow Lahey, *Immunity to Change: How to Overcome It and Unlock the Potential in Yourself and Your Organization* (Boston: Harvard Business School Press, 2009), 3–81.

6. National School Leaders Network, Spring 2011 newsletter, http://connectlead-succeed.org/impact/results.

7. Kegan, *In Over Our Heads*, 12–169; Kegan, "What 'Form' Transforms?" 38–70; Drago-Severson, *Helping Teachers Learn*, 21–35; Drago-Severson, *Leading Adult Learning*, 32–68.

8. Drago-Severson, *Leading Adult Learning*, 5–29; Donaldson, *How Leaders Learn*, 3–17; Kegan and Lahey, *Immunity to Change*, 5–6.

9. Ronald A. Heifetz, *Leadership Without Easy Answers* (Cambridge, MA: Harvard University Press, 1994), 1–17.

10. http://www.usatoday.com/news/education/story/2012-04-28/common-core-education/54583192/1.

11. Tony Wagner et al., *Change Leadership: A Practical Guide to Transforming Our Schools* (San Francisco: Jossey-Bass, 2006), 10–11; Aliki Irini Nicolaides, "Learning Their Way Through Ambiguity: Explorations of How Nine Developmentally

Mature Adults Make Sense of Ambiguity" (doctoral dissertation, Teachers College, Columbia University, 2008), 6–62.

12. Drago-Severson, *Leading Adult Learning*, 8; Kegan, *In Over Our Heads*, 331–337; Kegan, "What 'Form' Transforms?" 35–70; Kegan and Lahey, *Immunity to Change*, 3–63; David Clark McCallum Jr., "Exploring the Implications of a Hidden Diversity in Group Relations Conference Learning: A Developmental Perspective" (doctoral dissertation, Teachers College, Columbia University, 2008), 1–25; Nicolaides, "Learning Their Way," 7–62.

## Chapter 1

1. Laurent A. Daloz, *Effective Teaching and Mentoring: Realizing the Transformational Power of Adult Learning Experiences* (San Francisco: Jossey-Bass, 1986), 11–28; Carol Gilligan, Robert Kegan, and Theodore Sizer, "Memorial Minute: William Graves Perry Jr." *Harvard Gazette Archives*, http://www.news.harvard.edu/gazette/1999/05.27/mm.perry.html.

2. Michael Basseches, *Dialectical Thinking and Adult Development* (Norwood, NJ: Ablex Press, 1984), 2–36; Marcia B. Baxter-Magolda, *Knowing and Reasoning in College: Gender-Related Patterns in Students' Intellectual Development* (San Francisco: Jossey-Bass, 1992), 17–34; Marcia B. Baxter-Magolda, *Authoring Your Life: Developing an Internal Voice to Navigate Life's Challenges* (Sterling, VA: Stylus Publishing, 2009), 6–11; Mary Belenky et al., *Women's Ways of Knowing* (New York: Basic Books, 1986), 2–24; Carol Gilligan, *In a Different Voice: Psychological Theory and Women's Development* (Cambridge, MA: Harvard University Press, 1982), 14–42; Robert Kegan, *The Evolving Self: Problem and Process in Human Development* (Cambridge, MA: Harvard University Press, 1982), 25–73; Robert Kegan, *In Over Our Heads: The Mental Demands of Modern Life* (Cambridge, MA: Harvard University Press, 1994), 5–353; Robert Kegan, "What 'Form' Transforms?: A Constructive-Developmental Approach to Transformative Learning," in *Learning as Transformation: Critical Perspectives on a Theory in Progress*, eds. Jack Merizow and Associates (San Francisco: Jossey-Bass, 2000), 35–70; Patricia M. King and Karen Strohm Kitchener, *Developing Reflective Judgment* (San Francisco: Jossey-Bass, 1994), 1–18; Lee L. Knefelkamp and Timothy David-Lang, "Encountering Diversity on Campus and in the Classroom: Advancing Intellectual and Ethical Development," *Diversity Digest* 3, no. 2 (2000): 10; Lawrence Kohlberg, "Stage and Sequence: The Cognitive-Developmental Approach to Socialization," in *Handbook of Socialization Theory and Research*, ed. David A. Goslin (New York: Rand McNally, 1969), 347–480; Lawrence Kohlberg, *Stage and Sequence: The Cognitive Developmental Approach to Socialization: The Psychology of Moral Development* (San Francisco: Harper & Row, 1984), 6–23; Jean Piaget, *The Origins of Intelligence in Children* (New York: International Universities Press, 1952) 10–323; William G. Perry Jr., *Forms of Intellectual and Ethical Development in the College Years* (New York: Holt, Rinehart and Winston, 1970) 3–12.

3. Kegan, *The Evolving Self*, 15-73; Kegan, *In Over Our Heads*, 3–37.

4. Kegan, *In Over Our Heads*, 371.

5. David Clark McCallum Jr., "Exploring the Implications of a Hidden Diversity in Group Relations Conference Learning: A Developmental Perspective" (doctoral

dissertation, Teachers College, Columbia University, 2008), 2–70, 89–124; Knefelkamp and David-Lang, "Encountering Diversity," 10.

6. Eleanor Drago-Severson, *Leading Adult Learning: Supporting Adult Development in Our Schools* (Thousand Oaks, CA: Corwin Press, 2009), 36-58; Robert Kegan and Lisa Laskow Lahey, *Immunity to Change: How to Overcome It and Unlock the Potential in Yourself and Your Organization* (Boston: Harvard Business School Press, 2009), 8–22.

7. Lisa Boes, "Practicing Democracy" (doctoral dissertation, Harvard University, 2006), 14–53.

8. D. W. Winnicott, *The Maturation Processes and the Facilitating Environment* (New York: International Universities Press, 1965) 5–15.

9. Kegan, *The Evolving Self,* 1–15, 115.

10. Eleanor Drago-Severson, *Helping Teachers Learn: Principal Leadership for Adult Growth and Development* (Thousand Oaks, CA: Corwin Press, 2004), 21–36; Drago-Severson, *Leading Adult Learning,* 31–68; Kegan, *The Evolving Self,* 25–73; Kegan, *In Over Our Heads,* 15–351; Kegan, "What 'Form' Transforms?" 35–70.

11. Eleanor Drago-Severson, Jessica Blum-DeStefano, and Anila Asghar, *Leading and Learning for Growth* (Thousand Oaks, CA: Corwin Press, forthcoming), 15–33.

12. Ibid., 55–178.

## Chapter 2

1. *Merriam-Webster Online*, s.v. "care," http://www.merriam-webster.com/dictionary/care.

2. Ibid., s.v. "respect," http://www.merriam-webster.com/dictionary/respect.

3. Ibid., s.v. "trust," http://www.merriam-webster.com/dictionary/trust.

4. Ibid., s.v. "collaborate," http://www.merriam-webster.com/dictionary/collaboration.

5. Ibid., s.v. "intentional," http://www.merriam-webster.com/dictionary/intentionality.

6. Eleanor Drago-Severson, Jessica Blum-DeStefano, and Anila Asghar, *Leading and Learning for Growth* (Thousand Oaks, CA: Corwin Press, forthcoming), 1–36.

## Chapter 3

1. *Merriam-Webster Online*, s.v. "sense," http://www.merriam-webster.com/dictionary/sense.

2. Ibid., s.v. "listen," http://www.merriam-webster.com/dictionary/listen.

3. Ibid., s.v. "language," http://www.merriam-webster.com/dictionary/language.

4. Robert Kegan and Lisa Laskow Lahey, *How the Way We Talk Can Change the Way We Work* (San Francisco: Jossey-Bass, 2002).

5. Eleanor Drago-Severson, *Leading Adult Learning: Supporting Adult Development in Our Schools* (Thousand Oaks, CA: Corwin Press, 2009), 5–12.

6. *Merriam-Webster Online*, s.v. "see," http://www.merriam-webster.com/dictionary/see.

7. Eleanor Drago-Severson, Jessica Blum-DeStefano, and Anila Asghar, *Leading and Learning Together* (Thousand Oaks, CA: Corwin Press, forthcoming), 15–33.

8. Ibid., 15–45.

## Chapter 4

1. Eleanor Drago-Severson, *Helping Teachers Learn: Principal Leadership for Adult Growth and Development* (Thousand Oaks, CA: Corwin Press, 2004), 1–20; Eleanor Drago-Severson, *Leading Adult Learning: Supporting Adult Development in Our Schools* (Thousand Oaks, CA: Corwin Press, 2009), 3–30.

2. Drago-Severson, *Helping Teachers Learn*, 7–14; Drago-Severson, *Leading Adult Learning*, 3–36; Eleanor Drago-Severson, Jessica Blum-DeStefano, and Anila Asghar, *Leading and Learning Together* (Thousand Oaks, CA: Corwin Press, forthcoming), 5–28.

3. Drago-Severson, Blum-DeStefano, and Asghar, *Leading and Learning Together*, 15–45.

4. Drago-Severson, *Helping Teachers Learn*, 17–20; Drago-Severson, *Leading Adult Learning*, 5–27.

5. Ibid., 71–106.

6. Ibid., 223–231.

## Chapter 6

1. Richard H. Ackerman and Pat Maslin-Ostrowski, "The Wounded Leader," *Educational Leadership* 61, no. 7 (2004): 28–32; Monica Byrne-Jiménez and Margaret Terry Orr, *Developing Effective Principals Through Collaborative Inquiry* (New York: Teachers College Press, 2007), 1–45; Gordon A. Donaldson Jr., *How Leaders Learn: Cultivating Capacities for School Improvement* (New York: Teachers College Press, 2008), 2–17.

# Acknowledgments

*If I have seen further, it is by standing on the shoulders of giants.*

—ISAAC NEWTON

There are many wonderful, cherished, beautiful, and inspiring individuals—friends, colleagues, students, partners in thought, and family members—who have contributed to this book in meaningful and different ways. Their presence, gifts, and loving connection have helped to shape conditions for me to grow and give to others. I am keenly aware of the blessing of these precious connections and the important ways in which their bright lights, generous hearts, and lovely souls inspire, encourage, support, and strengthen me. This book is a tribute to them, to their teachings, to their modeling, to their ways of creating the conditions for growth. It is equally a tribute to all who have taught me how to create the conditions that support other people's growth, which in turn helps those people do the same for those in their care.

The lessons shared in these pages represent the collective contribution of many individuals. I hope that each of you has known and felt my deep gratitude long before you read about it here. This book is one way for me to express my appreciation for you by sharing your light with others. My hope is that others will find this work helpful to them in their quest to support adult development—for supporting adult development *is* leadership.

I'd like to begin by expressing heartfelt appreciation for a few friends, colleagues, and partners in thought who have contributed to this book in meaningful and different ways because of their influence in my life. I trust you know why I mention you here: Richard Ackerman, Dan Alpert, Anila Asghar, Jessica Blum-DeStefano, Ira Bogotch, Judith Brady, Maria Broderick, Tom Buffett, Warner Burke, Deanna Burney, Kirsten Busch, Caroline Chauncey, Robb Clousse, Betty Drago, John Drago, Bud Drago, Joe Drago, Paul Drago, Eleanor Duckworth, Jane Ellison, Susan Fuhrman, Howard Gardner, Sue Gaylor, Monica George-Fields, Tom James, Susan

Moore Johnson, Anne Jones, Robert Kegan, India Koopman, Daphne Layton, Sarah Levine, Neville Marks, Victoria Marsick, Pat Maslin-Ostrowski, David McCallum, Kathleen McCartney, Elizabeth Neale, Peter Neaman, Aliki Nicolaides, Julie Porter, Barbara Rapaport, Carolyn Riehl, Kate Scott, David Severson, and Steve Silverman.

Deep gratitude goes to *all* of the students and practicing and aspiring leaders who have helped me learn and whose courage, insight, and wisdom infuses this book. Thank you for the honor of learning with and from you, and for the trust with which you generously open your hearts and minds so that all of us can learn from your experiences, from your good work, and from your efforts to support adult development while growing your selves. Thank you for welcoming me into your schools, your teams, your districts, your coaching sessions, your professional learning communities, and your experiences. In particular, I would like to voice special gratitude to those whose reflections and wisdom appear in the examples shared in this book: Matt Aborn, Jed Lippard, Brooke McCaffrey, and Malka Schwarzmer. While I am unable to name each leader here, please know that the lessons shared in this book are reflections of all of you and what I have learned from being in your company. Please accept my heartfelt gratitude.

I have had the privilege of longer-term relationships with many practicing educators from different organizations. I am thankful for all that they have taught me and continue to teach me as we strive together to create conditions supportive of adult growth and leadership development. I offer warm gratitude for the organizations and the people behind and within them who have enabled my learning, including:

- The Cahn Fellows Program at Teachers College, Columbia University, and in particular, benefactor Chuck Cahn, director Krista Dunbar, and the principals, assistant principals, and teacher leaders in the program.
- The Executive Leadership Institute of New York City (ELI), and especially the leaders affiliated with the Advanced Leadership Program for Assistant Principals (ALPAP): the mentor principals, the assistant principals, ALPAP director Janet Aravena, Council of School Supervisors and Administrators (CSA) director Peter McNally, ELI executive director Dr. Eloise Messineo, and leadership coach Dr. Linda Gross Cheliotes.
- Dr. Elizabeth Neale and principals connected with the School Leaders Network.
- Allison Scheff, Pamela Pelletier, Dr. Hannah Sevian, and the Science Education Fellows of Boston, Massachusetts.

- Director Craig Richards and the aspiring leaders in the Summer Principals Academy Program at Teachers College.
- Executive Director David Chojnacki and educators who are members of the Near East South Asian Council of Overseas Schools (NESA).
- Learning Forward executive director Stephanie Hirsch, executive editor Tracy Crow, and members.
- Dr. Mary Anton-Oldenburg and members of her learning community at the Bowman School of Lexington, Massachusetts.
- Jed Lippard, Elizabeth Murray, and other educators at Prospect Hill Academy Charter School in Cambridge, Massachusetts.
- Dr. Peter McFarlane and the math and literacy coaches at Hugo Preparatory School in Harlem, New York.
- The former National Academy for Excellence in Teaching (NAfET) at Teachers College and its former director, Dr. Douglas Wood, as well as the schools served by NAfET.

Among the many students who have helped advance this work, I would especially like to thank those I have been privileged to teach and learn from at Teachers College and at Harvard's Graduate School of Education. Your teachings, insights, questions, and curiosity have made this work stronger. Thank you for teaching me.

Over the past twenty-five years, I have been blessed with the precious gift of learning from and with Professor Robert Kegan of Harvard's Graduate School of Education. During these years, I have been the beneficiary of Bob's extraordinary gifts as teacher, trusted advisor, wise mentor, thought partner and collaborator in research, cherished friend, and treasured colleague. I have also benefited from experiencing firsthand how Bob ingeniously goes about creating holding environments. Bob, no words can ever truly express how grateful I am for your friendship, your modeling, your brilliant teachings, and the gift that you are. Thank you from deep in my soul for all that you teach me, for sharing your gifts, and for helping me to understand better how to hold others, help them grow, and create conditions that support growth. You are inspiration and light.

Deepest gratitude also goes to India Koopman, my dear friend, insightful teacher, and thought partner. Thank you for your careful listening, enduring support, and presence, and for your care about this work and me. Your helpful questions, keen insights, and inspiring suggestions have made this book much better. I thank you, India, with all my heart, for the gifts of love that you give; for your presence, generosity, strength, wisdom, and patience; for your careful attention to ideas; and for your thoughtfulness. You are treasure.

I am very grateful for Jessica Blum-DeStefano and the gifts she gives to my work and to me. They are impossible to name, and even more impossible to describe. Thank you for your time, energy, love, care, insights, wisdom, and encouragement, and for the attention you devoted to thinking with me, especially when I could not see what you so clearly saw in the ways I work to create conditions for others to grow. Thank you for being a trusted thought partner and for sharing your insights. Thank you for your light throughout this process and for your heartfelt care and belief in this work. There's so much more I hope you know and feel of my gratitude. You are precious.

A deep and heartfelt expression of gratitude is a must for Caroline Chauncey, senior editor of Harvard Education Press. Thank you for your belief and *faith* in this work and me, for your enduring patience and gracious help, and for the many important contributions you have made to this book. It is so much stronger because of you, your wisdom, and your care.

I'd also like to express gratitude to the Harvard Education Press team for your thoughtful communications, leadership, and support during the final stages of this work. I thank you all deeply for your expertise in bringing this book to readers.

In closing, I end with where I began, by offering deep expressions of love to those who most shaped my life and what I am able to offer in support to others. My late father, Dr. Rosario Drago, and my mother, Mrs. Betty Drago, have been my guides and finest teachers. With extraordinary love, wisdom, joy, exemplary hard work, and care, they modeled loving, learning, and leadership that continues to inspire and hold me. It is on their shoulders that I continue to stand so that I might see a little further. A very special note to you, dearest Mom: you are incredibly beautiful. You, your courage, your presence, and your love strengthen me. You are *love*.

I thank my siblings and their families for their love and support over many years and for all you teach me.

In this collection of ideas and practices for holding others to support growth, how can I possibly speak to all that I feel and think and appreciate about the holding and support sustaining my life and work that comes from my husband and lifelong soulmate, David Severson? How does one go about thanking the sun for its warmth, nurturing, glow, and light? No words come close to capturing the depths of my love for you and breadth of my gratitude to you. Thank you for believing in me. Thank you for the impossible-to-describe sacrifices and compromises that you deliver to my life and work with joy and love. Thank you for the gift of you, your companionship, and your friendship every step—every day. David, thank you for your enduring love, for all that you teach me, for the many ways in which you help me to grow, and for your light in my life. You are my cherished love, angel, and touchstone. I love you.

# About the Author

ELEANOR DRAGO-SEVERSON is a professor of education leadership and adult learning and leadership at Columbia University's Teachers College. She earned her master's and doctoral degrees from Harvard, where she taught from 1997 to 2005. Her research and teaching center on leadership for supporting adult development in K–12 schools, adult basic education/English for speakers of other languages (ABE/ESOL), and university contexts. Her work is inspired by the idea that schools must be places where adults as well as children can grow. Ellie is the author of *Becoming Adult Learners: Principles and Practices for Effective Development* (Teachers College Press, 2004), *Helping Teachers Learn: Principal Leadership for Adult Growth and Development* (Corwin, 2004), and *Leading Adult Learning: Supporting Adult Development in Our School* (Corwin/Sage Press, 2009). *Helping Teachers Learn* was recognized as the 2004 Book of the Year from the National Staff Development Council (now Learning Forward). *Leading Adult Learning* was awarded Learning Forward's book of fall 2009. She is currently writing *Learning and Leading Together* (Corwin/Sage).

Ellie has served as teacher, program designer, director, consultant, and professional developer in a variety of educational contexts, including K–12 schools, adult education community centers, and universities. She also was a lead researcher, with Robert Kegan, on the Adult Development Team of the National Center for the Study of Adult Learning and Literacy (NCSALL) at Harvard University. She consults for coaches, leaders, and educational organizations on matters of personal and professional learning and development for superintendents, principals, and teachers, as well as on leadership supportive of adult growth domestically and internationally. Ellie has been awarded three distinguished teaching awards from Teachers College (2007), the Harvard Graduate School of Education's Morningstar Award (2005) for excellence in teaching, and Harvard Extension School's Dean's Award for Excellence in Teaching (1998).

She grew up in the Bronx and lives in New York City with her husband, David.

# Index